2025 Astrological Planner

This planner belongs to:

Name

e-mail

phone number

In case of an emergency, contact

✦ ✦ ✦

Regulus 2025 Astrological Planner

Produced by Paula Belluomini
and Richard Fidler.

Published by Regulus Publishing Ltd.

Astrological data generated in part
by Matrix Search Inc Software.
Astronomical data and information
about the visibility of the Eclipse:
<http://sunearth.gsf.nasa.gov/>.

Set for GMT
Lunations charts were calculated
using Natural House System.

No part of this publication may be
reproduced or transmitted in any form or by
any means, electronic or mechanical, without
prior authorization from Regulus Publishing.

ISBN 978-1-0683131-0-3

www.RegulusBooks.com

Regulus Publishing, UK
email: **reguluspublishing@gmail.com**

Learn more about the Astrologers:

Visit Paula Belluomini's website
www.astropaula.com

Visit Richard Fidler's website
www.richardfidler.com

TABLE OF CONTENTS

Your Astrological Planner 6
    Making the Most of Your Astrological Planner 6
    Calculating Your Own Transits Using the Ephemeris 7

Overview of the Year 2025 10

The Lunar Cycle 16

Lunations 2025 17

Eclipses in Astrology 18

Eclipses in 2025 19

Planetary Movements 20
    and Retrograde Periods in 2025

Astronomical Events 21
      Visible in the Sky
      Occultations by the Moon

Planetary Days and Planetary Hours 22

Planets 24

Signs of the Zodiac 28

Houses 32

Aspects 34

Astrological Planner 2025 36

Annotations 200

Space to Draw Your Own Chart 204

Legend 205

World Map with Time Zones 206

Your Astrological Planner

You are holding in your hands the Regulus Astrological Planner for 2025, a priceless sextant for navigating the tides of time, a map of the ebb and flow in the seasons of life. How much you can benefit from it really depends on your astrological creativity and acuity. Whether you're a astrological beginner or more advanced, it will provide you with valuable notes and reminders about what's going on in the heavens. It's perfect as a daily planner, working diary or as a journal for concise reflections and observations.

This planner uses Modern Tropical Astrology and provides information on the phases of the Moon, aspects between the planets, planet ingresses into new signs, retrograde and direct motion, and more.

All times are given in Greenwich Mean Time (GMT). Be sure to convert your local time to GMT so you'll know what time the event has occured in your time zone.

For example, South Africa is always 2 hours ahead of GMT, so if you are located in South Africa you need to subtract 2 hours from South African Standard Time to align with GMT. New York is on Eastern Standard Time when Daylight Savings Time is not in effect and is then 5 hours behind GMT. So if you are in New York and Daylight Savings Time is not in effect (EST) you need to add 5 hours to your local time to align with GMT. When Daylight Savings Time is in effect in New York (EDT) you need to add 4 hours to the local time to get GMT.

Bear in mind that British Standard Time is not the same thing as GMT. When Daylight Savings Time is in effect in the United Kingdom, it is an hour ahead of GMT, so one hour needs to be subtracted from the local clock time to get GMT.

Making the Most of Your Astrological Planner

At the most simple and basic level of engagement with your planner you can simply enjoy receiving a weekly heads-up on notable astrological events. Sometimes even seasoned and knowledgeable astrologers can lose track of basic but important things.

The comments that are provided at the commencement of every week are deliberately quite terse. They're essentially intended to point out some of the week's salient astrological events for your further consideration and reflection. They're the springboard to fuller insights and revelation rather than complete conclusions; they are only the first words, not the last. Use your astrological resources, references, acumen and intuition to embellish. Some of these weekly commentaries will point to distinct globally significant narratives you'll hear about in the news.

However, one of the most valuable features of this astrological planner is the ephemeris, the tables that provide basic data on the planets in their passage through the zodiac, and having this on hand means you can not only pay attention to what's happening in the sky generally, you can also keep an eye on your own personal transits. At the start of every month you'll find the ephemeris for that month along with a bird's eye view of the most notable astrological events. Wheel charts are shown for the New Moon and Full Moon in that month.

If you're watching your own personal transits, these general or globally active aspect combinations that are pointed out in the weekly commentary may alert you to particularly significant personal events.

Note that some of the weekly commentary refers to the 45 degree multiple aspects, the semi-square and sesquiquadrate, and these aspects are not listed in the planner's daily astro-data. We add these notes as a supplementary consideration.

Calculating Your Own Personal Transits Using the Ephemeris

Learning to calculate your own transits is perhaps the most important breakthrough in the journey of every astrologer. It's not particularly complicated, and yet it's endlessly fascinating and rewarding. This will be a very concise, but hopefully effective, description of the procedure.

In a nutshell, all you do is find aspects being formed between the transiting planetary positions and the planetary positions at birth. As a good general rule of thumb we're most interested in when these angles reach about 1 degree from exact. With conjunctions and oppositions the orb you use could be a little wider, but for the most part you'll find the relevant events tend to materialize right on time, when the angle is pretty close to exact.

Now, it happens to be very convenient that the most important and widely used aspects are all multiples of 30 degrees (except, technically, the conjunction of course). This is convenient because it means that whenever two planets occupy the same numbered degree of any two zodiac signs they are forming an aspect.

It's like playing Bingo! "I've got a transit here at 24 degrees – do we have any 24's in the birth chart?" Ah, Bingo! Transiting Mercury at 24° Aquarius is Sextile Natal Mars at 24° Aries (and so we may speculate that there will be lively discussions and debates, etc.).

Regulus 2025 Astrological Planner

Even if you're not very familiar with aspects just yet, rest assured that when the numbers match there's an aspect there; you just need to analyse the data and determine whether it's a conjunction, semi-sextile, sextile, square, trine, quincunx or opposition. With a little practice you'll soon know instantly which aspect it is.

From there you just let the symbols do the talking. Allow them to form sentences themselves. You can use the descriptions of the planets and aspects in this planner as a guide, or you can draw on other resources you might have access to. Planets in Transit by Robert Hand is a definitive reference for interpreting transits.

Look at the ephemeris for January 2025 on page 39. You'll see each planet has it's own column. It starts with Sun, then Moon, North Node of the Moon, Mercury, Venus, Mars etc. The zodiacal placements in this ephemeris are given for midnight GMT. The zodiac sign at the top of the column shows us which sign the planet is in at the start of the month. So, we can see that on the 1st of January 2025 the Sun was located at 10 degrees 48 minutes and 50 seconds Capricorn. For all practical purposes we can stick with the degrees only.

The Moon is the fastest moving of the planets. As a rule of thumb bear in mind the Moon moves approximately 1 degree every 2 hours. So, at midnight GMT on the 1st of January 2025 the Moon was located at 23 degrees, 54 minutes and 56 seconds. At 6:00am GMT that day the Moon will be approximately 3 degrees later. Again, we can stick to the nearest degree for most practical purposes and dispense with minutes and seconds.

So, considering that the Sun is located at 10 degrees Capricorn on the 1st of January, we could look for any planets in the example birth chart below, located at or near 10 degrees of any sign. We see the Ascendant is located at 11 degrees Capricorn and Saturn at 12 degrees Scorpio. So, this individual will have transiting Sun Conjunct Ascendant and then transiting Sun sextile natal Saturn at the very start of January 2025.

Note in the ephemeris on page 39 that transiting Mercury will be positioned at 21 degrees Sagittarius on the 2nd of January and then 22 degrees Sagittarius on the 3rd of January. Our subject has Moon at 21 degrees Taurus and Sun at 22 degrees Virgo. So, transiting Mercury forms aspects to the Moon and then Sun at the start of the month. More precisely, transiting Mercury is quincunx natal Moon and then square natal Sun. Around 6-7 January this relatively swift moving transiting Mercury will reach a conjunction with our subject's natal Neptune at 27 degrees Sagittarius, and thus our subject will be prone to "dreamy mind" experiences;

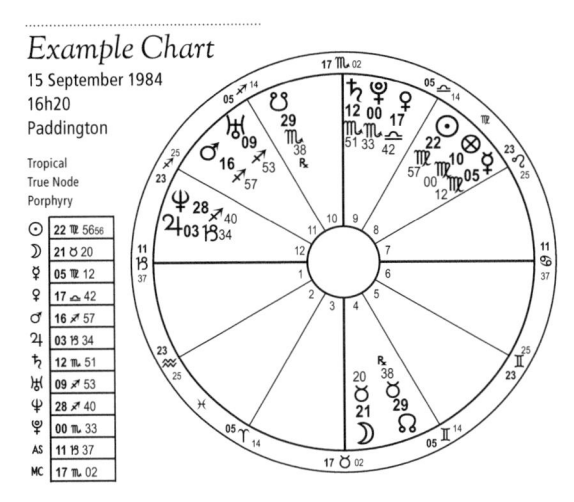

Example Chart
15 September 1984
16h20
Paddington

Tropical
True Node
Porphyry

☉ 22 ♍ 56 56
☽ 21 ♉ 20
☿ 05 ♍ 12
♀ 17 ♎ 42
♂ 16 ♐ 57
♃ 03 ♑ 34
♄ 12 ♏ 51
♅ 09 ♐ 53
♆ 28 ♐ 40
♇ 00 ♏ 33
AS 11 ♉ 37
MC 17 ♏ 02

abstract thinking, fuzzy logic, poetry, perhaps muddled accounting and vague communication, etc.

Mars starts the month at 1 degree 55 minutes Leo, but since Mars is retrograde, you'll see it's moving from there to 1 degree 35 Leo the next day, and then by the 7th of January Mars has moved back into Cancer. Look at our subject's natal chart placements. Pluto was located at 0 degrees Scorpio at the time of this person's birth, so when Mars in the first week of January moves back into 0 degrees Leo there will be an aspect, and it happens to be a square (which is potent). This is a very virulent energy and it implies that there will be assertiveness, determination and possible power struggles or fights.

Look at the ephemeris for January 2025, see that Saturn starts the month at 14 degrees 31 minutes Pisces. Saturn reaches 16 degrees Sagittarius on the 18th of January and will remain at that degree for about 10 days. Now, see that our subject's natal Mars is located at 16 degrees Sagittarius, and their natal Venus is at 17 degrees Libra. So, transiting Saturn will be aspecting this person's natal Mars and then Venus in the month of January 2025. Transiting Saturn will be square natal Mars and then quincunx natal Venus.

Our subject has natal Mercury at 5 degrees Virgo. Transiting Venus will reach 5 degrees Pisces on the 7th of January (at midnight on the 8th it's already at 5 degrees and 6 minutes Pisces). So, around that time our subject has transiting Venus opposition natal Mercury, and most likely there will be some sweet talk, "love letters" and friendly discussion. An interaction that is courteous. Expressing your views about or within a personal relationship.

These few examples should be just enough to help some intrepid astro-seekers to get cracking with exploring and magical wonder-world of transits.

Overview of the Year 2025

If there is a single event of special significance and importance in the year 2025 it's the conjunction of Saturn and Neptune near the first degree of tropical Aries. If you want to get very technical the conjunction does not become completely exact in 2025, but in July 2025 they come to within a fraction of a degree of an exact conjunction. It's a powerful alignment of significant factors. The first degree of tropical Aries is the place where the equinox occurs. This impact of this coming Saturn-Neptune conjunction, occurring as it does near the equinoctial point, is likely to be amplified and its effects may be more globally impactful than would otherwise have been the case.

The last time Saturn and Neptune formed a conjunction the Berlin Wall came tumbling down, and this of course was merely one notable localised symbolically resonant manifestation of the broader pattern, in that case the final dissolution of the Soviet Union. This pivotal historical event was linked to geopolitical power struggles that are once again simmering and threatening to reach a dangerous boiling point.

Neptune Conjunct Saturn dissolves and disintegrates. Things that were firm, collapse. This coming Saturn-Neptune conjunction almost certainly presages the redrawing of the world's maps in terms of states and sovereign territories.

But it would be a mistake, however, to assume that this coming Saturn-Neptune conjunction is essentially all about the most apparent border and territorial disputes on the world stage right now. That is certainly one area to watch, but there is a broader and more pervasive significance for society in this coming celestial omen. The degree of disillusionment regarding the state of the world and the way things are being done, and the clear and apparent inadequacy of the current system to truly address the legitimate rights and needs of people, will become a stark and unavoidable reality. This can manifest as a crisis, but hopefully one that leads to improvements. Things may become more humane only because they well and truly fell apart.

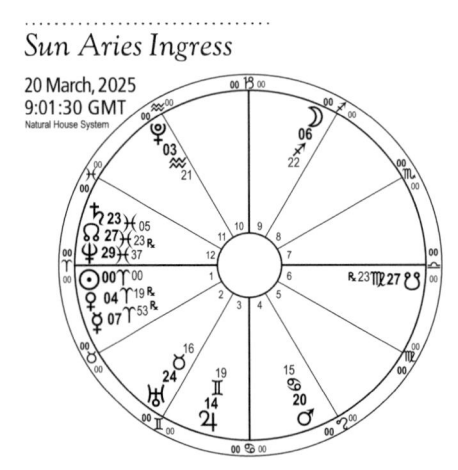

Sun Aries Ingress
20 March, 2025
9:01:30 GMT
Natural House System

Neptune is the most mystical and otherworldly of planets. It engages our most subtle and elusive psychological functions and triggers; it can induce mystical ecstasy or a total breakdown of coherence. Neptune can be chaotic. No single droplet is discernible in an ocean. As Neptune dissolves the usually rigid structures that give solidity, there could be events or discoveries that dramatically alter the way we view reality.

And speaking of oceans, legend has it that Neptune presides over that realm and in the context of this coming Saturn-Neptune conjunction, there could be some sort of maritime situation. Dirty or unruly waters, water supply disruption and floods. Some problems at sea, perhaps.

It is widely believed that a chart cast for the moment of the vernal equinox reveals the texture of the year ahead, and at the time of the equinox on the 20th of March 2025 Neptune is again brought into sharp focus since it will then be less than half a degree from the Sun. Mars will be trine Saturn and sextile Uranus, while there is an even tighter sextile of Saturn and Uranus.

This combination of influences seems to be indicative of strenuous efforts and rigorous work, but there is also the suggestion here of new innovative methodologies or technologies being employed. Adaptations to existing approaches can facilitate improved efficiency and a more rapid execution of tasks that once would have taken a far longer time to complete. On a more personal and intimate level the Moon being trine Venus and Mercury while Venus is sextile Pluto could speak of people devoting more time, care and attention to their personal relationships. There is a deeper appreciation of the value and

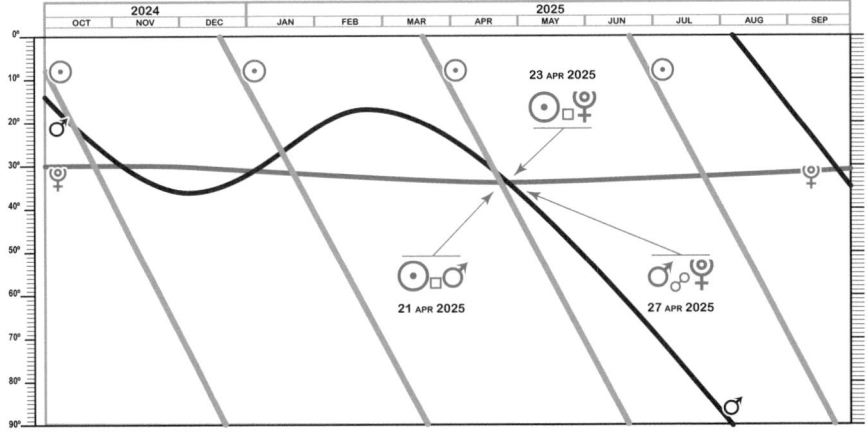

90° Graphic Ephemeris - Sun, Mars, Pluto T-Square

Regulus 2025 Astrological Planner

importance of friends and family and this can have a beneficial effect on mental and emotional well-being.

Towards the end of April 2025 Mars reaches an opposition to Pluto while both are square the Sun. This is one of the shorter term energy spikes that we should keep an eye on. It can bring conflict situations to a climax. It may even be that events around this time act as a potent trigger or catalyst for the dramatic social changes that appear to be imminent due to the looming Saturn-Neptune conjunction.

Jupiter will be square Saturn and Neptune around the very middle of June 2025. This will no doubt be a climactic moment in the year 2025. What happens then, and what is seeded or begins then will have a dramatic effect on the shape, and even the aspirations of society. It marks a fresh idealistic impetus, bogged down most likely in some manner. Perhaps a restorative impulse in the wake of collapsing systems.

June 2025 should be considered a particularly valuable opportunity to find solutions to things that are decaying, establish better principles to guide the way things get done in the world, and embark on a more altruistic and compassionate approach to societal systems. Necessity is the mother of invention.

This ray of hope for the month of June is reinforced by the fact that the Sun is relatively near Jupiter at the time of the Sun's ingress in Cancer (summer solstice in the Northern hemisphere) and then a few days later, on the 25th of June, there's a New Moon that occurs also very close to Jupiter. However, the "yod" configuration at the time of the solstice in June with Mars at the apex forming

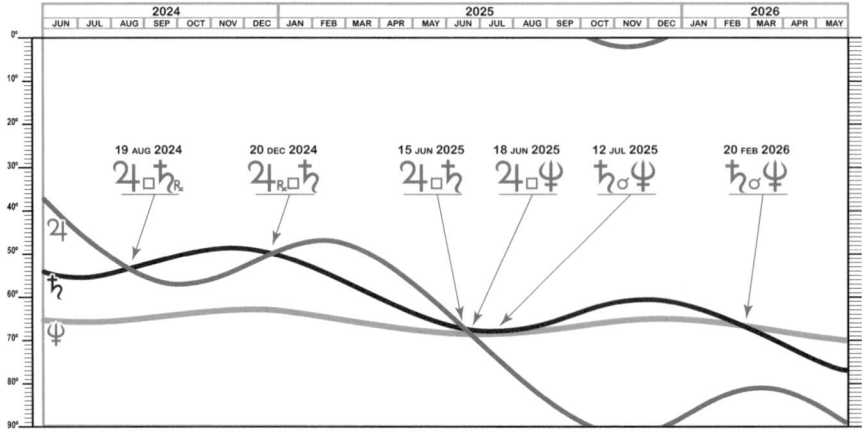

90° Graphic Ephemeris - Jupiter, Saturn & Neptune

Sun Cancer Ingress

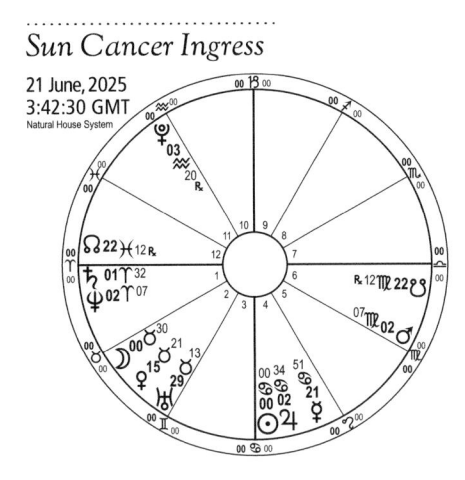

21 June, 2025
3:42:30 GMT
Natural House System

quincunx aspects to Saturn, Neptune and Pluto might be interpreted as some sort of veiled or sneaky aggressive act.

The idea that 2025 brings significant global changes is reinforced by the fact that there are several slow moving planets entering new signs of the zodiac; the year begins with Pluto in the first degree of Aquarius, Neptune enters Aries at the end of March, Saturn enters Aries in the last week of May, Jupiter enters Cancer in June and Uranus enters Gemini in July.

Around the end of July and early August Saturn, Uranus, Neptune and Pluto are all forming aspects to each other in the early degrees of their respective signs. In fact around this time Saturn and Neptune are both close to the midpoint of Uranus and Pluto. This looks like radical and probably sudden structural changes. There's an almost revolutionary quality to this combination; there may be strong social pressures or reactions to circumstances that have eroded the quality of people's lives.

A little later, during the second half of August, Jupiter forms a semi-square to Uranus which looks like an exciting breakthrough. New frontiers of knowledge or perhaps new frontiers in our exploration of the universe can occur. There is a greater openness to radical new viewpoints that free us from limiting traditional patterns of thought and belief.

The total lunar eclipse on the 7th of September occurs just slightly more than one degree from a semi-square to Pluto as well as forming a semi-square to the Uranus-Neptune midpoint. The fact that this lunar eclipse engages with the three outer planets makes it somewhat mysterious; there could be important global events occurring that are either distorted and obfuscated or they don't reach the public's awareness at all. Or, it could be that this eclipse is pointing to a strong spiritual or mystical impulse of some kind.

The partial solar eclipse of 21 September occurs in close opposition to Saturn and Neptune, and this may well turn out to be one of the most important and potent amplifications of the Saturn-Neptune process that plays such a dominant role in the year 2025.

Regulus 2025 Astrological Planner

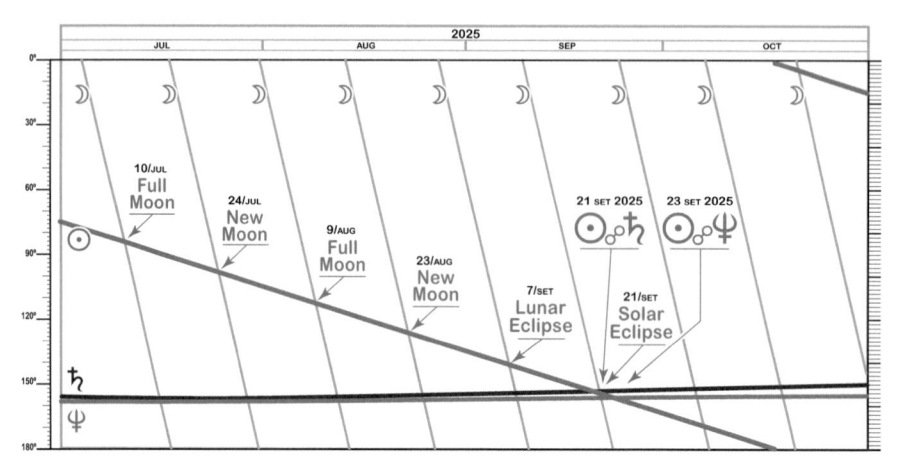

90° Graphic Ephemeris - Solar Eclipse opposite Saturn & Neptune

At the time of the Sun's ingress into Libra on the 22nd of September (autumn equinox in the Northern hemisphere) Mars is square Pluto and also forming a so-called "yod" configuration with the outer planets Uranus and Neptune. This hints at some sort of forceful and aggressive energy in the quarter that follows, and there may be something veiled about it, so that people don't know quite who or what is responsible. It hints at strong determination and energy directed towards uncommon or unconventional objectives.

During November Jupiter forms a trine to Saturn at 25 degrees Cancer and Pisces respectively. This would suggest a phase of relative equilibrium and constructive progress in social projects and some improvement in social cohesion. Obstacles and delays to economic progress are overcome and there is a sound vision charting the way forward.

Sun Libra Ingress
22 September, 2025
19:19:30 GMT
Natural House System

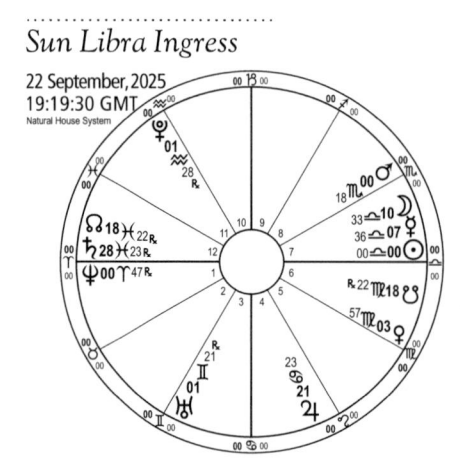

At the time of the Sun's ingress into Capricorn (the Northern hemisphere's mid-winter solstice) Venus is square Saturn and Neptune while also forming a quincunx aspect to Uranus. Personal and romantic relationships are subject to disruptions and separations. On a more impersonal and social level, the trine of Jupiter and Saturn promises economic recovery

14

Sun Capricorn Ingress

21 December, 2025
15:03 GMT
Natural House System

Overall it's hard not to be concerned about what the year 2025 will bring us, especially in light of the world's rather precarious current state. We may not be able to rely as fully as before on the traditional systems and structures that normally keep society functioning more or less smoothly. This may confront us with the need to take fuller personal responsibility for our health and our basic welfare.

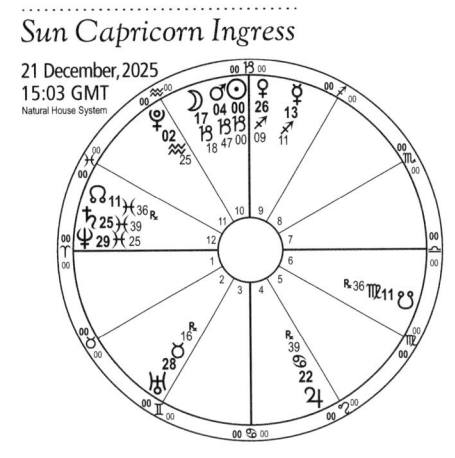

in the months immediately after the solstice.

The silver lining here is the fact that when the inherent fragility of social systems and structures is laid bare it all but forces a fundamental revision of our social institutions and our assumptions about how things ought to be done. Changes that have become long overdue may eventually be implemented, hopefully in a manner that ensures greater protection and safeguards for the well-being of regular people. There could, in fact, be a profound transformation in the value systems that inspire and direct decisions by those controlling the levers of society. It is not improbable that a more spiritual and humane society will emerge from the problems we are likely to be confronting in 2025.

The Lunar Cycle

The phases of the Moon

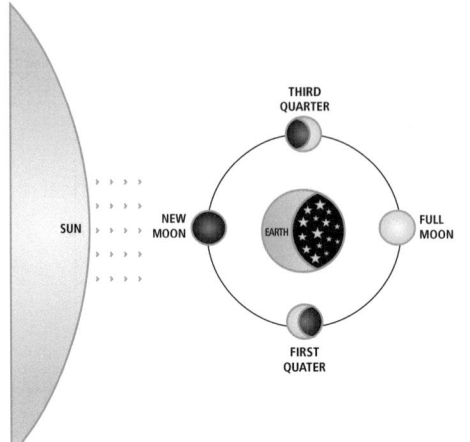

The phases of the Moon are the result of the relationship between the Sun and the Moon. Every week the Moon forms a so called "hard aspect" with the Sun, either a conjunction (New Moon), a square (First Quarter or Third Quarter) or an opposition (Full Moon). These aspects mark the quarterly phases of the Moon cycle. Each of these junctures in the lunar cycle sets the tone for the coming days.

The **New Moon** is a period of subjective or inner focus. Fantasy and reality blend together, making this period a propitious time to analyze dreams, meditate and discover new inner pathways. New plans and intentions can emerge from this introspective period.

During the **First Quarter** it is appropriate to review and adjust the plans created during the New Moon, and so there may be a sense of urgency. The 90 degree angle between the Sun and the Moon results in a tense situation that requires decision and the courage to discard what is no longer working.

The **Full Moon** brings fruition to developing projects and processes, whether it is a professional project, a romantic relationship or an analytical problem. The situation reaches a peak phase, a climax, resolution or important revelation.

During the **Last Quarter** the results of past efforts are revealed. Alternatively, we begin a process of cleansing and disintegration in preparation for the new cycle that is about to begin at the next New Moon.

The **Waxing** Period of the Moon occurs between the New and the Full Moon. As the increase in light suggests, this is a time for expansion in our projects and endeavors. Growth and nourishment are some of the key words associated with this period.

The **Waning** Period of the Moon occurs between the Full and the New Moon. The waning appearance of the Moon suggests a time of introversion, contraction and purification. This is an appropriate time to clear away the old and make room for the new.

Lunations 2025

First Quarter	Full Moon	Last Quarter	New Moon	First Quarter
16 ♈ 56 Jan 6	24 ♋ 00 Jan 13	02 ♏ 03 Jan 21	09 ♒ 51 Jan 29	
16 ♉ 46 Feb 5	24 ♌ 06 Feb 12	02 ♐ 20 Feb 20	09 ♓ 41 Feb 28	
16 ♊ 21 Mar 6	23 ♍ 59 Mar 14	02 ♑ 05 Mar 22	08 ♈ 53 Mar 29	
15 ♋ 33 Apr 5	23 ♎ 20 Apr 13	01 ♒ 12 Apr 21	07 ♉ 47 Apr 27	
14 ♌ 21 May 4	22 ♏ 13 May 12	29 ♒ 43 May 20	06 ♊ 06 May 27	
12 ♍ 50 Jun 3	20 ♐ 39 Jun 11	27 ♓ 48 Jun 18	04 ♋ 08 Jun 25	
11 ♎ 10 Jul 2	18 ♑ 50 Jul 10	25 ♈ 40 Jul 18	02 ♌ 08 Jul 24	
09 ♏ 32 Aug 1	17 ♒ 00 Aug 9	23 ♉ 36 Aug 16	00 ♍ 23 Aug 23	08 ♐ 07 Aug 31
	15 ♓ 24 Sep 7	21 ♊ 52 Sep 14	28 ♍ 59 Sep 21	07 ♑ 06 Sep 29
	14 ♈ 08 Oct 7	20 ♋ 40 Oct 13	28 ♎ 22 Oct 21	06 ♒ 30 Oct 29
	13 ♉ 23 Nov 5	20 ♌ 05 Nov 12	28 ♏ 12 Nov 20	06 ♓ 18 Nov 28
	13 ♊ 04 Dec 4	20 ♍ 04 Dec 11	28 ♐ 25 Dec 20	06 ♈ 17 Dec 27
	13 ♋ 02 Jan 3	20 ♎ 25 Jan 10	28 ♑ 44 Jan 18	06 ♉ 14 Jan 26

Regulus 2025 Astrological Planner

Eclipses in Astrology

The Moon and Earth form long, conical shadows that project into space, called the umbra and penumbra. Eclipses occur when the Sun, Moon and Earth are in alignment and these shadows reach the Earth's surface during a New Moon (Solar Eclipse) – or the Moon's surface during a Full Moon (Lunar Eclipse).

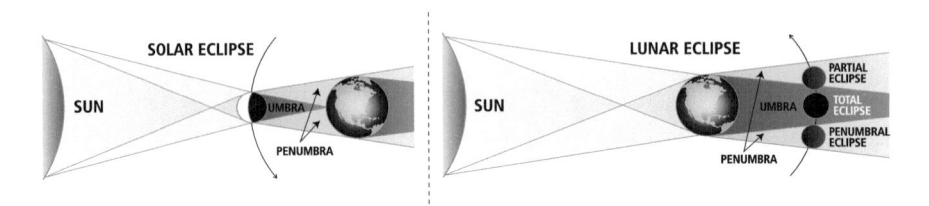

The Lunar Nodes represent the intersection between the Moon's orbit and the Sun's apparent path (the Ecliptic). They are stationary for 2 to 3 months twice a year – during which Eclipses occur, in Solar and Lunar pairs, normally 4 per year.

Our ancient astrological ancestors, the Chaldeans, discovered a repetitive pattern of Eclipses called the Saros Cycle, which is a sequence of Eclipses that occur every 18 years ± 10 days.

Eclipses have a distinct effect on human beings, even more intense if we are located on their path. During Lunar Eclipses, the shadows projected represent our subconscious, requiring of us to confront our fears, unresolved past situations or old traumas that may rise to the surface without warning.

Solar Eclipses, despite being less emotional than Lunar Eclipses, affect our lives in a more concrete way, culminating in circumstances that require definitive actions that will have long-term effects. Actions and decisions at these times have profound repercussions.

Eclipses are related to endings and new beginnings, and can represent losses or separations, moving to distant places or changing marital status. The changes represented by Eclipses can be related to any area of our lives, so take a look at the house in your natal chart where the Eclipse occurs for indications regarding which areas of your life will be affected.

Other important dates are the lunations that occur 90 days after the Eclipse and form a square to the degree at which the Eclipse occurred. On this date (±1 week) the unfolding events will often be a culmination of what was triggered during the Eclipse.

Eclipses in 2025

Drawings are visual representations and may not follow the Eclipse path exactly.

Total Lunar Eclipse

🌑 **23 ♏ 59**

March 14 - 06:58:44 UTC

Nature: Total
Umbral Mag. : 1.1784
Saros Series: 123 - 53 of 73

Visibility: Pacific Ocean, Americas, Western Europe, West Africa

Partial Solar Eclipse

☀ **08 ♈ 53**

March 29 - 10:48:36 UTC

Nature: Partial - Magnitude: 0.9376
Saros Series: 149 - 21 of 71

Visibility: Northeastern United States, Eastern Canada, Greenland, Europe, northwest Africa, and northern Russia.

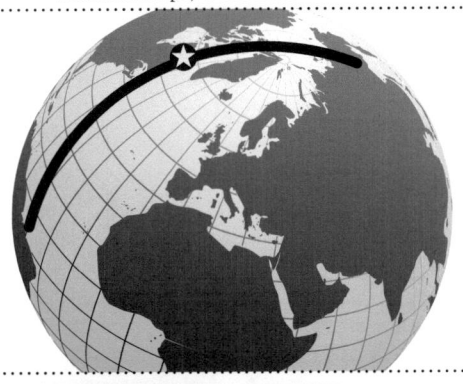

Total Lunar Eclipse

🌑 **15 ♓ 24**

Sept 7 - 18:11:43 UTC

Nature: Total
Umbral Mag. : 1.3619
Saros Series: 128 - 41 of 71

Visibility: Asia, Australia and East Africa, setting over East Asia and New Zealand.

Partial Solar Eclipse

☀ **28 ♍ 59**

Sept 21 - 19:43:04 UTC

Nature: Partial - Magnitude: 0.8550
Saros Series: 154 - Membro: 7 of 71

Visibility: Most of Oceania and Antarctica, with up to 73% visible coverage in New Zealand.

2025

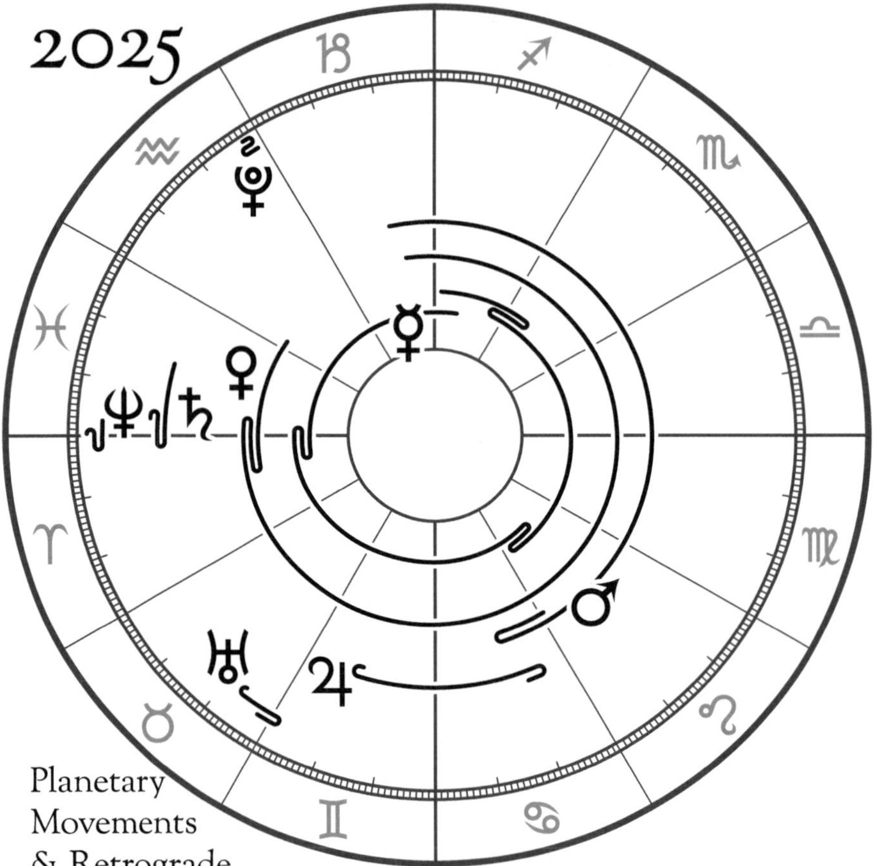

Planetary Movements & Retrograde Periods

All planets except the Sun and the Moon go retrograde from time to time. These periods do not always dramatically affect our daily lives, but are times when we can review concepts related to the areas of life ruled by that planet.

RETROGRADE PERIODS FOR THE PLANETS IN 2025

☿℞ Mar **15** **09**♈35	☿D Apr **7** **26**♓50	♃D Feb **4** **11**♊17	♃℞ Nov **11** **25**♋09
☿℞ Jul **17** **15**♌35	☿D Aug **11** **04**♌15	♄℞ Jul **12** **01**♈56	♄D Nov **27** **25**♓09
☿℞ Nov **9** **06**♐52	☿D Nov **29** **20**♏42	♅D Jan **30** **23**♉16	♅℞ Sep **5** **01**♊28
♀℞ Mar **1** **10**♈50	♀D Apr **12** **24**♓37	♆℞ Jul **4** **02**♈11	♆D Dec **10** **29**♓22
♂℞ Dec **06/24** **06**♌10	♂D Feb **23** **17**♋01	♇℞ May **4** **03**♒49	♇D Oct **13** **01**♒22

THIS YEAR THE PLANETS START AND END AT THE FOLLOWING POSITIONS (GMT)

	☿	♀	♂	♃	♄	♅	♆	♇
Jan 1	**19**♐52	**27**♒43	**01**♌55℞	**13**♊13℞	**14**♓31	**23**♉38℞	**27**♓18	**01**♒04
Dec 31	**28**♐39	**09**♑12	**12**♑41	**21**♋21℞	**26**♓10	**27**♉57℞	**29**♓30	**02**♒43

Astronomical Events

Perihelion Earth is closest to the Sun	Jan 4
Quadrantids Meteor Shower Look at the direction of Boötes Constellation	Jan 3, 4 peak
Mars in Opposition to the Sun Closest to Earth and totally illuminated	Jan 16
Sun and Saturn in Conjunction Saturn at 1.5° North in Latitude from Sun	Mar 12 10:29 GMT
Spring Equinox (Northern Hemisphere) Sun over Equator in Tropical Aries	Mar 20 9:01 GMT
Lyrid Meteor Shower Look at the direction of Lyra Constellation	Apr 22, 23 peak
Eta-Aquarid Meteor Shower Radiant from Aquarius Constellation	May 6, 7 peak
Summer Solstice (Northern Hemisphere) Sun at 23°44' N. in Tropical Cancer	Jun 21 2:42 GMT
Aphelion Earth is furthest from the Sun	Jul 3
Delta Aquarid Meteor Shower Radiant from Aquarius Constellation	Jul 28, 29 peak
Perseid Meteor Shower Radiant from Perseus Constellation	Aug 12, 13 peak
Saturn in Opposition to the Sun Closest to Earth and totally illuminated	Sep 21
Autumn Equinox (Northern Hemisphere) Sun over Equator in Tropical Libra	Sep 22 18:19 GMT
Netune in Opposition to the Sun Closest to Earth and totally illuminated	Sep 23
Draconid Meteor Shower Radiant from Draco Constellation	Oct 7 peak
Orionid Meteor Shower Look at the direction of Orion Constellation	Oct 21, 22 peak
Taurid Meteor Shower Look at the direction of Taurus Constellation	Nov 4, 5 peak
Leonid Meteor Shower Look at the direction of Leo Constellation	Nov 17, 18 peak
Uranus in Opposition to the Sun Closest to Earth and totally illuminated	Nov 21
Jupiter in Opposition to the Sun Closest to Earth and totally illuminated	Dec 7
Geminid Meteor Shower Look at the direction of Gemini Constellation	Dec 13 peak
Ursid Meteor Shower Look at the direction of Ursa Minor Constellation	Dez 21, 22 peak
Winter Solstice (Northern Hemisphere) Sun a 23°44' S. in Tropical Capricorn	Dez 21 12:03 BZT

Occultations are when the Moon aligns precisely in front of another Planet creating a perfect conjunction.

OCCULTATIONS by the Moon

☽☌♄	Jan 4	14♓49
☽☌♂℞	Jan 14	26♋59
☽☌♄	Feb 1	17♓27
☽☌♂℞	Feb 9	18♋20
☽☌☿	Mar 1	26♓35
☽☌♂	Mar 8	18♋00
☽☌♂	Jun 1	21♌18
☽☌♂	Jun 29	07♍13
☽☌♂	Jul 28	24♍19
☽☌♀	Sep 19	29♌59

Visible in the Sky in 2025

Morning and Evening Twilight

☿ - Mercury

Evening	*Morning*
March 8 Grt. Elongation - 18.2° E	March 8 Grt. Elongation - 27.4° W
July 4 Grt. Elongation - 25.9° E	Aug 19 Grt. Elongation - 18.6° W
October 29 Grt. Elongation - 23.9° E	October 29 Grt. Elongation - 20.7° W

♀ - Venus

Evening	*Morning*
January 9 Grt. Elongation - 47.2° E	May 31 Grt. Elongation - 45.9° W

♂ - Mars

Opposition

January 16

Best time for visibility

♃ - Jupiter

Conjunction	*Opposition*
June 24 Not visible	January 10, 2026 Best time for visibility

♄ - Saturn

Conjunction	*Opposition*
March 12 Not visible	September 21 Best time for visibility

Mercury is visible near the horizon during its greatest elongation, and can be seen for several days on either side of this date. It is best seen ~45 minutes after dusk when evening or before dawn when morning.

Venus is the brightest star, and each appearance lasts for several months. During its greatest elongation, Venus rises approximately 3 hours before the Sun (Morning Star) and sets about 3 hours after the Sun (Evening Star).

Mars reaches opposition on January 16, 2025, the best date for observation, but is visible most of the year.

Planetary Days and Planetary Hours

The days of the week were actually named after the seven planets of ancient astrology. This is very obvious in many languages. Although it's not often discussed in modern astrology books it is a deeply rooted and ancient astrological principle that the energy or quality of the week days are actually colored by the planets they are named after.

- ☉ - Sunday is ruled by the Sun
- ☽ - Monday is ruled by the Moon
- ♂ - Tuesday is ruled by Mars
- ☿ - Wednesday is ruled by Mercury
- ♃ - Thursday is ruled by Jupiter
- ♀ - Friday is ruled by Venus
- ♄ - Saturday is ruled by Saturn

It is, for example, ideal to perform Mercurial activities on a Wednesday. Therefor a Wednesday should be good for delivering messages, making phone-calls, embarking on relatively short journeys, learning and generally being adaptable, mobile and communicative. Friday, being ruled by Venus, should be auspicious for marriage, social engagements, sensuous pleasures and beautification. Tuesdays, being Mars ruled, would be suitable for vigorous and dynamic activities such as wars, disputes or activities requiring aggression, cutting or scorching (the fateful date of 11 September 2001 was a Tuesday, no less). It would appear that Moondays ought to be domesticated, dreamy and docile days, good for mothering and sailing and visiting the pub. Common day to day life.

This planetary day principle is one of many which are held in common by both the Western and Vedic astrological systems. Vedic astrology emphasizes this idea quite a bit more than does western astrology, and in that system the planets are almost invariably listed in the weekday order; Sun, then Moon, then Mars, then Mercury, Jupiter, Venus and, finally, Saturn. The sabbath. The stoppage. The end.

Vedic astrology employs prayers, mantras, rituals, gemstones and other remedial measures more regularly and systematically than is done in the west. The planetary weekday scheme is much used in this context. So, for example, if one is purchasing, or going to commence wearing a gem ruled by Mercury, and/or reciting mantras of Mercury, one would tend to do so on a Wednesday (ideally under a Waxing Moon, etc.). In a very similar vein western practitioners of ceremonial magic use the same scheme to choose appropriate times for rituals, or the making or consecration of talismans, and so on.

It is furthermore true that both Western and Vedic astrology divide each of these planetary weekdays into 24 planetary hours in much the same way, and it is believed that the first hour of a day is governed by the same planet that governs that same particular weekday. So, for example, the first hour of Sunday would be the Sun Hour, the first hour of a Tuesday would be Mars Hour, and so on. The first hour is usually said to commence at sunrise, and the amount of time between sunrise and sunset will be equally divided among the first twelve planetary hours of the day. The final twelve planetary hours will be evenly distributed within the time between sunset and the following sunrise. Therefor, a planetary hour may be somewhat longer or shorter than our usual clock time hours.

The planetary hours follow a set sequence, different to the weekday order. After the ruler of the weekday has enjoyed the first hour after sunrise, the following sequence is followed; Saturn, Jupiter, Mars, Sun, Venus, Mercury, Moon.

So, on a Friday, the first hour after sunrise belongs to Venus, next is Mercury Hour, then Moon Hour, then Saturn Hour, then Jupiter, and so on.

The following tabulation should be of help.

	Sunday	Monday	Tuesday	Wednesday	Thursday	Friday	Saturday
1	Sun	Moon	Mars	Mercury	Jupiter	Venus	Saturn
2	Venus	Saturn	Sun	Moon	Mars	Mercury	Jupiter
3	Mercury	Jupiter	Venus	Saturn	Sun	Moon	Mars
4	Moon	Mars	Mercury	Jupiter	Venus	Saturn	Sun
5	Saturn	Sun	Moon	Mars	Mercury	Jupiter	Venus
6	Jupiter	Venus	Saturn	Sun	Moon	Mars	Mercury
7	Mars	Mercury	Jupiter	Venus	Saturn	Sun	Moon
8	Sun	Moon	Mars	Mercury	Jupiter	Venus	Saturn
9	Venus	Saturn	Sun	Moon	Mars	Mercury	Jupiter
10	Mercury	Jupiter	Venus	Saturn	Sun	Moon	Mars
11	Moon	Mars	Mercury	Jupiter	Venus	Saturn	Sun
12	Saturn	Sun	Moon	Mars	Mercury	Jupiter	Venus
13	Jupiter	Venus	Saturn	Sun	Moon	Mars	Mercury
14	Mars	Mercury	Jupiter	Venus	Saturn	Sun	Moon
15	Sun	Moon	Mars	Mercury	Jupiter	Venus	Saturn
16	Venus	Saturn	Sun	Moon	Mars	Mercury	Jupiter
17	Mercury	Jupiter	Venus	Saturn	Sun	Moon	Mars
18	Moon	Mars	Mercury	Jupiter	Venus	Saturn	Sun
19	Saturn	Sun	Moon	Mars	Mercury	Jupiter	Venus
20	Jupiter	Venus	Saturn	Sun	Moon	Mars	Mercury
21	Mars	Mercury	Jupiter	Venus	Saturn	Sun	Moon
22	Sun	Moon	Mars	Mercury	Jupiter	Venus	Saturn
23	Venus	Saturn	Sun	Moon	Mars	Mercury	Jupiter
24	Mercury	Jupiter	Venus	Saturn	Sun	Moon	Mars

The Planets

The Sun

Rulership: Leo | Detriment: Aquarius | Exaltation: Aries | Fall: Libra

The Sun is quite obviously the vital core of the Solar System. Your astrological inner Sun may similarly be seen as the vital core of your being. We may even call it your Soul. The Sun represents your identity, and it is often seen as a barometer of one's vitality, confidence and capacity for positions of authority and leadership. The Sun may be associated with the government and officials, as well as all regal and dignified persons.

Positive: Self-esteem; leadership, creativity, and love radiating from the solar plexus.

Negative: Pride, arrogance, egocentricity, excessive desire to be unique and special.

Astronomical Facts: The Sun, the central star of the Solar System, has 8 Planets in its orbit. In order: Mercury, Venus, Earth, Mars, Jupiter, Saturn, Uranus and Neptune. In the Asteroid Belt between Mars and Jupiter there is the dwarf planet Ceres, and another binary dwarf planet, Pluto, after Neptune. The Sun, seen from Earth, takes approximately one year to go around the Zodiac, staying in each sign for approximately one month. The Sun does not retrograde and advances approximately 1° per day.

The Moon

Rulership: Cancer | Detriment: Capricorn | Exaltation: Taurus | Fall: Scorpio

The Moon is the archetypal Mother, and represents women in general. It is associated with feelings, instincts, emotional sensitivity, nurturing, nourishing, the home, and family life. The Moon represents familiar environments, our past (often as memories and emotional attachments), and the most basic and instinctive levels of our awareness. The habits and automatic responses that largely shape our personalities are essentially lunar.

Positive: Nurturing, inclusion, empathy, fluidity of feelings, positive family relationships.

Negative: Over-sensitivity and insecurity, negativity, alienation, shyness and inhibition

Astronomical Facts: The Moon, Earth's natural satellite, is ¼ the size of the planet it orbits and is 384,400 km from Earth. The Moon, seen from Earth, takes approximately 1 month to orbit the Zodiac, staying in each sign for approximately 2.5 days. The Moon does not retrograde and advances on average approximately 13° per day. With an orbital period of 27.32 days and a synodic period of 29.53 days.

Mercury

Rulership: Gemini & Virgo | Detriment: Sagittarius & Pisces | Exaltation: Virgo | Fall: Pisces

Mercury is a clever little youth, associated with intelligence, learning, communication, and mobility (short journeys). Mercury is eloquent and associated with all little detailed things. Letters, paperwork, news and information, and negotiations are all associated with Mercury. There is often a "mercantile" orientation to Mercury. Anything tiny, diminutive, speckled, variegated and rapid.

Positive: Intellectuality, analytic method, logic, ease and charm, sociability, clear communication

Negative: Superficiality, thoughtless and tactless in their speech, repeatedly changing interests, gossip, plagiarism.

Astronomical Facts: Mercury, the first planet in the Solar System, is 58 million km from the Sun and takes less than 3 months to orbit the Sun. It retrogrades between 20 and 24 days 3 times a year (18%). It has a Sidereal period of 87.97 days and a Synodic period of 115.88 days.

Venus

Rulership: Taurus & Libra | Detriment: Scorpio & Aries | Exaltation: Pisces | Fall: Virgo

Venus is well known in mythology as the goddess of love and beauty, and this is also largely the astrological connotation. Venus is by nature sweet, gentle, comfortable, harmonious and peaceful. She is associated with romance, as well as more platonic affection and friendship. Venus is attractive, friendly, sociable and charming and likes fashion, art and decoration.

Positive: Magnetism and attractiveness, pleasant and likeable manner, solidarity and cooperation.

Negative: Greed and envy, discord and malice, seduction, laziness and sleaziness.

Astronomical Facts: Venus, the second planet in the Solar System, is at an average distance of 108.2 million km from the Sun and takes less than 2/3 of a year to orbit the Sun. It retrogrades between 40 and 43 days once every 1 ½ years (7.7%). It has a Sidereal period of 224.7 days and a Synodic period of 583.9 days.

Mars

Rulership: Aries & Scorpio | Detriment: Libra & Taurus | Exaltation: Capricorn | Fall: Cancer

Mars, the God of War and slaughter, is symbolised by the shield and sword, and the physical planet itself has a reddish hue to it. This quite aptly expresses the aggressiveness and vigour of the planet, which inflames passion and urges one to act and pursue objectives through daring and self-assertion. The energy of Mars is hot, sharp, and piercing. Ideally Mars, the archetypal warrior, is a dynamic energizer. At worst he incites violence and reckless actions, and therefore accidents and disruption are associated with the planet.

Positive: Courageous, defender of principles, protector of the weak, independence and dynamism

Negative: Very aggressive, seeks and causes conflicts; destroyer of life and beauty; brutal and pernicious.

Astronomical Facts: Mars, the fourth planet in the Solar System, is at an average distance of 227.9 million km from the Sun and takes approximately 2 years to orbit the Sun. It retrogrades between 58 and 81 days every 2 years (9.5%). It has a Sidereal period of 687 days and a Synodic period of 779.9 days.

Jupiter

Rulership: Sagittarius & Pisces | Detriment: Gemini & Virgo | Exaltation: Cancer | Fall: Capricorn

Jupiter, the King of the Gods, also known as Zeus in mythology, is a big and beneficent personage in the planetary family. Wise, wealthy and jovial. Jupiter brings good fortune, expansion, growth and faith wherever he is located or to whatever he influences. Jupiter is associated with long-distance journeys and faraway people and places. He presides over religious beliefs, and moral or ethical values, as well as those social institutions that provide care and protection, or preserve and disseminate knowledge.

Positive: Trust and faith; optimism, wisdom and ethical principles; benefactor and abundant provider.

Negative: Limitless exaggeration; promises more than it can deliver; moral preaching and deception.

Astronomical Facts: Jupiter, the fifth and largest planet in the Solar System, is at an average distance of approx. 741 million km (4.95 AU) from the Sun and takes approximately 11.9 years to orbit the Sun (and the Zodiac), staying in each sign for approximately 1 year. It retrogrades 4 months each year (33%). It advances approximately 30° per year (40° direct, 10° retrograde). With a Sidereal period of 11.89 years and a Synodic period of 399 days.

Saturn

Rulership: Capricorn & Aquarius | Detriment: Cancer & Leo | Exaltation: Libra | Fall: Aries

Saturn in mythology, the Lord of Time, is Kronos. God of Agriculture, the founder of cities and civilization, Saturn is often associated with the role of father, or more generally, the idea of an elder or authority figure. Saturn furthermore has a bearing on our own social status and standing, our work and our professional goals, our worldly duties, and generally the structure of our lives. We especially tend to look to the parent of the same sex as ourselves to help us define our social roles and responsibilities.

Positive: Peace through order, control and balance, preservation and distribution, realism and discernment.

Negative: Coldness, lack of emotions; dry and unexpressive; secluded, depressed, disinterested.

Astronomical Facts: Saturn, the sixth planet in the Solar System, is at an average distance of approx. 1.4 billion km (9.6 AU) from the Sun and takes approximately 29 years to orbit the Sun (and the Zodiac), staying in each sign for approximately 2 and a half years. It retrogrades 4 ½ months each year (37.5%). It advances approximately 12° to 15° per year (18°-21° direct, 6°-7° retrograde).

Uranus

Uranus has been called an "awakener", and also a "rebel", and the effect of Uranus tends to be sudden, startling and dazzling. Uranus is brilliant and innovative, and it is a peculiar astronomical fact that the axial tilt of Uranus is extremely irregular, compared to the other planets.

Uranus "electrifies", inducing an accelerated tempo of events and experiences. At best Uranus is progressive and triggers liberating realisations. At worst, its influence causes chaotic, wayward unpredictability and volatility.

Astronomical Facts: Uranus, the seventh planet in the Solar System, is at an average distance of approx. 2.88 billion km (19.2 AU) from the Sun and takes approximately 84 years to orbit the Sun (and the Zodiac), staying in each sign for approximately 7 years. It retrogrades for about 5.1 months each year (42%). It advances approximately 4° per year (8° direct, 4° retrograde). It has a Sidereal period of 84.02 years and a Synodic period of 370 days.

Neptune

Neptune is associated with the illusive world of imagination, fantasy, dreams, intoxication, psychic experiences, and mystical or otherworldly phenomena. Spirituality, compassion and empathy are also regularly associated with this planet. Neptune produces sensitivity and vulnerability on various levels, but a strong and positively expressed Neptune will contribute to sensitivity and compassion for others, making Neptunian types empathic by nature.

Astronomical Facts: Neptune, the eighth planet in the Solar System, is at an average distance of approx. 4.5 billion km (30 AU) from the Sun and takes approximately 165 years to orbit the Sun (and the Zodiac), staying in each sign for approximately 14 years. It retrogrades for about 5.2 months each year (43%). It advances approximately 2.25° per year (5° direct, 2.75° retrograde). With a Sidereal period of 164.79 years and a Synodic period of 367.4 days.

Pluto*

The astrological Pluto is associated with transformation, or what could be described as a death-rebirth process. Pluto energy is deep, powerful, and volcanic, and it often seems to produce a purging effect. Pluto destroys in order to renew, represents the recovery of buried emotions and the power of transformation that can bring healing, upliftment, and regeneration to society.

Astronomical Facts: Pluto, the only planet in the Solar System to be a binary, is at an average distance of approx. 5.9 billion km (39.5 AU) from the Sun, with the most elliptical orbit of the Planets and takes about 248 years to go around the Sun (and the Zodiac), its stay in each sign is varied approximately 31 years in Taurus, but only 11 years in Scorpio. It retrogrades for about 5.3 months each year (44%). It advances approximately 2.25° per year (5° direct, 2.75° retrograde).

*Unlike Uranus and Neptune, which are gas giants, Pluto inhabits the remote trans-Neptunian region of the Solar System called the Kuiper Belt, where many small objects orbit. In 2006, with the discovery of other objects apparently as large or larger than Pluto in this region, Pluto was classified as a dwarf planet, as was Ceres (located in the asteroid belt between Mars and Jupiter), which was reclassified from an asteroid to a dwarf planet. During its 75 years as a planet in the Solar System, Pluto gained a notable astrological reputation through transits and generational expressions, thus maintaining its astrological attributions.

The Signs of the Zodiac

♈ Aries (21 March to 20 April)
Ruling Planet: Mars | Polarity: Masculine | Element: Fire | Modality: Cardinal.

Aries is the first sign of the zodiac, representing the pure impulse to be, to begin, to be born, and to do. Aries is the "big bang". The vigorous first impulse that gets things started. It is associated with qualities of impatience and assertiveness upon the environment. Aries is dynamic and pioneering, impulsive and impetuous. In a sense, Aries is the infant of the zodiac, bursting into the world in direct, open and unambiguous self-affirmation. But they have eleven further stages of "self-unfolding" still to be assimilated and integrated. Rams are known for butting heads with other Rams, and this aptly depicts the competitive spirit of Aries who rushes headlong into things, without much planning or forethought. Aries belongs to the dynamic Cardinal Cross and the feisty Fire Triplicity.

♉ Taurus (21 April to 21 May)
Ruling Planet: Venus | Polarity: Feminine | Element: Earth | Modality: Fixed.

The Bull is a solid and voluptuous bulk of creature: determined, slow, sure, and steady in their movement. They tend to calmly go about the pleasurable tasks of fulfilling their basic needs, like self- nourishment and procreation. The Bull is a symbol of material abundance and earthy fertility. Taurus is associated with property and financial matters, and tends to be possessive and materialistic. If Aries is the newborn infant, Taurus is a baby settling into the physical world, stabilising and anchoring itself, and growing in strength and stability. Taurus belongs to the Fixed Cross and Earth Triplicity, and is ruled by the beautiful, sensuous and amorous planet Venus.

♊ Gemini (22 May to 21 June)
Ruling Planet: Marcury | Polarity: Masculine | Element: Ar | Modality: Mutable.

The image of the young Twins represents the youthful curiosity and communicativeness of the sign Gemini.Gemini represents basic literacy, the process of learning to interact with the people and things in one's immediate environment. It also represents our ability to physically travel over relatively short distances. It is associated with the desire to learn, mimic, and pick up the lingo used in the environment, and represents multiplicity and diversity, as well as physical and mental dexterity and mobility. Gemini belongs to the Mutable Cross, and the Air Triplicity, and is ruled by the clever and versatile planet Mercury.

♋ Cancer (22 June to 22 July)
Ruling Planet: Moon | Polarity: Feminine | Element: Water | Modality: Cardinal.

A Crab is a ravenous but careful creature, retreating into its shell at the slightest sign of danger. This sign is extremely sensitive and has a great need for safety, and yet the prominent claws might represent acquisitiveness and tenacity. The crab is wary of intrusions from the outside, but is protective and caring towards those that are familiar and part of its intimate sphere. Cancer is the Cardinal-Water sign of the zodiac, and is ruled by the archetypal mother of the planetary family, the Moon. This private and domestic inner life needs to be healthy and secure for public and professional potentials associated with Capricorn, the opposite sign, to thrive. Family units or households constitute the building blocks, and are in a sense the foundation of the larger social order; a town, nation or civilization.

♌ Leo (23 July to 22 August)
Ruling Planet: Sun | Polarity: Masculine | Element: Fire | Modality: Fixed.

The Lion is the "King of the Jungle": a symbol of authority, majesty and power, representing the blossoming of the individual's creative vitality. Leo is ruled by the Sun, the most radiant of the "planets" (the Sun is a luminar) and this again represents the power, vitality and individual grandeur associated with this sign. Even so, Leo is perhaps the most truly generous sign, since it is the natural instinct of a "king" to patronise his subjects. Leo needs to be acknowledged, and cannot bear to go unnoticed. Leo belongs to the Fixed Cross and Fire Triplicity and could thus be considered the most stable and steadily focused of the Fire signs, while perhaps being the most lively, energetic and volatile of the Fixed signs.

♍ Virgo (23 August to 22 September)
Ruling Planet: Marcury | Polarity: Feminine | Element: Earth | Modality: Mutable.

The symbol of a virgin represents the idea of pristine purity and perfection. Virgo is often depicted as a woman holding ears of wheat, which hints at a knowledge of sowing, harvesting, food processing and agriculture, and more generally, practical techniques and efficiency in all its forms. Practicality, efficiency, service, precision and the proper functioning of the body - these are among the outstanding themes of the sign. Virgo is ruled by the intellectual planet Mercury, giving this sign mental attributes but, as Virgo is the Mutable-Earth sign of the zodiac, the mind tends to focus on practical techniques that accomplish concrete work, rather than vague and remote abstractions, or communication for its own sake (as one may encounter in Gemini, the other sign ruled by Mercury).

Libra (23 September to 23 October)

Ruling Planet: Venus | Polarity: Masculine | Element: Air | Modality: Cardinal.

Libra is the middle-point of the zodiac, dividing it into two equal halves, like the even symmetry of the balance, and is thus opposite the first sign, Aries, on the zodiac wheel. If the key phrase for Aries is "I Am", then Libra's would be "We Are". A union of two equal, opposite and (ideally or potentially) mutually complementary entities. It represents a type of initiation into the collective, socially-orientated half of the zodiac that follows. Libra is ruled by the planet Venus, and this suggests qualities of grace and gentleness, a love of beauty and harmony, and therefore artistic inclinations. Despite the friendly, courteous and amicable attributes associated with this sign, it does belong to the dynamic Cardinal Cross, and the Masculine Airy Triplicity. Libra is the match for Aries in terms of enthusiastic and direct competitiveness.

Scorpio (23 Oct. to 22 Nov.)

Ruling Planet: Mars | Polarity: Feminine | Element: Water | Modality: Fixe.

Scorpions have a reputation for being dangerous and are also rather elusive creatures, hiding under rocks or in other dark crevices. Some of the deeper, darker, more mysterious and secret facets of life (such as death, sex and the occult) are associated with the 8th sign of the zodiac. Scorpio belongs to the Fixed Cross and the Feminine Water Triplicity, and represents emotional intensity, which might be expressed as great concentration and focus. Obviously these attributes can be useful, and Scorpio can achieve great things through this capacity for intense commitment and determination. This same quality, however, can make for a type of obsessive or fanatical preoccupation with an idea or feeling, so that it warps and distorts reality (especially where fear or paranoia are driving this obsessive focus).

Sagittarius (23 Nov. to 21 Dec.)

Ruling Planet: Jupiter | Polarity: Masculine | Element: Fire | Modality: Mutable.

The Sagittarian Centaur is usually depicted as aiming his arrow high at a distant goal. The sign Sagittarius represents idealism and aspiration, a lifting of one's gaze towards higher things and a wider horizon. Sagittarius is associated with mental and physical exploration, and this can manifest as the quest for philosophical truth or, on a more physical level, journeys to foreign lands. Sagittarius is ruled by the expansive planet Jupiter, the largest and luckiest planet in the solar system. This sign frequently demonstrates an intuitive and visionary streak, expressing itself through art, science or other culturally vital knowledge. Sagittarius belongs to the Mutable Cross, and the Fiery Triplicity. Similarly to the other Fire signs, Sagittarius is optimistic, enthusiastic and forthright, but is probably the most mobile, and certainly the most moral, of them all.

Capricorn (22 Dec. to 20 Jan.)

Ruling Planet: Saturn | Polarity: Feminine | Element: Earth | Modality: Cardinal.
The Goat is an adept mountain climber, toughened and hardy, able to withstand the cold winds and rocky terrain of worldly ambition. Calculated steps get you to the top, and relentless determination combined with careful initiative ensures eventual success. Capricorn is associated with career goals, social status, financial security, and dynamic practicality. It represents a relatively mature stage of development in which responsibility can be shouldered for projects that will affect many people, such as in the realms of politics and big business. This requires worldly experience and a combination of discipline and dynamism. Capricorn is the Cardinal sign of the Earthy Triplicity, and as such is capable of greater initiative and confidence than the other Earth signs.

Aquarius (21 Jan. to 17 Feb.)

Ruling Planet: Saturn | Polarity: Masculine | Element: Ar | Modality: Fixed.
The sign Aquarius is depicted as the Water Bearer: a man pouring forth water from a jar or urn. This sign represents a socially idealistic phase that follows from the socially conscious, ambitious practicality of Capricorn. It is significant, however, that Saturn, the planet of structure, rules both Capricorn and Aquarius. Capricorn is the earthy (materialistic) and Aquarius the airy (communicative) expression of Saturn's energy. Aquarius is very much associated with knowledge and the arts and sciences that express social ideals and humanity's collective pool of knowledge and culture. Aquarius is the Fixed Air sign of the zodiac, which combines the ideas of holding (fixed) with communication (air), hence the association with collective social values and communication systems and channels that maintain the collective unity of a group.

Pisces (18 Feb. to 20 March)

Ruling Planet: Jupiter | Polarity: Feminine | Element: Water | Modality: Mutable.
Pisces is the final sign of the zodiac, representing the closure and ending of the process begun in Aries. It represents a return and surrender to the "cosmic ocean" or "primordial soup". In Aquarius, humanity's collective unity is realised, but in Pisces there is a realisation of unity that encompasses all that is. Pisces is therefore associated with a distinctly indiscriminate tendency. Though this nebulous way of being makes for an ability to deal with abstract and paradoxical ideas, and gives the potential to feel the relatedness of all things and beings on a level that transcends thought and concepts as we normally experience them. Jupiter is the traditional planetary ruler of Pisces, though Neptune has become associated with it in modern times. This sign belongs to the Mutable Cross and Water Triplicity.

The Houses in Astrology

1st House - The Ascending sign to the east marks the cusp of the first house, which represents the being and life itself. The first House is the House of the Self, which gives identity to the native, how they see the world, and one's outstanding personal characteristics. It is often associated with the physical appearance and body (health) in general. Any planet in the 1st House is greatly enhanced in strength and importance in the chart as a whole. It represents qualities and attributes we embody or radiate to the world. This may prove exceptionally true of a planet close to the Ascendant. The 1st House is the pinnacle of the chart, the ultimate synthesis of the whole being and therefore a strong 1st House (and 1st House ruler) improves the entire chart. Of course, the reverse also holds true.

2nd House - Represents the native's values, how they deal with money and the ability to attract or repel material goods. It is associated with money, property and material assets. Western astrology doesn't usually offer much more than this on the 2nd House, but Vedic astrology further associates the 2nd House with speech (Taurus rules the throat and neck and ears), and by extension, orally transmitted knowledge (for example, early education), what you eat, as well as the "lustre of the face".

3rd House - Rules brothers and sisters, cousins, or family members of similar age, and neighbours, as well as routine outings and short trips. It is associated with routine day to day encounters and communications, the mind and basic education, as well as our dexterity and ability to interact effectively with people and our environment.

4th House - Represents the parents, the home, family, residence and the domestic environment. It reveals the characteristics of private life, the deepest emotions, and the end of life. It portrays the roots of existence, genes, ancestry, and the parents. The 4th House is our inner foundation, our psychological and emotional basis. The Sun is in the region of the 4th House around midnight. It is, ideally, a place of rest, peace and recuperation.

5th House - Represents children, pregnancy and the conditions of the offspring, relating to what provides a social and joyful atmosphere with children. It reveals the creative potential of the person, also related to sports, competitive spirit, games and financial speculation. The fifth house symbolises love, passion and courtship, as well as infidelity and love scandals. It also symbolises vacations, banquets, theatre, movies, spontaneous enjoyment, and things we do with or for heartfelt pleasure.

6th House - Represents daily work, routine tasks, matters related to health maintenance, medicine and illness. Which includes regular physical exercise, hygiene, diet, and the administration of medicines. The 6th House represents enemies, crises, illnesses, unforeseen obstacles, accidents and injuries, weaknesses and afflictions. It also rules hard work, the lower clergy, servants, employees, tenants, and pets.

7th House - This area of the chart is primarily associated with relationships, marriage and partnerships. All face-to-face encounters, including consultations or confrontations with others. Planets and signs in the 7th House describe our approach to, and experience of, relationships, as well as indicating the type of person to whom we are attracted in partnership, consultation or competition. These significant others will tend to literally have the planets/sign in your 7th House prominent in their charts.

8th House - Refers to matters related to death, loss, decay, inactivity, and the fear related to these themes. It has an association with certain deep and dark facets of life, such as death, sex, crime and the occult. Since the 8th House is the 2nd House from the 7th House, it reflects joint resources, each other's money, financial obligations, loans, taxes, charges, interest, and banks, as well as making use of and multiplying the resources of others. Known as the House of sexual communion, it represents our ability to master our own emotions and know ourselves deeply.

9th House - Represents that which is related to foreign countries, long journeys, adventures and other languages. The 9th House describes our moral, ethical and religious beliefs, as well as higher education. It also describes qualities such as noble aspiration, and an interest in religion and philosophy. Associated with the divinatory arts and astrology, the 9th house is the conscious spiritual side of the individual. This is the house of social sciences, laws, courts, judges, and lawyers.

10th House - Represents the career, the individual's ultimate goal and long-term plans. It describes our social status, reputation, and profession. Planets are powerfully and prominently positioned here and tend to mould our ambitions and describe the type of activities we are suited for, or likely to pursue. This House is commonly associated with authority figures and bosses. Planets in the 10th House are often associated with one's career, probably since we are to a great extent identified by our social standing and, in a sense, planets in the 10th also have a more general tendency to define our identity, or what we could term our public persona.

11th House - This House shows our friendships and group activities. Planets and signs in the 11th House will describe our typical patterns in group activities, including the types of groups or clubs we might belong to. The 11th House is often referred to as the house of hopes and wishes, and in this regard may describe major or long-term life goals. The 11th House can also represent gains, and it has an important bearing in the ability to earn wealth.

12th House - The 12th House is associated with spirituality, seclusion and sacrifice. As the last of the Houses it represents endings, renunciation, surrender, withdrawal and rest. It is often regarded as a place of misfortune, difficulty, secret enemies, losses, confinement and obscurity. Prisons, hospitals and charitable institutions are ruled by this house. This House carries an important spiritual connotation, and relates to one's inner life and also that which is hidden and unconscious. The 12th House can greatly enhance sensitivity and empathy, but also sometimes indicates confusion and a sense of hopelessness and secrecy.

Aspects

Aspects are geometric angles formed by planets based on their respective zodiacal or longitudal positions. The most widely used aspects are multiples of 30 degrees (with the exception of the conjunction), but the 45 degree multiple aspects are also important.

30 Degree Multiple Aspects

☌ **Conjunction** 0 degrees

Planets forming a conjunction are powerfully united in their expression. The conjunction is the most powerful of the all the aspects.

⚺ **Semi-Sextile** 30 degrees

The semi-sextile is arguably the weakest and subtlest of the aspects. The effect may be almost subliminal. It is possible that the semi-sextile will manifest through or affect financial matters.

✶ **Sextile** 60 degrees

The sextile aspect is considered relatively easy and enables planets to interact without much tension. It is also true that the sextile aspect can manifest through or influence day-to-day neighbourly interactions, friendships and group activities.

□ **Square** 90 degrees

The square aspect tends to be potent and indicates a vigorous and energetic connection between planets. It is possible for this to be a bit too stimulating and there could be an abrupt manifestation of the planetary combination. It is also possible that the square aspect will manifest specifically in and through the domestic and professional arenas of life.

△ **Trine** 120 degrees

The trine aspect is generally regarded as the most harmonious of all the aspects. It enables the planets connected by this angle to interact in a manner that is inspired, creative and spontaneous.

⚻ **Quincunx (Inconjunct)** 150 degrees

The quincunx aspect is considered relatively weak, but also somewhat awkward. Planets meeting through this angle may struggle to find a comfortable way of interacting. The quincunx may specifically manifest in and through health related matters, jobs, service and financial obligations between people.

☍   **Opposition**   180 degrees

The opposition aspect is very powerful, rivalling the conjunction in potency. Planets are brought into a very direct and intense interaction. The opposition may specifically manifest in and through partnerships and important one-to-one interactions with others.

45 Degree Multiple Aspects

∠   **Semi-Square**   45 degrees

⚼   **Sesquiquadrate**   135 degrees

These two 45 degree multiple aspects are basically similar. They're related to the same family of aspects as the opposition and square and they share some of the solidity and intensity of those aspects. They are widely underestimated and they are capable of bringing things into concrete manifestation.

January 2025

Day	☉	☽	True ☊	☿	♀	♂	♃	♄	♅	♆	♇
01	10 ♑ 48 50	23 ♑ 54 56	00 ♈ 53 ℞	19 ♐ 52 D	27 ♒ 43 D	01 ♌ 55 ℞	13 ♊ 13 ℞	14 ♓ 31 D	23 ♉ 38 ℞	27 ♓ 18 D	01 ♒ 04 D
02	11 50 00	07 ♒ 27 28	00 42	21 10	28 47	01 35	13 07	14 36	23 37	27 19	01 06
03	12 51 11	21 09 57	00 34	22 29	29 51	01 15	13 00	14 41	23 35	27 20	01 08
04	13 52 21	04 ♓ 59 50	00 29	23 50	00 ♓ 55	00 54	12 54	14 45	23 34	27 20	01 09
05	14 53 31	18 55 12	00 26	25 12	01 58	00 32	12 49	14 50	23 33	27 21	01 11
06	15 54 41	02 ♈ 54 49	00 26 D	26 35	03 01	00 10	12 43	14 55	23 31	27 22	01 13
07	16 55 50	16 57 58	00 26 ℞	27 58	04 04	29 ♋ 48	12 37	15 00	23 30	27 23	01 15
08	17 56 59	01 ♉ 04 06	00 26	29 23	05 06	29 25	12 32	15 05	23 29	27 24	01 17
09	18 58 07	15 12 19	00 23	00 ♑ 48	06 08	29 02	12 27	15 10	23 28	27 26	01 19
10	19 59 15	29 20 53	00 18	02 14	07 09	28 38	12 22	15 15	23 27	27 27	01 21
11	21 00 23	13 ♊ 27 03	00 10	03 41	08 10	28 15	12 17	15 21	23 26	27 28	01 23
12	22 01 30	27 27 05	29 ♓ 59	05 09	09 11	27 51	12 12	15 26	23 25	27 29	01 25
13	23 02 36	11 ♋ 16 46	29 48	06 37	10 11	27 27	12 07	15 31	23 24	27 30	01 27
14	24 03 43	24 52 04	29 36	08 05	11 11	27 03	12 03	15 37	23 23	27 31	01 28
15	25 04 48	08 ♌ 09 46	29 26	09 35	12 10	26 39	11 59	15 42	23 22	27 33	01 30
16	26 05 54	21 08 06	29 18	11 05	13 09	26 15	11 55	15 48	23 21	27 34	01 32
17	27 06 58	03 ♍ 46 56	29 12	12 35	14 07	25 51	11 51	15 54	23 21	27 35	01 34
18	28 08 03	16 07 50	29 09	14 06	15 05	25 27	11 48	15 59	23 20	27 37	01 36
19	29 09 07	28 13 47	29 08	15 38	16 02	25 04	11 44	16 05	23 19	27 38	01 38
20	00 ♒ 10 11	10 ♎ 08 53	29 08 D	17 10	16 59	24 40	11 41	16 11	23 19	27 39	01 40
21	01 11 14	21 58 04	29 09	18 43	17 55	24 17	11 38	16 17	23 18	27 41	01 42
22	02 12 17	03 ♏ 46 38	29 09 ℞	20 16	18 50	23 54	11 35	16 23	23 18	27 42	01 44
23	03 13 20	15 40 03	29 08	21 50	19 45	23 31	11 32	16 29	23 17	27 44	01 46
24	04 14 22	27 43 34	29 05	23 24	20 39	23 09	11 30	16 35	23 17	27 45	01 48
25	05 15 24	10 ♐ 01 50	29 00	24 59	21 33	22 47	11 28	16 41	23 17	27 47	01 50
26	06 16 25	22 38 34	28 53	26 35	22 26	22 25	11 26	16 47	23 16	27 48	01 52
27	07 17 26	05 ♑ 36 06	28 44	28 11	23 18	22 04	11 24	16 53	23 16	27 50	01 54
28	08 18 26	18 55 05	28 35	29 48	24 09	21 44	11 22	17 00	23 16	27 51	01 56
29	09 19 25	02 ♒ 34 18	28 26	01 ♒ 26	25 00	21 24	11 21	17 06	23 16	27 53	01 57
30	10 20 23	16 30 46	28 18	03 04	25 50	21 05	11 20	17 12	23 16	27 55	01 59
31	11 21 20	00 ♓ 40 12	28 13	04 43	26 39	20 46	11 19	17 19	23 16 D	27 56	02 01

Declination

Day	☉	☽	True ☊	☿	♀	♂	♃	♄	♅	♆	♇
1	-22°57′	-24°15′	+00°19′	-22°04′	-13°22′	+23°36′	+21°47′	-07°54′	+18°26′	-02°15′	-23°07′
3	-22°46′	-14°42′	+00°13′	-22°30′	-12°29′	+23°49′	+21°46′	-07°50′	+18°25′	-02°14′	-23°06′
5	-22°33′	-02°00′	+00°11′	-22°53′	-11°35′	+24°02′	+21°45′	-07°46′	+18°25′	-02°13′	-23°05′
7	-22°18′	+11°12′	+00°11′	-23°13′	-10°40′	+24°16′	+21°44′	-07°42′	+18°24′	-02°13′	-23°04′
9	-22°01′	+22°11′	+00°08′	-23°28′	-09°45′	+24°28′	+21°43′	-07°38′	+18°24′	-02°12′	-23°04′
11	-21°43′	+28°03′	+00°02′	-23°39′	-08°49′	+24°41′	+21°42′	-07°34′	+18°23′	-02°11′	-23°03′
13	-21°23′	+26°58′	-00°07′	-23°45′	-07°53′	+24°52′	+21°41′	-07°29′	+18°23′	-02°10′	-23°02′
15	-21°01′	+19°51′	-00°15′	-23°47′	-06°56′	+25°04′	+21°40′	-07°25′	+18°22′	-02°09′	-23°02′
17	-20°38′	+09°23′	-00°20′	-23°43′	-06°00′	+25°14′	+21°40′	-07°20′	+18°22′	-02°08′	-23°01′
19	-20°13′	-02°05′	-00°21′	-23°35′	-05°03′	+25°24′	+21°39′	-07°16′	+18°22′	-02°06′	-23°00′
21	-19°47′	-13°00′	-00°20′	-23°21′	-04°06′	+25°33′	+21°39′	-07°11′	+18°22′	-02°05′	-22°59′
23	-19°19′	-22°06′	-00°21′	-23°01′	-03°10′	+25°41′	+21°39′	-07°06′	+18°21′	-02°04′	-22°59′
25	-18°50′	-27°41′	-00°26′	-22°37′	-02°13′	+25°48′	+21°39′	-07°01′	+18°21′	-02°03′	-22°58′
27	-18°19′	-27°49′	-00°32′	-22°06′	-01°18′	+25°55′	+21°39′	-06°56′	+18°21′	-02°01′	-22°57′
29	-17°47′	-21°36′	-00°39′	-21°30′	-00°22′	+26°00′	+21°39′	-06°51′	+18°21′	-02°00′	-22°57′
31	-17°14′	-10°19′	-00°43′	-20°48′	+00°32′	+26°04′	+21°39′	-06°46′	+18°21′	-01°59′	-22°56′

January, 2025

Degree of
Key Aspects

3 Jan 2025
♂℞ ☍ ♇ 1♌08 1♒08

4 Jan 2025
☉ ⚹ ♄ 14♑50 14♓50

6 Jan 2025
☿ □ ♆ 27♐23 27♓23

12 Jan 2025
♂℞ △ ♆ 27♋30 27♓30

13 Jan 2025
☉ △ ♅℞ 23♑24 23♉24

14 Jan 2025
♀ □ ♃℞ 12♓00 12♊00

16 Jan 2025
☉ ☍ ♂℞ 26♑13 26♋13

17 Jan 2025
☉ ⚹ ♆ 27♑36 27♓36

19 Jan 2025
♀ ☌ ♄ 16♓05 16♓05
☿ ⚹ ♄ 16♑07 16♓07
☿ ⚹ ♀ 16♑41 16♓41

21 Jan 2025
☉ ☌ ♇ 1♒43 1♒43

23 Jan 2025
♂℞ ⚹ ♅℞ 23♋17 23♉17
☿ ☍ ♂℞ 23♑12 23♋12
☿ △ ♅℞ 23♑17 23♉17

25 Jan 2025
♀ △ ♂℞ 22♓25 22♋25

26 Jan 2025
☿ ⚹ ♆ 27♑49 27♓49
♀ ⚹ ♅℞ 23♓16 23♉16

29 Jan 2025
☿ ☌ ♇ 1♒58 1♒58

30 Jan 2025
♅D 23♉16
☉ △ ♃℞ 11♒19 11♊19

CAPRICORN

Sunday	Monday	Tuesday
29	30	31
5 ☽ voc 14:30 ☽→♈ 19:01 ☽⚹♅ 7:56 ☽□☿ 11:57 ☽☌♆ 14:30 ☽△♂ 19:25 ☽⚹♇ 21:06	6 First Quarter 16♈56 ♂→♋ 10:43 ☿□♆ 13:56 ☽⚹♃ 16:38 ☽□☉ 23:56	**7** ☽ voc 21:16 ☽→♉ 22:11 ☽△☿ 20:49 ☽□♂ 21:16
12 ☽ voc 0:03 ☽→♋ 4:24 ☽□♆ 0:03 ☽☍☿ 14:53 ♂△♆ 21:15 ☽△♀ 21:56	13 Full Moon 24♋00 ☽△♄ 7:30 ☉△♅ 8:13 ☽⚹♅ 21:21 ☽☍☉ 22:27	**14** ☽ voc 4:45 ☽→♌ 9:12 ☽☌♂ 3:48 ☽△♆ 4:45 ☽☍♇ 11:53 ♀□♃ 19:48
19 ☽ voc 2:01 ☽→♏ 3:33 ♀☌♄ 1:26 ☽△☉ 2:01 ☽△♇ 6:51 ☿⚹♄ 7:38 ☿⚹♀ 16:31 ☉→♒ 20:00	**20** ☽△♃ 3:06 ☽□☿ 16:22	21 ☽ voc 4:33 ☽→♏ 16:20 Last Quarter 02♏03 ☽□♂ 4:33 ☉☌♇ 12:29 ☽□♇ 19:50 ☽□☉ 20:31
26 ☽ voc 9:39 ☽→♑ 13:42 ☽□♆ 9:39 ♀⚹♅ 23:11	**27** ☽⚹♄ 20:33	**28** ☽ voc 15:48 ☽→♒ 19:31 ☿→♒ 2:52 ☽☍♂ 4:52 ☽△♅ 7:42 ☽⚹♀ 9:53 ☽⚹♆ 15:48 ☽☌☿ 21:45 ☽☌♇ 22:56

GMT

13 January, 2025
22:27 GMT

Full Moon

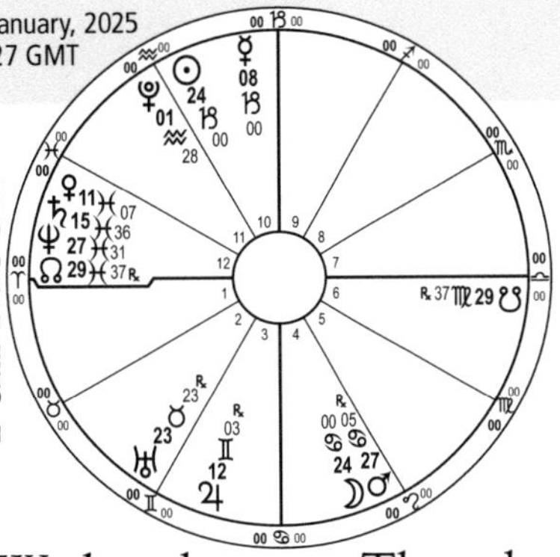

29 January, 2025
12:36 GMT

New Moon

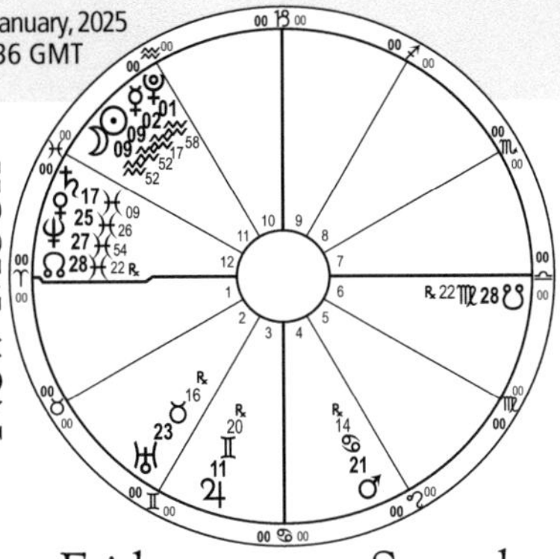

Wednesday	Thursday	Friday	Saturday
1 New Year ☽ voc 6:02 ☽→♒ 10:49 ☽⚹♆ 6:02 ☽☌♇ 12:44 ☽☍♂ 13:53	**2** ☽△♃ 9:51 ☽⚹☿ 2:33	**3** ☽ voc 4:13 ☽→♓ 15:21 ♀→♓ 3:24 ☽□♅ 4:13 ♂☍♇ 7:19 ☽☌♀ 16:20	**4** ☽□♃ 13:33 ☽⚹☉ 16:31 ☽☌♄ 16:56 ☉⚹♄ 22:36
8 ☽□♇ 0:22 ☽⚹♀ 7:23 ☿→♑ 10:30 ☽⚹♄ 23:56	**9** ☽ voc 22:50 ☽△☉ 6:53 ☽☌♅ 14:00 ☽⚹♆ 20:46 ☽⚹♂ 22:50	**10** ☽→♊ 1:06 ☽△♇ 3:24 ☽□♀ 14:18 ☽☌♃ 22:01	**11** ☽□♄ 3:15
15 ☽⚹♃ 6:58	**16** ☽ voc 4:10 ☽→♍ 16:46 ☉☍♂ 2:38 ☽□♅ 4:10	**17** ☉⚹♆ 11:20 ☽□♃ 15:33 ☽△☿ 19:27 ☽☍♀ 21:46 ☽☍♄ 23:43	**18** ☽△♅ 14:13 ☽⚹♂ 17:52 ☽☍♆ 22:48
22	**23** ☽△♄ 1:39 ☽△♀ 8:50 ☽⚹☿ 14:10 ♂⚹♅ 15:09 ☽△♂ 15:12 ☽☍♅ 15:12 ☿☍♂ 20:49 ☿△♅ 22:07	**24** ☽ voc 0:03 ☽→♏ 4:29 ☽△♆ 0:03 ☽⚹♇ 8:01 ☽⚹☉ 13:55	**25** ☽☍♃ 2:45 ☽□♄ 12:51 ☽□♀ 23:34 ♀△♂ 23:54
Chinese New Year: Serpent ● New Moon 09♒51 ☿☌♇ 7:52 ☽☌☉ 12:36 ☽△♃ 15:08	**30** ☽ voc 11:29 ☽→♓ 22:52 ☽□♅ 11:29 ♅ SD 15:51 ☉△♃ 22:59	**31** ☽□♃ 17:52	**1**

AQUARIUS

♑ Capricorn

At the time of the New Moon on the 30th of December the Sun and Moon are both sesquiquadrate Uranus which describes a restless and excitable energy. Moreover, Mercury is forming a sesquiquadrate aspect to Mars which is somewhat similar: vigorous mental energy and impatience in communication.

On the 3rd of January a retrograde Mars backs into an opposition to Pluto. This can be a brutally assertive energy, simmering tensions can erupt into open confrontations. At best this combination can stimulate decisiveness and intense efforts that can drive projects forward.

As Venus prepares to enter tropical Pisces at the very beginning of January, she finds herself at the midpoint of Neptune and Pluto which paints a picture of mystical and otherworldly artistic visions, or something like a supernatural love.

☉ Sunday

29

☽ VOC 23:34

☽ Monday

30

☽☌☿ 3:01
☽⚹♀ 20:03
☽□♆ 23:34

☽→♑ 4:37

● New Moon
09♑44

♂ Tuesday

31

☽☌☉ 22:27

☽⚹♄ 7:02
☽△♅ 23:30

40   GMT

January 2025

☿ Wednesday

1 January

☽VOC   6:02
☽→♒   10:49

Happy New Year!

☽✶♆   6:02
☽☌♇   12:44
☽☍♂   13:53

♃ Thursday

2

☽△♃   9:51

♀ Friday

3

☽VOC   4:13
☽→♓   15:21

☽✶☿   2:33
♀→♓   3:24
☽□♅   4:13
♂☍♇   7:19
☽☌♀   16:20

♄ Saturday

4

☽□♃   13:33
☽✶☉   16:31
☽☌♄   16:56
☉✶♄   22:36

Regulus 2025 Astrological Planner   41

♑ Capricorn

The Moon arrives at a square to the Sun on Monday the 6th. At this time Mercury and Neptune happen to be forming a tight square which speaks of muddled and ineffective communication. Facts and figures get washed away in a tide of fantasy, distraction or wishful thinking. Read the fine print before you sign. Better yet, sip on a cocktail and read devotional poetry and stay away from accounting or anything requiring accurate attention to technical details.

Retrograde Mars re-enters the sign Cancer where it will remain until he re-enters Leo on the 18th of April.

Mercury ingresses into Capricorn on the 8th of January, so important and high level communications are sent and delivered. Breaking news and gossip becomes public.

☉ Sunday
5

☽ VOC 14:30
☽→♈ 19:01

☽ Monday
6

☽⚹♅ 7:56
☽□☿ 11:57
☽☌♆ 14:30
☽△♂ 19:25
☽⚹♇ 21:06

◐
First Quarter
16♈56

♂ Tuesday
7

♂→♋ 10:43
☿□♆ 13:56
☽⚹♃ 16:38
☽□☉ 23:56

☽ VOC 21:16
☽→♉ 22:11

☽△☿ 20:49
☽□♂ 21:16

42   GMT

January 2025

☿ Wednesday
8

☽□♇	0:22
☽⚹♀	7:23
☿→♑	10:30
☽⚹♄	23:56

♃ Thursday
9

☽VOC 22:50

☽△☉	6:53
☽☌♅	14:00
☽⚹♆	20:46
☽⚹♂	22:50

♀ Friday
10

☽→♊ 1:06

☽△♇	3:24
☽□♀	14:18
☽☌♃	22:01

♄ Saturday
11

☽□♄ 3:15

Regulus 2025 Astrological Planner 43

♑ Capricorn

On Sunday the 12th of January Mars is trine Neptune. Compassion and spiritual values motivate actions. We'll see inspired sacrificial efforts and mesmerising displays of artistry and prowess. At the time of the Full Moon on the 13th the Sun and Moon will be trine and sextile Uranus respectively. Thinking is fresh, new and novel and the vibe is electric and excited. There is support for freedom, liberty and innovation.

The mood is sensual, lavish and extravagant by the time Venus squares Jupiter on the 14th of January. There are parties, celebrations (with hangovers and indigestion a possible consequence). Money may be wasted on self-indulgent whims.

The Sun and Mars arrive at an exact opposition on Thursday the 16th of January as the Sun approaches a sextile to Neptune which becomes exact on the following day. There's the spirit of competitiveness and an urge to act decisively, but also a recognized need for self-sacrifice for the sake of greater good.

☉ Sunday

12

☽ VOC 0:03
☽→♋ 4:24

☽☐♆ 0:03
☽☍☿ 14:53
♂△♆ 21:15
☽△♀ 21:56

☽ Monday

13

○
Full Moon
24♋00

☽△♄ 7:30
☉△♅ 8:13
☽✶♅ 21:21
☽☍☉ 22:27

♂ Tuesday

14

☽ VOC 4:45
☽→♌ 9:12

☽☌♂ 3:48
☽△♆ 4:45
☽☍☿ 11:53
♀☐♃ 19:48

GMT

January 2025

☿ Wednesday
15

☽✶♃	6:58

♃ Thursday
16

☽VOC	4:10
☽→♍	16:46

☉☌♂	2:38
☽□♅	4:10

♀ Friday
17

☉✶♆	11:20
☽□♃	15:33
☽△☿	19:27
☽☌♀	21:46
☽☌♄	23:43

♄ Saturday
18

☽△♅	14:13
☽✶♂	17:52
☽☌♆	22:48

Regulus 2025 Astrological Planner

♒ Aquarius

Congratulations Aquarians!

Venus and Saturn form a conjunction on Sunday which speaks of distance between lovers and friends and critical changes in personal relationships. Then we have a third quarter Sun Moon square with the Sun at the time conjunct Pluto. This can be a potent and explosive release of energy. There may even be a significant development on the world stage: power and authority is wielded forcefully.

On Thursday, Mercury, Mars and Uranus conspire to speed things up, bringing a barrage of news and information. Communication is assertive and there is ingenuity and clever execution of bold actions.

Venus is trine Mars on Saturday and the spirit is friendly and gregarious. Lovers are energised and chemistry is crackling. Vibrant artistic creativity, parties and revelry.

☉ Sunday
19

☽ VOC 2:01
☽→♎ 3:33

♀☌♄ 1:26
☽△☉ 2:01
☽△♇ 6:51
☿⚹♄ 7:38
☿⚹♀ 16:31
☉→♒ 20:00

☽ Monday
20

☽△♃ 3:06
☽□☿ 16:22

♂ Tuesday
21

☽ VOC 4:33
☽→♏ 16:20

◐
Last Quarter
02 ♏ 03

☽□♂ 4:33
☉☌♇ 12:29
☽□♇ 19:50
☽□☉ 20:31

46 GMT

January 2025

☿ Wednesday
22

♃ Thursday
23

☽△♄ 1:39
☽△♀ 8:50
☽⚹☿ 14:10
♂⚹♅ 15:09
☽△♂ 15:12
☽☍♅ 15:12
☿☍♂ 20:49
♀△♅ 22:07

♀ Friday
24

☽VOC 0:03
☽→♐ 4:29

☽△♆ 0:03
☽⚹♇ 8:01
☽⚹☉ 13:55

♄ Saturday
25

☽☍♃ 2:45
☽□♄ 12:51
☽□♀ 23:34
♀△♂ 23:54

Regulus 2025 Astrological Planner 47

♒ Aquarius

On Sunday the 26th of January Venus makes a sextile to Uranus while she is close to the Saturn-Neptune midpoint. This might describe a need to accept limitations in relationships, while being open, flexible and less possessive.

Mercury enters Aquarius on the 28th of January and arrives at a conjunction with Pluto the following day. On the 29th there's a New Moon that occurs not very far from this Mercury-Pluto conjunction, bringing it into sharper focus. Power is wielded through communication, there is deep probing analysis and investigation. Propaganda could be potent now; there's a cunning manipulation of people's opinions and perceptions.

This New Moon is also trine Jupiter which suggests that there is receptivity to good counsel and people are inspired by morally upright goals and plans.

Uranus turns direct on Thursday, and this can result in sudden and surprising unleashing of pent-up energy.

☉ Sunday 26

☽ VOC	9:39
☽→♑	13:42

☽ Monday 27

☽□♆	9:39
♀✶♅	23:11

♂ Tuesday 28

☽✶♄	20:33
☽ VOC	15:48
☽→♒	19:31
☿→♒	2:52
☽☍♂	4:52
☽△♅	7:42
☽✶♀	9:53
☽✶♆	15:48
☽☌☿	21:45
☽☌♇	22:56

48   GMT

January 2025

☿ **Wednesday**

29

● New Moon
09 ♒ 51

Chinese New Year: Snake

☿ ☌ ♇	7:52
☽ ☌ ☉	12:36
☽ △ ♃	15:08

♃ **Thursday**

30

☽ VOC	11:29
☽ → ♓	22:52

☽ □ ♅	11:29
♅ SD	15:51
☉ △ ♃	22:59

♀ **Friday**

31

☽ □ ♃	17:52

♄ **Saturday**

1 February

☽ VOC	22:06

☽ ☌ ♄	4:09
☽ △ ♂	9:01
☽ ✶ ♅	13:54
♀ ☌ ♆	16:33
☽ ☌ ♆	21:48
☽ ☌ ♀	22:06

Regulus 2025 Astrological Planner

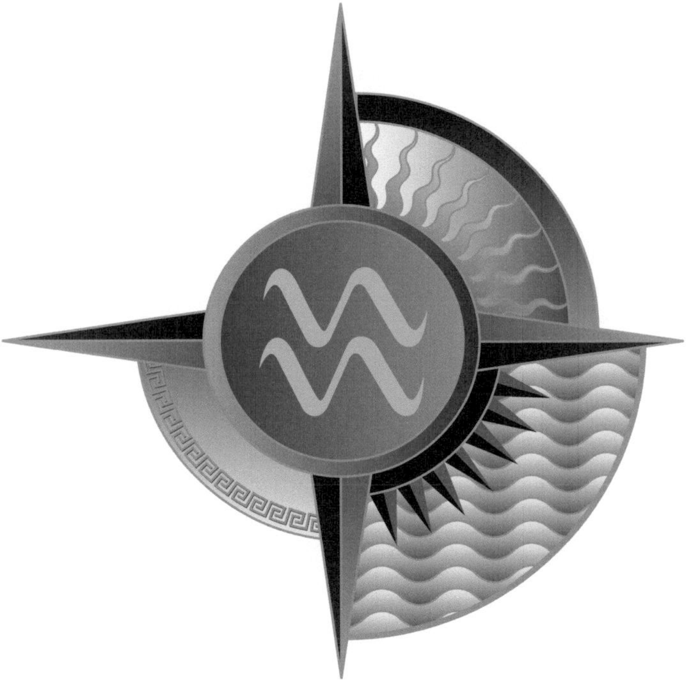

Ephemeris for February 2025, set at Midnight GMT.

February 2025

Day	☉	☽	True ☊	☿	♀	♂	♃	♄	♅	♆	♇
01	12 ♒ 22 16	14 ♓ 57 40	28 ♓ 10 R	06 ♒ 23 D	27 ♓ 27 D	20 ♋ 28 R	11 ♊ 18 R	17 ♓ 25 D	23 ♉ 16 D	27 ♓ 58 D	02 ♒ 03 D
02	13 23 10	29 18 20	28 09 D	08 03	28 14	20 10	11 17	17 32	23 16	28 00	02 05
03	14 24 04	13 ♈ 38 05	28 10	09 44	29 00	19 54	11 17	17 39	23 16	28 02	02 07
04	15 24 55	27 53 48	28 11	11 26	29 45	19 38	11 17	17 45	23 16	28 03	02 09
05	16 25 46	12 ♉ 03 24	28 12	13 08	00 ♈ 29	19 22	11 17 D	17 52	23 16	28 05	02 11
06	17 26 35	26 05 30	28 12 R	14 52	01 13	19 08	11 17	17 58	23 17	28 07	02 13
07	18 27 23	09 ♊ 59 08	28 10	16 36	01 55	18 54	11 17	18 05	23 17	28 09	02 15
08	19 28 09	23 43 22	28 06	18 20	02 35	18 41	11 18	18 12	23 18	28 11	02 16
09	20 28 54	07 ♋ 17 10	28 01	20 06	03 15	18 29	11 19	18 19	23 18	28 13	02 18
10	21 29 37	20 39 20	27 55	21 52	03 53	18 18	11 20	18 26	23 19	28 14	02 20
11	22 30 19	03 ♌ 48 37	27 48	23 39	04 30	18 07	11 21	18 33	23 19	28 16	02 22
12	23 30 59	16 44 01	27 43	25 27	05 06	17 57	11 23	18 40	23 20	28 18	02 24
13	24 31 38	29 24 59	27 38	27 16	05 40	17 48	11 24	18 46	23 20	28 20	02 26
14	25 32 15	11 ♍ 51 42	27 35	29 05	06 13	17 40	11 26	18 53	23 21	28 22	02 27
15	26 32 51	24 05 14	27 34	00 ♓ 54	06 44	17 33	11 28	19 00	23 22	28 24	02 29
16	27 33 26	06 ♎ 07 34	27 34 D	02 45	07 14	17 26	11 30	19 08	23 23	28 26	02 31
17	28 33 59	18 01 34	27 36	04 36	07 42	17 20	11 33	19 15	23 24	28 28	02 33
18	29 34 31	29 50 51	27 38	06 27	08 08	17 15	11 35	19 22	23 25	28 30	02 35
19	00 ♓ 35 02	11 ♏ 39 43	27 39	08 18	08 33	17 11	11 38	19 29	23 26	28 32	02 36
20	01 35 31	23 32 56	27 41	10 10	08 56	17 07	11 41	19 36	23 27	28 34	02 38
21	02 36 00	05 ♐ 35 25	27 41 R	12 01	09 17	17 04	11 44	19 43	23 28	28 36	02 40
22	03 36 27	17 52 05	27 40	13 53	09 36	17 03	11 48	19 50	23 29	28 39	02 42
23	04 36 52	00 ♑ 27 26	27 38	15 43	09 53	17 01	11 51	19 58	23 30	28 41	02 43
24	05 37 16	13 25 03	27 35	17 33	10 07	17 01	11 55	20 05	23 31	28 43	02 45
25	06 37 39	26 47 11	27 32	19 22	10 20	17 01 D	11 59	20 12	23 33	28 45	02 47
26	07 38 01	10 ♒ 34 12	27 29	21 09	10 31	17 02	12 03	20 19	23 34	28 47	02 48
27	08 38 20	24 44 17	27 26	22 54	10 39	17 04	12 07	20 27	23 35	28 49	02 50
28	09 38 38	09 ♓ 13 20	27 25	24 37	10 45	17 07	12 12	20 34	23 37	28 51	02 52
01	10 38 54	23 55 25	27 24	26 17	10 49	17 10	12 16	20 41	23 38	28 54	02 53

Declination

Day	☉	☽	True ☊	☿	♀	♂	♃	♄	♅	♆	♇
1	-16°57'	-03°38'	-00°44'	-20°25'	+00°59'	+26°06'	+21°39'	-06°43'	+18°21'	-01°58'	-22°56'
3	-16°22'	+09°56'	-00°43'	-19°34'	+01°53'	+26°09'	+21°39'	-06°38'	+18°21'	-01°57'	-22°55'
5	-15°46'	+21°21'	-00°43'	-18°37'	+02°45'	+26°12'	+21°40'	-06°33'	+18°22'	-01°55'	-22°54'
7	-15°08'	+27°50'	-00°45'	-17°35'	+03°36'	+26°13'	+21°40'	-06°27'	+18°22'	-01°54'	-22°54'
9	-14°30'	+27°39'	-00°49'	-16°27'	+04°25'	+26°14'	+21°41'	-06°22'	+18°22'	-01°52'	-22°53'
11	-13°51'	+21°21'	-00°54'	-15°13'	+05°13'	+26°14'	+21°42'	-06°16'	+18°22'	-01°51'	-22°52'
13	-13°11'	+11°15'	-00°58'	-13°53'	+05°59'	+26°13'	+21°42'	-06°11'	+18°23'	-01°49'	-22°52'
15	-12°30'	-00°15'	-00°59'	-12°28'	+06°43'	+26°12'	+21°43'	-06°05'	+18°23'	-01°47'	-22°51'
17	-11°48'	-11°27'	-00°57'	-10°57'	+07°25'	+26°10'	+21°44'	-06°00'	+18°24'	-01°46'	-22°50'
19	-11°05'	-20°56'	-00°56'	-09°22'	+08°04'	+26°08'	+21°46'	-05°54'	+18°24'	-01°44'	-22°50'
21	-10°22'	-27°10'	-00°56'	-07°43'	+08°41'	+26°05'	+21°47'	-05°48'	+18°25'	-01°42'	-22°49'
23	-09°38'	-28°25'	-00°57'	-06°01'	+09°14'	+26°02'	+21°48'	-05°43'	+18°25'	-01°41'	-22°49'
25	-08°54'	-23°28'	-01°00'	-04°17'	+09°44'	+25°58'	+21°50'	-05°37'	+18°26'	-01°39'	-22°48'
27	-08°09'	-12°54'	-01°01'	-02°33'	+10°10'	+25°54'	+21°51'	-05°31'	+18°27'	-01°37'	-22°48'
28	-07°46'	-06°13'	-01°02'	-01°42'	+10°21'	+25°52'	+21°52'	-05°28'	+18°27'	-01°36'	-22°47'

Regulus 2025 Astrological Planner · 51

February, 2025

Degree of
Key Aspects

1 Feb 2025
♀ ☌ ♆ 27♓59 27♓59

3 Feb 2025
☿ △ ♃℞ 11♒17 11♊17

4 Feb 2025
♃D 11♊17

7 Feb 2025
♀ ⚹ ♇ 2♈16 2♒16

9 Feb 2025
☉ ☌ ☿ 21♒00 21♒00
♂℞ △ ♄ 18♋23 18♓23

10 Feb 2025
☿ □ ♅ 23♒19 23♉19

11 Feb 2025
☉ □ ♅ 23♒20 23♉20

20 Feb 2025
☿ □ ♃ 11♓44 11♊44

23 Feb 2025
☿ △ ♂℞ 17♓01 17♋01

24 Feb 2025
♂D 17♋01

25 Feb 2025
☿ ☌ ♄ 20♓16 20♓16

27 Feb 2025
☿ ⚹ ♅ 23♓36 23♉36

Sunday	Monday	Tuesday
26	27 AQUARIUS	28
2 ☽→♈ 1:10 ☽⚹♇ 4:40 ☽⚹☿ 16:35 ☽⚹♃ 20:03	3 ☽ voc 10:19 ☽⚹☉ 1:23 ☽□♂ 10:19 ☿△♃ 21:51	4 ☽→♉ 3:33 ☽□♇ 7:12 ♀→♈ 7:57 ♃ SD 9:28
9 ☿☌☉ 12:08 ♂△♄ 13:14 ☽☌♂ 19:47 ☽△♄ 19:56	10 ☽ voc 13:49 ☽→♌ 17:00 ☽⚹♅ 4:49 ☽△♆ 13:49 ☿□♅ 19:27 ☽☍♇ 21:20	11 ☽△♀ 1:21 ☽⚹♃ 13:59 ☉□♅ 19:30
16 ☽☍♀ 2:19 ☽△♃ 10:51 ☽□♂ 22:36	17 ☽ voc 23:24 ☽△☉ 23:24	18 ☽→♏ 0:19 ☽□♇ 5:34 ☉→♓ 10:06 ☽△☿ 15:55
23 ☽⚹☉ 8:26 ☿△♂ 16:58 ☽□♀ 17:52	24 ♂ SD 1:51 ☽☍♂ 6:32 ☽⚹☿ 8:41 ☽⚹♄ 12:10 ☽△♅ 18:14	25 ☽ voc 3:28 ☽→♒ 5:40 ☽⚹♆ 3:28 ☽☌♇ 10:32 ☿☌♄ 12:02 ☽⚹♀ 23:54

GMT

12 February, 2025
13:54 GMT

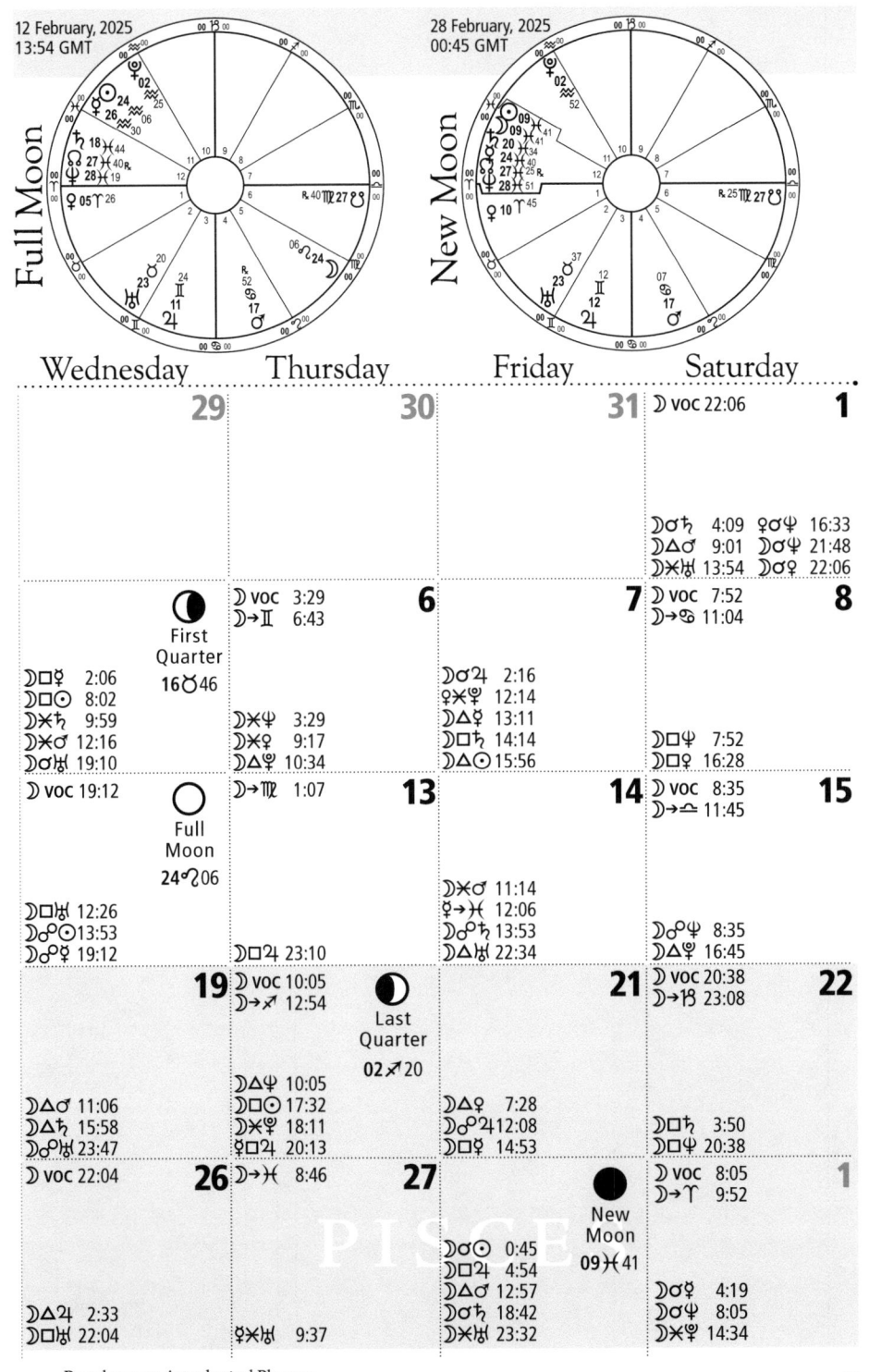

Full Moon

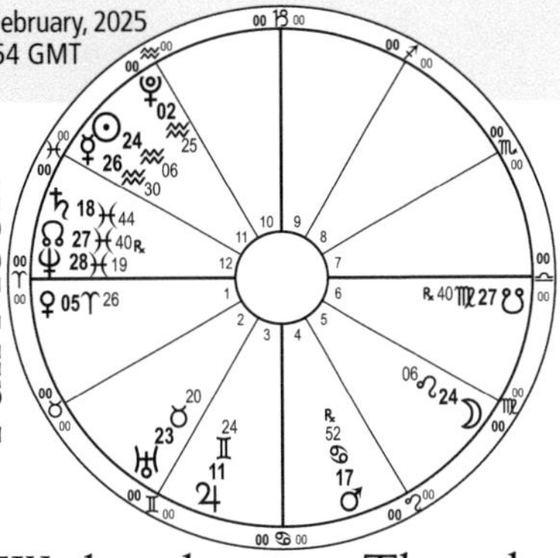

28 February, 2025
00:45 GMT

New Moon

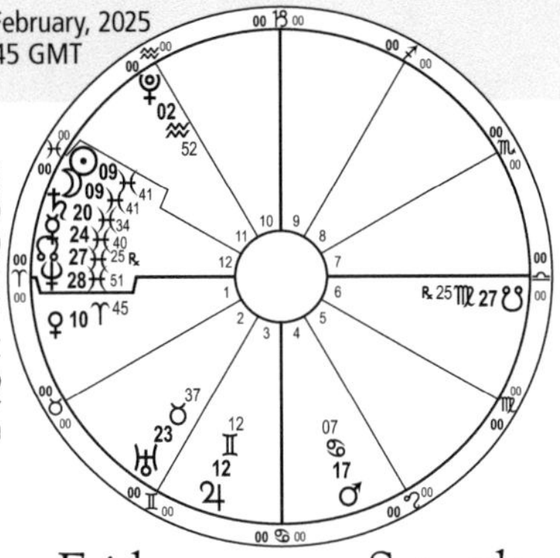

Wednesday	Thursday	Friday	Saturday
29	30	31	1 ☽ voc 22:06 ☽☌♄ 4:09 ☽△♂ 9:01 ☽⚹♅ 13:54 ♀☌♆ 16:33 ☽☌♆ 21:48 ☽☌♀ 22:06
First Quarter 16♉46 ☽□☿ 2:06 ☽□☉ 8:02 ☽⚹♄ 9:59 ☽⚹♂ 12:16 ☽☌♅ 19:10	6 ☽ voc 3:29 ☽→♊ 6:43 ☽⚹♆ 3:29 ☽⚹♀ 9:17 ☽△♇ 10:34	7 ☽☌♃ 2:16 ♀⚹♇ 12:14 ☽△☿ 13:11 ☽□♄ 14:14 ☽△☉ 15:56	8 ☽ voc 7:52 ☽→♋ 11:04 ☽□♆ 7:52 ☽□♀ 16:28
☽ voc 19:12 Full Moon 24♌06 ☽□♅ 12:26 ☽☍☉ 13:53 ☽☍☿ 19:12	13 ☽→♍ 1:07 ☽□♃ 23:10	14 ☽⚹♂ 11:14 ☿→♓ 12:06 ☽☍♄ 13:53 ☽△♅ 22:34	15 ☽ voc 8:35 ☽→♎ 11:45 ☽☍♆ 8:35 ☽△♇ 16:45
19 ☽△♂ 11:06 ☽△♄ 15:58 ☽☍♅ 23:47	☽ voc 10:05 ☽→♐ 12:54 Last Quarter 02♐20 ☽△♆ 10:05 ☽□☉ 17:32 ☽⚹♇ 18:11 ☿□♃ 20:13	21 ☽△♀ 7:28 ☽☍♃ 12:08 ☽□☿ 14:53	22 ☽ voc 20:38 ☽→♑ 23:08 ☽□♄ 3:50 ☽□♆ 20:38
26 ☽ voc 22:04 ☽△♃ 2:33 ☽□♅ 22:04	27 ☽→♓ 8:46 ♀⚹♅ 9:37	New Moon 09♓41 ☽☌☉ 0:45 ☽□♃ 4:54 ☽△♂ 12:57 ☽☌♄ 18:42 ☽⚹♅ 23:32	1 ☽ voc 8:05 ☽→♈ 9:52 ☽☌☿ 4:19 ☽☌♆ 8:05 ☽⚹♇ 14:34

PISCES

♒ Aquarius

Venus is conjunct Neptune on the 1st of February at 27° of Pisces. Love and beauty is intoxicating but it can also be beguiling and confusing.

On Monday the 3rd of February Mercury forms a trine to Jupiter as Jupiter turns direct. Moral and philosophical concepts are lucidly articulated. Communication is sincere and sound agreements can be made.

Venus enters Aries on the 4th of February and the First Quarter Sun-Moon square occurs on the following day. Venus is located close to the Sun-Moon midpoint at the time of the Sun-Moon square, so all considered, there's a fresh new impulse in matters related to Venus, such as love and friendship. New relationships may be formed and existing ones re-energised. This idea is reinforced by the approaching sextile of Venus and Pluto on the 7th of February.

◉ Sunday   ☽→♈   1:10

2

       ☽✶♆   4:40
       ☽✶♀   16:35
       ☽✶♃   20:03

☽ Monday   ☽ VOC   10:19

3

       ☽✶☉   1:23
       ☽□♂   10:19
       ☿△♃   21:51

♂ Tuesday   ☽→♉   3:33

4

       ☽□♇   7:12
       ♀→♈   7:57
       ♃ SD   9:28

GMT

February 2025

☿ Wednesday
5

◐
First Quarter
16♉46

☽□☿	2:06
☽□☉	8:02
☽⚹♄	9:59
☽⚹♂	12:16
☽☌♅	19:10

♃ Thursday
6

☽ VOC	3:29
☽→♊	6:43

☽⚹♆	3:29
☽⚹♀	9:17
☽△♇	10:34

♀ Friday
7

☽☌♃	2:16
♀⚹♇	12:14
☽△☿	13:11
☽□♄	14:14
☽△☉	15:56

♄ Saturday
8

☽ VOC	7:52
☽→♋	11:04

☽□♆	7:52
☽□♀	16:28

Regulus 2025 Astrological Planner

♒ Aquarius

On Sunday the Sun and Mercury form a conjunction lending a formal and official tone to news, messages and communications. Mars is trine Saturn on the same day which is purposeful, practical and hard-working. No time for nonsense.

The Full Moon on the 12th of February at 24° of Leo creates a t-square with Uranus, producing excitement, impulsivity, originality and a spirit of defiant independence. Events develop rapidly, suddenly and abruptly. Those with planets or angles on those degrees (23°-25° of Fixed signs) will be restless and edgy.

Mercury enters Pisces on the 14th of February. Information is lost or its meaning is confounding. Communication is subtle, elusive or secretive.

☉ Sunday

9

☿σ☉	12:08
♂△♄	13:14
☽σσ	19:47
☽△♄	19:56

☽ Monday

10

☽VOC	13:49
☽→♌	17:00

☽⚹♅	4:49
☽△♆	13:49
☿□♅	19:27
☽☍♇	21:20

♂ Tuesday

11

☽△♀	1:21
☽⚹♃	13:59
☉□♅	19:30

GMT

February 2025

☿ Wednesday
12

☽ VOC 19:12

○
Full Moon
24 ♌ 06

☽□♅ 12:26
☽☌☉ 13:53
☽☌☿ 19:12

♃ Thursday
13

☽→♍ 1:07

☽□♃ 23:10

♀ Friday
14

☽⚹♂ 11:14
☿→♓ 12:06
☽☌♄ 13:53
☽△♅ 22:34

♄ Saturday
15

☽ VOC 8:35
☽→♎ 11:45

☽☌♆ 8:35
☽△⚷ 16:45

Regulus 2025 Astrological Planner 57

♓ Pisces

Congratulations Pisceans!

Venus is semi-square Uranus on the 18th of February. Social and romantic interactions occur suddenly and surprisingly and there may be an unconventional quality to it.

At the time of the Third Quarter Sun-Moon square at 2° Sagittarius Mars is in close opposition to the Sun-Moon midpoint, and so we can expect some unruly and aggressive energy. At best this combination is energising in a productive way, providing the vigor to get things done.

Mercury is square Jupiter on the 20th of February and so ideas and plans are big and bold. There's some danger of exaggeration or miscalculation, even if in essence the ideas are good.

☉ Sunday
16

☽☌☍☿ 2:19
☽△♃ 10:51
☽□♂ 22:36

☽ Monday
17

☽ voc 23:24

☽△☉ 23:24

♂ Tuesday
18

☽→♏ 0:19

☽□♅ 5:34
☉→♓ 10:06
☽△♀ 15:55

GMT

February 2025

☿ Wednesday

19

☽△♂ 11:06
☽△♄ 15:58
☽☍♅ 23:47

♃ Thursday

20

☽ voc 10:05
☽→♐ 12:54

◐
Last Quarter
02♐20

☽△♆ 10:05
☽□☉ 17:32
☽⚹♇ 18:11
☿□♃ 20:13

♀ Friday

21

☽△♀ 7:28
☽☍♃ 12:08
☽□☿ 14:53

♄ Saturday

22

☽ voc 20:38
☽→♑ 23:08

☽□♄ 3:50
☽□♆ 20:38

Regulus 2025 Astrological Planner 59

♓ Pisces

Mercury forms a trine to Mars on Sunday the 23rd of February as Mars prepares to turn direct on the following day. Discussion is forthright and spirited. Views and opinions are expressed with penetrating incisiveness. With Mars turning direct there can be drive and motivation and a spilling over of pent-up aggressive energy.

On the following day, Mercury reaches a conjunction with Saturn which suggests grave and serious communication, or no communication at all. At best, this energy facilitates the execution of tedious and painstaking mental tasks. At worst it represents fault finding and nitpicking.

On Thursday the 27th of February Mercury forms a sextile aspect to Uranus, bringing fresh new ideas and perspective. On the following day we have the New Moon at 9° Pisces forming a square to Jupiter and a wide conjunction with Saturn. There's a restless drive to expand which is constrained by limiting circumstances.

☉ Sunday
23

☽✶☉	8:26
☿△♂	16:58
☽□♀	17:52

☽ Monday
24

♂ SD	1:51
☽☍♂	6:32
☽✶♀	8:41
☽✶♄	12:10
☽△♅	18:14
☽ VOC	3:28
☽→♒	5:40

♂ Tuesday
25

☽✶♆	3:28
☽☌♇	10:32
☿☌♄	12:02
☽✶♀	23:54

GMT

February 2025

☿ **Wednesday** ☽VOC 22:04

26

☽△♃ 2:33
☽□♅ 22:04

♃ **Thursday** ☽→♓ 8:46

27

☿⚹♅ 9:37

♀ **Friday**

28

● New Moon
09♓41

☽☌☉ 0:45
☽□♃ 4:54
☽△♂ 12:57
☽☌♄ 18:42
☽⚹♅ 23:32

♄ **Saturday** ☽VOC 8:05
☽→♈ 9:52

1 Março

☽☌☿ 4:19
☽☌♆ 8:05
☽⚹♇ 14:34

Regulus 2025 Astrological Planner   61

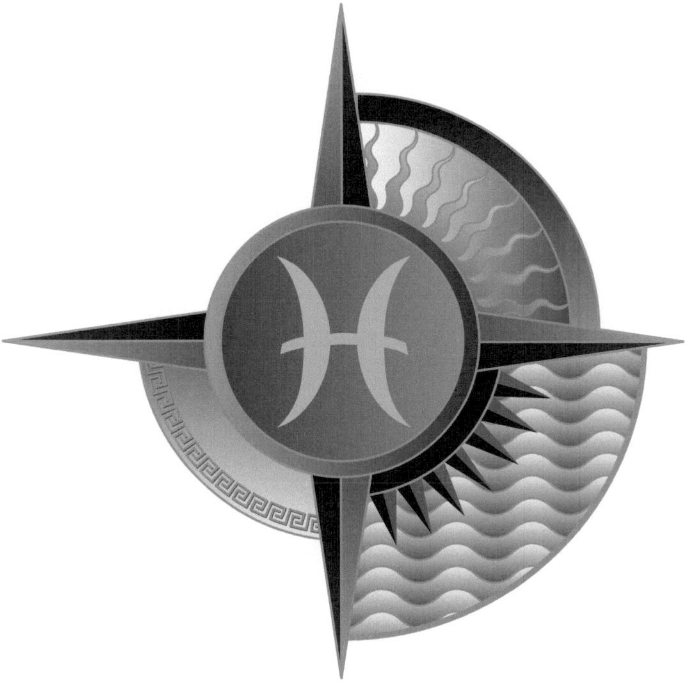

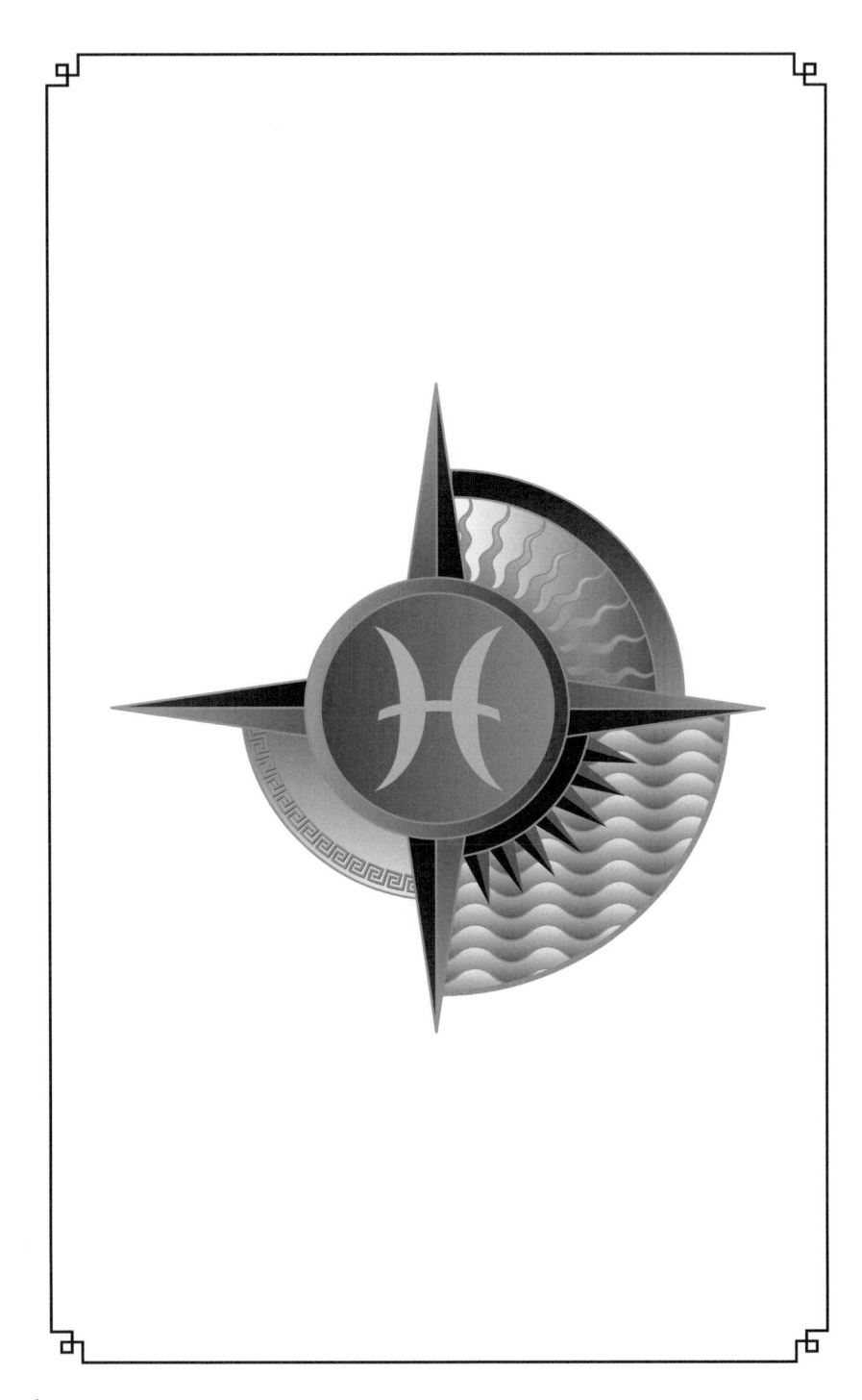

Ephemeris for March 2025, set at Midnight GMT.

March 2025

Day	☉	☽	True ☊	☿	♀	♂	♃	♄	♅	♆	♇
01	10 ♓ 38 54	23 ♓ 55 25	27 ♓ 24 R	26 ♓ 17 D	10 ♈ 49 D	17 ♋ 10 D	12 ♊ 16 D	20 ♓ 41 D	23 ♉ 38 D	28 ♓ 54 D	02 ♒ 53 D
02	11 39 09	08 ♈ 43 27	27 24 D	27 54	10 50	17 14	12 21	20 49	23 40	28 56	02 55
03	12 39 21	23 30 11	27 25	29 26	10 49 R	17 18	12 26	20 56	23 41	28 58	02 56
04	13 39 32	08 ♉ 09 12	27 26	00 ♈ 54	10 45	17 24	12 31	21 03	23 43	29 00	02 58
05	14 39 40	22 35 30	27 27	02 17	10 39	17 29	12 37	21 11	23 45	29 02	02 59
06	15 39 46	06 ♊ 45 51	27 28	03 34	10 31	17 36	12 42	21 18	23 46	29 05	03 01
07	16 39 51	20 38 38	27 28 R	04 45	10 19	17 43	12 48	21 26	23 48	29 07	03 03
08	17 39 53	04 ♋ 13 34	27 28	05 49	10 06	17 51	12 54	21 33	23 50	29 09	03 04
09	18 39 53	17 31 16	27 27	06 46	09 49	18 00	13 00	21 40	23 52	29 11	03 05
10	19 39 50	00 ♌ 32 56	27 26	07 35	09 31	18 09	13 06	21 48	23 54	29 14	03 07
11	20 39 46	13 19 57	27 25	08 16	09 10	18 18	13 12	21 55	23 56	29 16	03 08
12	21 39 39	25 53 45	27 24	08 49	08 46	18 29	13 19	22 03	23 58	29 18	03 10
13	22 39 30	08 ♍ 15 49	27 24	09 13	08 21	18 39	13 26	22 10	24 00	29 20	03 11
14	23 39 20	20 27 37	27 23	09 28	07 53	18 51	13 32	22 17	24 02	29 23	03 13
15	24 39 07	02 ♎ 30 41	27 23 D	09 35	07 24	19 02	13 39	22 25	24 04	29 25	03 14
16	25 38 52	14 26 51	27 23	09 33 R	06 52	19 15	13 46	22 32	24 06	29 27	03 15
17	26 38 36	26 18 11	27 23	09 23	06 20	19 28	13 54	22 40	24 08	29 29	03 16
18	27 38 17	08 ♏ 07 16	27 23 R	09 05	05 45	19 41	14 01	22 47	24 10	29 32	03 18
19	28 37 57	19 57 04	27 23	08 39	05 10	19 55	14 09	22 54	24 13	29 34	03 19
20	29 37 35	01 ♐ 51 07	27 23	08 07	04 33	20 09	14 16	23 02	24 15	29 36	03 20
21	00 ♈ 37 12	13 53 21	27 23	07 29	03 56	20 24	14 24	23 09	24 17	29 38	03 21
22	01 36 47	26 08 00	27 23	06 46	03 19	20 40	14 32	23 16	24 20	29 41	03 23
23	02 36 20	08 ♑ 39 23	27 23 D	05 58	02 41	20 55	14 40	23 24	24 22	29 43	03 24
24	03 35 51	21 31 38	27 23	05 08	02 03	21 12	14 48	23 31	24 24	29 45	03 25
25	04 35 20	04 ♒ 48 07	27 24	04 16	01 26	21 28	14 57	23 39	24 27	29 48	03 26
26	05 34 48	18 30 58	27 24	03 23	00 49	21 45	15 05	23 46	24 30	29 50	03 27
27	06 34 14	02 ♓ 40 26	27 25	02 30	00 13	22 03	15 14	23 53	24 32	29 52	03 28
28	07 33 38	17 14 17	27 26	01 39	29 ♓ 38	22 21	15 22	24 00	24 35	29 54	03 29
29	08 32 59	02 ♈ 07 36	27 26 R	00 50	29 04	22 39	15 31	24 08	24 37	29 57	03 30
30	09 32 19	17 12 59	27 25	00 04	28 32	22 58	15 40	24 15	24 40	29 59	03 31
31	10 31 37	02 ♉ 21 26	27 24	29 ♓ 22	28 01	23 17	15 49	24 22	24 43	00 ♈ 01	03 32

Declination

Day	☉	☽	True ☊	☿	♀	♂	♃	♄	♅	♆	♇
1	-07°23'	+00°51'	-01°02'	-00°51'	+10°32'	+25°50'	+21°53'	-05°25'	+18°28'	-01°35'	-22°47'
3	-06°37'	+14°29'	-01°01'	+00°47'	+10°49'	+25°45'	+21°54'	-05°20'	+18°28'	-01°34'	-22°47'
5	-05°51'	+24°39'	-01°00'	+02°19'	+11°01'	+25°40'	+21°56'	-05°14'	+18°29'	-01°32'	-22°46'
7	-05°04'	+28°42'	-01°01'	+03°40'	+11°08'	+25°34'	+21°58'	-05°08'	+18°30'	-01°30'	-22°46'
9	-04°17'	+25°57'	-01°01'	+04°50'	+11°09'	+25°29'	+22°00'	-05°02'	+18°31'	-01°28'	-22°46'
11	-03°30'	+18°00'	-01°03'	+05°46'	+11°05'	+25°22'	+22°02'	-04°56'	+18°32'	-01°27'	-22°45'
13	-02°43'	+07°15'	-01°03'	+06°25'	+10°54'	+25°16'	+22°04'	-04°51'	+18°33'	-01°25'	-22°45'
15	-01°56'	-04°19'	-01°03'	+06°46'	+10°37'	+25°09'	+22°06'	-04°45'	+18°34'	-01°23'	-22°44'
17	-01°08'	-15°05'	-01°03'	+06°49'	+10°15'	+25°02'	+22°08'	-04°39'	+18°35'	-01°21'	-22°44'
19	-00°21'	-23°37'	-01°02'	+06°34'	+09°47'	+24°55'	+22°10'	-04°33'	+18°37'	-01°19'	-22°44'
21	+00°27'	-28°17'	-01°02'	+06°03'	+09°14'	+24°47'	+22°12'	-04°28'	+18°38'	-01°18'	-22°44'
23	+01°14'	-27°36'	-01°02'	+05°17'	+08°37'	+24°39'	+22°14'	-04°22'	+18°39'	-01°16'	-22°43'
25	+02°01'	-20°57'	-01°02'	+04°20'	+07°58'	+24°30'	+22°16'	-04°16'	+18°40'	-01°14'	-22°43'
27	+02°48'	-09°20'	-01°01'	+03°18'	+07°16'	+24°21'	+22°19'	-04°11'	+18°41'	-01°12'	-22°43'
29	+03°35'	+04°51'	-01°01'	+02°14'	+06°33'	+24°12'	+22°21'	-04°05'	+18°43'	-01°10'	-22°43'
31	+04°22'	+18°10'	-01°02'	+01°13'	+05°50'	+24°03'	+22°23'	-03°59'	+18°44'	-01°09'	-22°43'

Regulus 2025 Astrological Planner 63

March, 2025

Degree of
Key Aspects

2 Mar 2025
♀℞ 10♈50
☿ ☌ ♆ 28♓57 28♓57
☉ □ ♃ 12♓25 12♊25

5 Mar 2025
☿ ⚹ ♇ 3♈00 3♒00

8 Mar 2025
☉ △ ♂ 17♓53 17♋53

11 Mar 2025
☿ ☌ ♀℞ 8♈48 8♈48

12 Mar 2025
☉ ☌ ♄ 22♓06 22♓06

14 Mar 2025
☉ ⚹ ♅ 24♓02 24♉02

15 Mar 2025
☿℞ 9♈35

19 Mar 2025
☉ ☌ ♆ 29♓36 29♓36

21 Mar 2025
♀℞ ⚹ ♇ 3♈23 3♒23

23 Mar 2025
☉ ☌ ♀℞ 2♈39 2♈39
☉ ⚹ ♇ 3♈25 3♒25

24 Mar 2025
☉ ☌ ☿℞ 4♈25 4♈25

25 Mar 2025
☿℞ ⚹ ♇ 3♈27 3♒27

27 Mar 2025
♀℞ ☌ ♆ 29♓53 29♓53

30 Mar 2025
☿℞ ☌ ♆ 29♓59 29♓59

PISCES

Sunday	Monday	Tuesday
2 ☽ voc 13:52 ♀ SR 0:36 ☽☌♀ 3:25 ☽⚹♃ 5:55 ☽□♂ 13:52 ☿☌♆ 16:22 ☉□♃ 18:18	**3** ☽→♉ 10:36 ☿→♈ 9:03 ☽□♇ 15:27	**4** ☽⚹☉ 9:47 ☽⚹♂ 15:25 ☽⚹♄ 21:37
9 ☽ voc 21:32 ☽→♌ 22:59 ☽☌♂ 0:52 ☽△☉ 2:16 ☽△♄ 7:40 ☽⚹♅ 11:39 ☽△♆ 21:32	**10** ☽☍♇ 4:47 ☽△☿ 13:56 ☽△♀ 16:20 ☽⚹♃ 23:46	**11** ☽ voc 20:16 ☽□♅ 20:16 ☿☌♀ 22:54
16 ☽ voc 9:53 ☽□♂ 9:53	**17** ☽→♏ 7:30 ☽□♇ 14:11	**18** ☽△♂ 23:56
23 ♀☌☉ 1:07 ☉⚹♇ 19:32 ☽☍♂ 23:22	**24** ☽ voc 15:00 ☽→♒ 15:24 ☽⚹♄ 3:41 ☽△♅ 5:17 ☽⚹♆ 15:00 ☽⚹♀ 18:14 ☿☌☉ 19:48 ☽☌♇ 21:34 ☽⚹☿ 23:06 ☽⚹☉ 23:35	**25** ☽△♃ 18:00 ☿⚹♇ 22:02
30 ☽ voc 9:18 ☽→♉ 20:15 ☿→♓ 2:18 ☿☌♆ 2:46 ☽□♂ 9:18 ♆→♈ 11:59	**31**	**1**

Charts cast with Natural House System in GMT

Lunar Eclipse
14 March, 2025
5:59 GMT

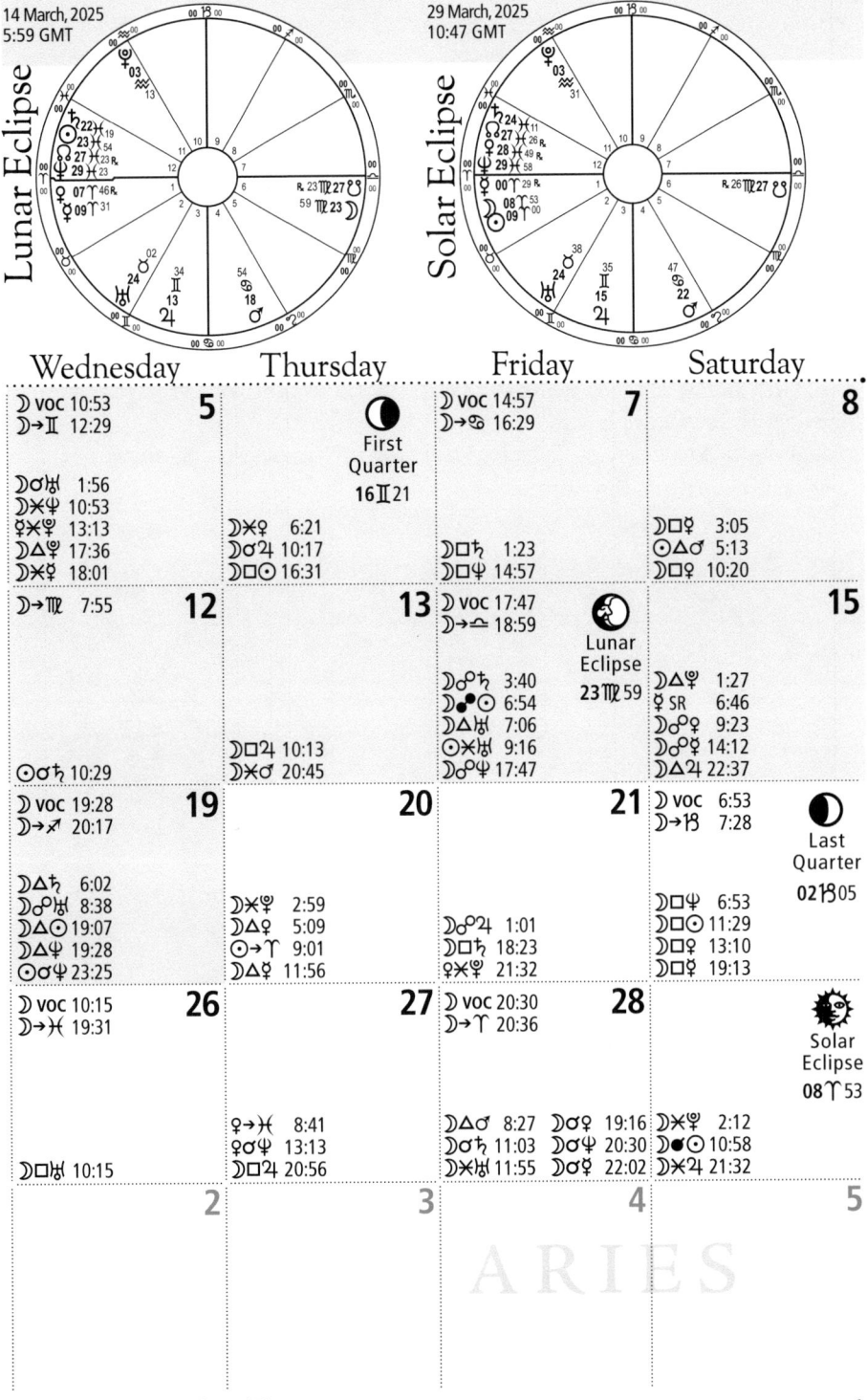

Solar Eclipse
29 March, 2025
10:47 GMT

Wednesday	Thursday	Friday	Saturday
5 ☽ voc 10:53 ☽→♊ 12:29 ☽☌♅ 1:56 ☽⚹♆ 10:53 ☿☌♇ 13:13 ☽△♇ 17:36 ☽⚹♀ 18:01	**6** ◐ First Quarter 16♊21 ☽⚹☿ 6:21 ☽☌♃ 10:17 ☽☐☉ 16:31	**7** ☽ voc 14:57 ☽→♋ 16:29 ☽☐♄ 1:23 ☽☐♆ 14:57	**8** ☽☐☿ 3:05 ☉△♂ 5:13 ☽☐♀ 10:20
12 ☽→♍ 7:55 ☉☌♄ 10:29	**13** ☽☐♃ 10:13 ☽⚹♂ 20:45	**14** ☽ voc 17:47 ☽→♎ 18:59 ☽☌♄ 3:40 ☽●☉ 6:54 ☽△♅ 7:06 ☉⚹♆ 9:16 ☽☌♆ 17:47 Lunar Eclipse 23♍59	**15** ☽△♇ 1:27 ☿ SR 6:46 ☽☌♀ 9:23 ☽☌☿ 14:12 ☽△♃ 22:37
19 ☽ voc 19:28 ☽→♐ 20:17 ☽△♄ 6:02 ☽☌♅ 8:38 ☽△☉ 19:07 ☽△♆ 19:28 ☉☌♀ 23:25	**20** ☽⚹♇ 2:59 ☽△♀ 5:09 ☉→♈ 9:01 ☽△☿ 11:56	**21** ☽☌♃ 1:01 ☽☐♄ 18:23 ♀⚹♆ 21:32	**22** ☽ voc 6:53 ☽→♑ 7:28 ☽☐♆ 6:53 ☽☐☉ 11:29 ☽☐♀ 13:10 ☽☐☿ 19:13 ◑ Last Quarter 02♑05
26 ☽ voc 10:15 ☽→♓ 19:31 ☽☐♅ 10:15	**27** ♀→♓ 8:41 ♀☌♆ 13:13 ☽☐♃ 20:56	**28** ☽ voc 20:30 ☽→♈ 20:36 ☽△♂ 8:27 ☽☌♆ 11:03 ☽⚹♅ 11:55	**29** ☽☌♀ 19:16 ☽☌♆ 20:30 ☽☌☿ 22:02 ☽⚹♇ 2:12 ☽●☉ 10:58 ☽⚹♃ 21:32 Solar Eclipse 08♈53
2	3	4	5

ARIES

Regulus 2025 Astrological Planner

65

♓ Pisces

Venus turns retrograde on the 2nd of March while at 10° Aries. There is a change of gear in the realm of personal relationships. On the same day Mercury and Neptune arrive at a conjunction, and communication is vague and fuzzy. There is potential here for misinterpretation and miscalculation. Mercury combining with Neptune can also indicate abstract ideas, poetry, and information or texts about spiritual realities.

On Monday the 3rd of March Mercury enters Aries and brings a surge of new information into the public sphere. Then Mercury forms a sextile to Pluto on the 5th of March and there's deep analysis and research. Penetrating and insightful discussions can occur.

The Sun is trine Mars on Saturday the 8th of March. This energy is vigorous, courageous, assertive and enthusiastic.

☉ Sunday

2

☽ VOC 13:52

♀ SR   0:36
☽ ☌ ♀   3:25
☽ ⚹ ♃   5:55
☽ □ ♂   13:52
☿ ☌ ♆   16:22
☉ □ ♃   18:18

☽ Monday

3

☽ → ♉   10:36

☿ → ♈   9:03
☽ □ ♇   15:27

♂ Tuesday

4

☽ ⚹ ☉   9:47
☽ ⚹ ♂   15:25
☽ ⚹ ♄   21:37

GMT

March 2025

☿ **Wednesday**
5

☽VOC 10:53
☽→♊ 12:29

☽☌♅ 1:56
☽⚹♆ 10:53
☿⚹♇ 13:13
☽△⚷ 17:36
☽⚹☿ 18:01

♃ **Thursday**
6

◐
First Quarter
16♊21

☽⚹♀ 6:21
☽☌♃ 10:17
☽□☉ 16:31

♀ **Friday**
7

☽VOC 14:57
☽→♋ 16:29

☽□♄ 1:23
☽□♆ 14:57

♄ **Saturday**
8

☽□☿ 3:05
☉△♂ 5:13
☽□♀ 10:20
☽☌♂ 0:52
☽△☉ 2:16

Regulus 2025 Astrological Planner   67

♓ Pisces

On Tuesday the 11th of March Mercury and Venus form a conjunction at 8° of Aries and so there will be sweet talk and love letters. Relationship dynamics are analysed and discussed.

On Thursday there's a Lunar Eclipse with the Moon at 23° Virgo. Saturn is very close to the Sun and opposite the Moon at this time, making this a serious and somber eclipse. This opposition also engages with Uranus, which implies that there is enthusiasm for new, novel and creative ideas. At best, all of this could describe the implementation of new systems and methods that yield concrete, practical results, improving on approaches and methods of the past.

Mercury turns retrograde on Saturday the 15th of March and remains retrograde until the 7th of April. During this period keep reviewing ongoing plans and dedicate your attention to unfinished business. Expect delays.

☉ Sunday

9

☽ VOC 21:32
☽→♌ 22:59

☽ Monday

10

☽△♄ 7:40
☽✶♅ 11:39
☽△♆ 21:32

♂ Tuesday

11

☽☌♀ 4:47
☽△☿ 13:56
☽△♀ 16:20
☽✶♃ 23:46

☽ VOC 20:16

☽□♅ 20:16
☿☌♀ 22:54

---

68   GMT

March 2025

Mercury is retrograde from March 15th (☿ᴿ 9°35'♈) through April 7th (☿ᴰ 26°50'♓).

☿ Wednesday

12

☽→♍   7:55

☉☌♄   10:29

♃ Thursday

13

☽□♃   10:13
☽⚹♂   20:45

♀ Friday

14

☽VOC   17:47
☽→♎   18:59

Lunar Eclipse
23 ♍ 59

☽☍♄   3:40
☽☌☊☉   6:54
☽△♅   7:06
☉⚹♅   9:16
☽☍♆   17:47

♄ Saturday

15

☽△♆   1:27
☿ SR   6:46
☽☌♀   9:23
☽☌☿   14:12
☽△♃   22:37

♈ Aries

Congratulations Arians! The Sun arrives at a conjunction with Neptune on the 19th of March, just prior to the Spring Equinox on the 20th of March. There's a yearning for spiritual or mystical experiences. Some may try to achieve this through getting intoxicated or engaging in some kind of escapist behaviour. The proximity of Neptune to the Sun at the day of equinox may in fact indicate that the world is in for a year of fantasies and dreams. There's a lack of focus and clear purpose.

Venus forms a sextile to Pluto on the 21st of March making social and romantic interactions deep and intense, and perhaps prone to expressions of jealousy. The Third Quarter Sun-Moon square at 2° Capricorn also highlights Venus which is backing to a conjunction with the Sun. The Venus-Sun conjunction becomes exact on Sunday the 23rd. Friendship and romance gains greater priority, new relationships are formed and existing relationships are invigorated.

☉ Sunday ☽VOC 9:53
16

☽ Monday ☽□♂ 9:53
☽→♏ 7:30
17

♂ Tuesday ☽□♇ 14:11
18

☽△♂ 23:56

Mercury is retrograde from March 15th (☿℞ 9°35'♈) through April 7th (☿D 26°50'♓).

☿ Wednesday

19

☽VOC 19:28
☽→♐ 20:17

☽△♄ 6:02
☽☍♅ 8:38
☽△☉ 19:07
☽△♆ 19:28
☉☌♆ 23:25

♃ Thursday

20

Spring Equinox

☽⚹♇ 2:59
☽△♀ 5:09
☉→♈ 9:01
☽△☿ 11:56

♀ Friday

21

☽☍♃ 1:01
☽□♄ 18:23
♀⚹♇ 21:32

♄ Saturday

22

☽VOC 6:53
☽→♑ 7:28

Last Quarter
02♑05

☽□♆ 6:53
☽□☉ 11:29
☽□♀ 13:10
☽□☿ 19:13

♈ Aries

On Monday the 24th of March retrograde Mercury will be conjunct the Sun, lending a formal and official tone to news, messages and communications. Add to this the fact that Mercury is forming a sextile to Pluto on the 25th and we get a narrative of deep analysis and research. Penetrating and insightful discussions can occur.

On Thursday the 27th of March retrograde Venus backs into Pisces and makes a conjunction to Neptune. Love and beauty is intoxicating but it can also be beguiling and confusing.

On Saturday the 29th of March there's a Partial Solar Eclipse at 8° Aries. This Sun-Moon conjunction forms a semi-square aspect to Uranus. This is live-wire energy. Events occur suddenly, abruptly and surprisingly. There's a love of the new and the novel and there may be expressions of self-will and defiance.

☉ Sunday
23

♀☌☉	1:07
☉⚹♇	19:32
☽☍♂	23:22

☽ Monday
24

☽ VOC	15:00
☽→♒	15:24

☽⚹♄	3:41
☽△♅	5:17
☽⚹♆	15:00
☽⚹♀	18:14
☿☌☉	19:48
☽☌♇	21:34
☽⚹♀	23:06
☽⚹☉	23:35

♂ Tuesday
25

☽△♃	18:00
☿⚹♇	22:02

72   GMT

March 2025

Mercury is retrograde from March 15th (☿℞ 9°35'♈) through April 7th (☿D 26°50'♓).

☿ **Wednesday**
26

☽ VOC 10:15
☽→♓ 19:31

☽□♅ 10:15

♃ **Thursday**
27

♀→♓ 8:41
♀☌♆ 13:13
☽□♃ 20:56

♀ **Friday**
28

☽ VOC 20:30
☽→♈ 20:36

☽△♂ 8:27
☽☌♄ 11:03
☽✶♅ 11:55
☽☌♀ 19:16
☽☌♆ 20:30
☽☌☿ 22:02

♄ **Saturday**
29

Solar Eclipse
08 ♈ 53

☽✶♇ 2:12
☽●☉ 10:48
☽✶♃ 21:32

Regulus 2025 Astrological Planner 73

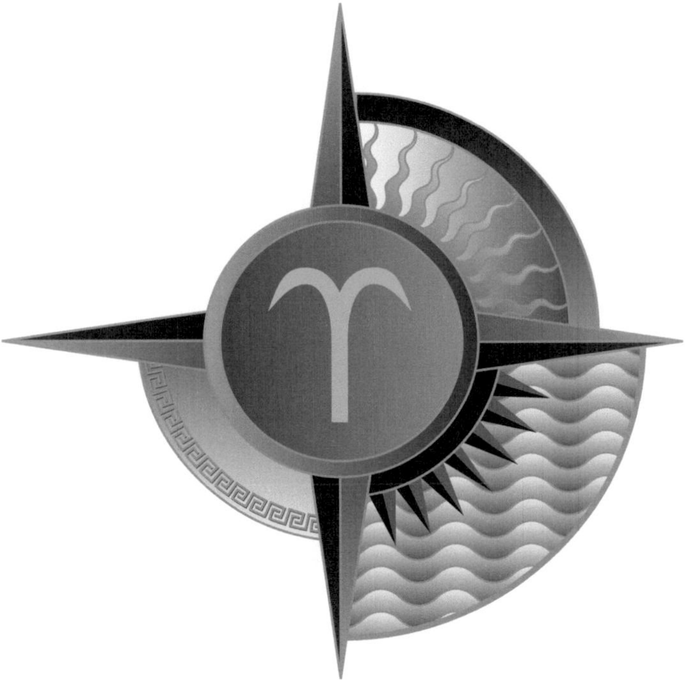

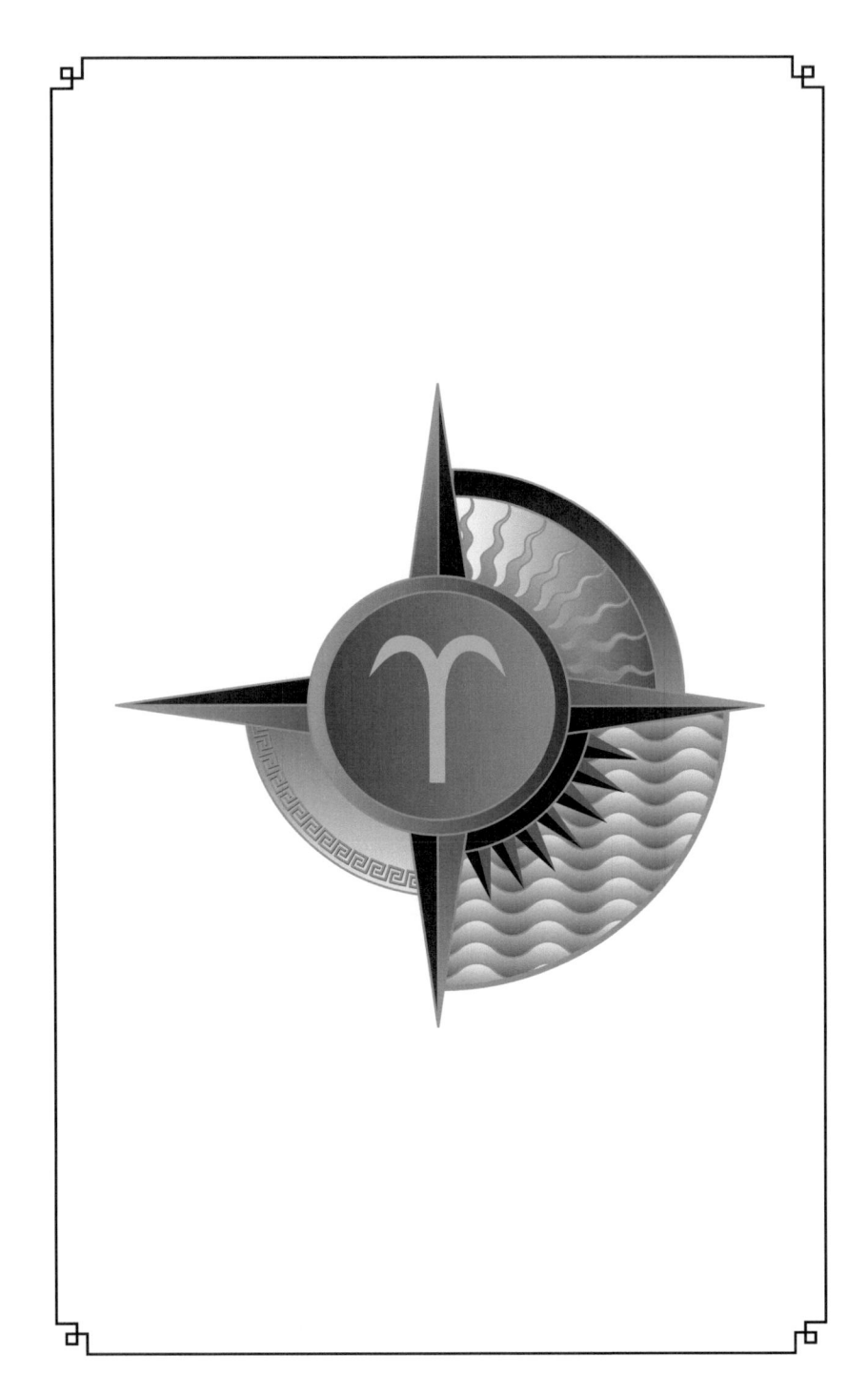

Ephemeris for April 2025, set at Midnight GMT.

April 2025

Day	☉	☽	True ☊	☿	♀	♂	♃	♄	♅	♆	♇
01	11 ♈ 30 53	17 ♉ 23 34	27 ♓ 22 R	28 ♓ 45 R	27 ♓ 32 R	23 ♋ 36 D	15 ♊ 59 D	24 ♓ 29 D	24 ♉ 45 D	00 ♈ 03 D	03 ♒ 33 D
02	12 30 07	02 ♊ 11 05	27 21	28 12	27 05	23 56	16 08	24 37	24 48	00 06	03 34
03	13 29 18	16 37 53	27 19	27 45	26 40	24 16	16 18	24 44	24 51	00 08	03 35
04	14 28 27	00 ♋ 40 29	27 18	27 23	26 17	24 36	16 27	24 51	24 54	00 10	03 36
05	15 27 34	14 18 00	27 17	27 06	25 56	24 57	16 37	24 58	24 57	00 12	03 37
06	16 26 38	27 31 33	27 18 D	26 55	25 38	25 19	16 47	25 05	25 00	00 14	03 38
07	17 25 40	10 ♌ 23 40	27 19	26 50	25 22	25 40	16 56	25 12	25 02	00 17	03 38
08	18 24 40	22 57 36	27 20	26 50 D	25 08	26 02	17 07	25 19	25 05	00 19	03 39
09	19 23 38	05 ♍ 16 50	27 21	26 56	24 57	26 24	17 17	25 26	25 08	00 21	03 40
10	20 22 33	17 24 45	27 23	27 07	24 49	26 46	17 27	25 33	25 11	00 23	03 41
11	21 21 26	29 24 23	27 23 R	27 22	24 43	27 09	17 37	25 40	25 14	00 25	03 41
12	22 20 17	11 ♎ 18 24	27 22	27 43	24 39	27 32	17 48	25 47	25 17	00 28	03 42
13	23 19 06	23 09 07	27 20	28 08	24 37	27 55	17 58	25 54	25 20	00 30	03 42
14	24 17 52	04 ♏ 58 38	27 17	28 38	24 39 D	28 19	18 09	26 01	25 24	00 32	03 43
15	25 16 38	16 48 55	27 12	29 11	24 42	28 43	18 19	26 08	25 27	00 34	03 44
16	26 15 21	28 41 59	27 06	29 49	24 48	29 07	18 30	26 14	25 30	00 36	03 44
17	27 14 02	10 ♐ 40 05	27 02	00 ♈ 31	24 56	29 31	18 41	26 21	25 33	00 38	03 45
18	28 12 42	22 45 51	26 57	01 16	25 06	29 56	18 52	26 28	25 36	00 40	03 45
19	29 11 20	05 ♑ 02 16	26 54	02 05	25 18	00 ♌ 20	19 03	26 34	25 39	00 42	03 46
20	00 ♉ 09 56	17 32 44	26 51	02 57	25 33	00 45	19 14	26 41	25 43	00 44	03 46
21	01 08 31	00 ♒ 20 49	26 51	03 52	25 49	01 11	19 26	26 48	25 46	00 46	03 46
22	02 07 04	13 30 05	26 51 D	04 50	26 07	01 36	19 37	26 54	25 49	00 48	03 47
23	03 05 35	27 03 33	26 52	05 51	26 28	02 02	19 48	27 01	25 52	00 50	03 47
24	04 04 05	11 ♓ 03 01	26 54	06 55	26 50	02 28	20 00	27 07	25 56	00 52	03 48
25	05 02 33	25 28 26	26 55	08 01	27 13	02 54	20 11	27 14	25 59	00 54	03 48
26	06 00 59	10 ♈ 17 03	26 54 R	09 10	27 39	03 20	20 23	27 20	26 02	00 56	03 48
27	06 59 24	25 23 06	26 52	10 22	28 06	03 47	20 35	27 26	26 06	00 58	03 48
28	07 57 47	10 ♉ 38 03	26 47	11 36	28 35	04 14	20 46	27 32	26 09	01 00	03 48
29	08 56 08	25 51 34	26 41	12 52	29 05	04 41	20 58	27 39	26 12	01 02	03 49
30	09 54 28	10 ♊ 53 16	26 35	14 10	29 36	05 08	21 10	27 45	26 16	01 04	03 49

Declination

Day	☉	☽	True ☊	☿	♀	♂	♃	♄	♅	♆	♇
1	+04°45'	+23°17'	-01°03'	+00°45'	+05°29'	+23°58'	+22°24'	-03°57'	+18°45'	-01°08'	-22°43'
3	+05°31'	+28°33'	-01°04'	-00°06'	+04°47'	+23°47'	+22°27'	-03°51'	+18°46'	-01°06'	-22°43'
5	+06°17'	+26°35'	-01°05'	-00°48'	+04°08'	+23°37'	+22°29'	-03°46'	+18°48'	-01°04'	-22°43'
7	+07°02'	+19°06'	-01°04'	-01°20'	+03°31'	+23°26'	+22°31'	-03°40'	+18°49'	-01°03'	-22°43'
9	+07°47'	+08°39'	-01°03'	-01°42'	+02°58'	+23°15'	+22°33'	-03°35'	+18°50'	-01°01'	-22°43'
11	+08°31'	-02°48'	-01°03'	-01°53'	+02°29'	+23°03'	+22°35'	-03°30'	+18°52'	-00°59'	-22°43'
13	+09°14'	-13°43'	-01°05'	-01°54'	+02°03'	+22°51'	+22°38'	-03°24'	+18°53'	-00°58'	-22°43'
15	+09°57'	-22°37'	-01°08'	-01°46'	+01°41'	+22°39'	+22°40'	-03°19'	+18°55'	-00°56'	-22°43'
17	+10°40'	-27°53'	-01°12'	-01°30'	+01°23'	+22°26'	+22°42'	-03°14'	+18°56'	-00°54'	-22°43'
19	+11°21'	-27°59'	-01°14'	-01°05'	+01°10'	+22°13'	+22°44'	-03°09'	+18°58'	-00°53'	-22°43'
21	+12°02'	-22°25'	-01°15'	-00°32'	+01°00'	+21°59'	+22°46'	-03°04'	+19°00'	-00°51'	-22°43'
23	+12°43'	-11°57'	-01°14'	+00°07'	+00°54'	+21°45'	+22°48'	-02°59'	+19°01'	-00°50'	-22°43'
25	+13°22'	+01°36'	-01°13'	+00°52'	+00°52'	+21°30'	+22°50'	-02°54'	+19°03'	-00°48'	-22°44'
27	+14°00'	+15°23'	-01°16'	+01°44'	+00°54'	+21°16'	+22°52'	-02°50'	+19°04'	-00°47'	-22°44'
29	+14°38'	+25°29'	-01°20'	+02°41'	+00°58'	+21°00'	+22°54'	-02°45'	+19°06'	-00°45'	-22°44'

Regulus 2025 Astrological Planner

April, 2025

Degree of
Key Aspects

4 Apr 2025			
♄ ⚹ ♅	24♓56	24♉56	
♂ ⚹ ♅	24♋57	24♉57	
5 Apr 2025			
♂ △ ♄	24♋58	24♓58	
6 Apr 2025			
☉ ⚹ ♃	16♈51	16♊51	
♀℞ △ ♂	25♓29	25♋29	
7 Apr 2025			
♀℞ ☌ ♄	25♓15	25♓15	
☿D	26♓50		
8 Apr 2025			
♀℞ ⚹ ♅	25♓06	25♉06	
13 Apr 2025			
♀D	24♓37		
17 Apr 2025			
☿ ☌ ♆	0♈38	0♈38	
19 Apr 2025			
♂ △ ♆	0♌44	0♈44	
20 Apr 2025			
♀ ⚹ ♅	25♓45	25♉45	
☿ ⚹ ♇	3♈46	3♒46	
21 Apr 2025			
☉ □ ♂	1♉12	1♌12	
23 Apr 2025			
☉ □ ♇	3♉47	3♒47	
25 Apr 2025			
♀ ☌ ♄	27♓14	27♓14	
27 Apr 2025			
♂ ☍ ♇	3♌48	3♒48	

ARIES

Sunday	Monday	Tuesday
30	**31**	**1** ☽ voc 17:42 ☽→♊ 20:25 ☽⚹♂ 10:14 ☽⚹♀ 15:54 ☽⚹♄ 11:33 ☽⚹☿ 17:42 ☽☌♅ 11:55 ☽⚹♆ 20:34
6 ☽→♌ 4:34 ☽△♆ 5:02 ☉⚹♃ 9:44 ☽☍♇ 11:19 ♀△♂ 12:13	**7** ♀☌♄ 11:01 ☿ SD 11:07 ☽⚹♃ 12:36 ☽△☉ 14:30	**8** ☽ voc 4:08 ☽→♍ 13:40 ☽□♅ 4:08 ♀⚹♅ 4:48
☽ voc 10:00 ☽→♏ 13:54 Full Moon 23♎20 ☽☍☉ 0:22 ♀ SD 1:02 ☽□♂ 10:00 ☽□♇ 21:26	**14**	**15** ☽△♀ 16:03 ☽☍♅ 17:31 ☽△♄ 19:00
☽ voc 17:21 ☽→♒ 23:21 Last Quarter 01♒12 ☽⚹♀ 15:23 ☽△♅ 15:26 ☽⚹♄ 17:21 ♀⚹♅ 18:20 ☿⚹♇ 21:39	**21** ☽⚹♆ 0:47 ☉□♂ 1:34 ☽☍♂ 1:35 ☽□☉ 1:35 ☽☌♇ 6:19 ☽⚹☿ 7:00	**22** ☽ voc 21:55 ☽△♃ 11:04 ☽□♅ 21:55
☽→♉ 7:17 New Moon 07♉47 ♂☍♇ 1:05 ☽□♇ 13:16 ☽□♂ 13:38 ☽☌☉ 19:31	**28**	**29** ☽ voc 5:17 ☽→♊ 6:34 ☽☌♅ 0:33 ☽⚹♄ 2:51 ☽⚹♀ 5:17 ☽⚹♆ 8:14 ☽△♇ 12:39 ☽⚹♂ 14:28

Charts cast with Natural House System in GMT

12 April, 2025
22:23 GMT

Full Moon

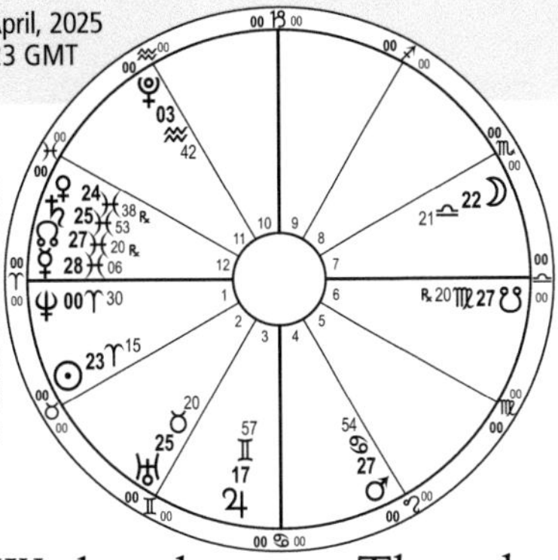

27 April, 2025
19:30 GMT

New Moon

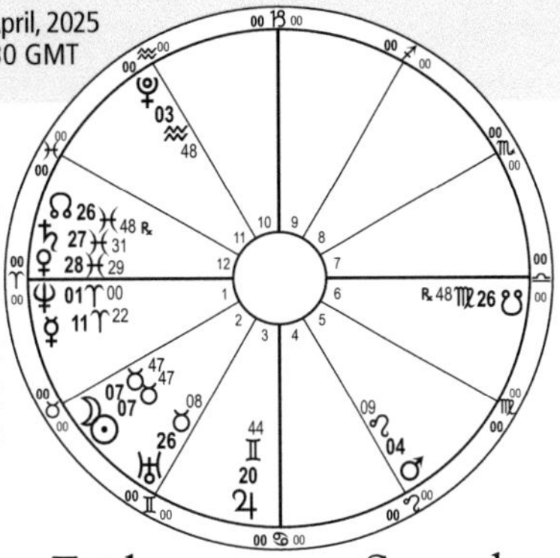

Wednesday	Thursday	Friday	Saturday
2 ☽△♇ 2:16 ☽⚹☉ 18:20 ☽☌♃ 23:25	**3** ☽ voc 18:26 ☽→♋ 22:50 ☽☐♄ 13:52 ☽☐♀ 16:36 ☽☐☿ 18:26 ☽☐♆ 23:07	**4** ◐ First Quarter 15♋33 ♄⚹♅ 16:25 ♂⚹♅ 23:04	**5** ☽ voc 22:54 ♂△♄ 1:07 ☽☐☉ 2:14 ☽⚹♅ 19:20 ☽△♄ 19:29 ☽☌♂ 19:49 ☽△♀ 20:36 ☽△☿ 22:54
9	**10** ☽ voc 19:49 ☽☐♃ 0:04 ☽☍♀ 14:39 ☽△♅ 15:36 ☽☍♄ 16:25 ☽⚹♂ 19:19 ☽☍☿ 19:49	**11** ☽→♎ 1:12 ☽☍♆ 2:03 ☽△♇ 8:37	**12** ☽△♃ 13:20
16 ☽ voc 2:23 ☽→♐ 2:37 ☽△♂ 0:51 ☽△☿ 2:23 ☽△♆ 3:50 ☿→♈ 6:25 ☽⚹♇ 10:08	**17** ☿☌♆ 4:11 ☽☍♃ 16:11	**18** ☽ voc 11:38 ☽→♑ 14:12 ♂→♌ 4:21 ☽☐♀ 4:40 ☽☐♄ 7:20 ☽△☉ 11:38 ☽☐♆ 15:33 ☽☐☿ 17:50	**19** ☉→♉ 19:56 ♂△♆ 22:52
23 ☽→♓ 5:06 ☽⚹☉ 11:14 ☉☐♇ 17:10	**24** ☽☐♃ 15:10	**25** ☽ voc 2:57 ☽→♈ 7:24 ♀☌♄ 0:02 ☽⚹♅ 0:50 ☽☌♄ 2:53 ☽☌♀ 2:57 ☽☌♆ 8:53 ☽△♂ 12:29 ☽⚹♇ 13:34 ☽☌☿ 22:04	**26** ☽ voc 16:18 ☽⚹♃ 16:18
30 ☽⚹☿ 5:50 ☽☌♃ 16:58 ♀→♈ 17:16	1	2	3

TAURUS

♈ Aries

On Sunday the 30th of March Mercury backs into Pisces and forms a conjunction with Neptune. Communication is vague and there is the potential here for misinterpretation and miscalculation. Mercury-Neptune can also indicate abstract ideas, poetry, and information about spiritual realities.

On the same day Neptune ingresses into Aries for the first time in 165 years, which is approximately the time Neptune takes to go around the zodiac. Refer to the introductory overview of 2025 for more information about this transit.

Later this week Mars will form a trine aspect to Saturn at 24° Cancer and Pisces respectively, with both Mars and Saturn sextile Uranus (so Uranus is located at the Mars-Saturn midpoint). This looks like hard work and an intense effort involving the application of new and innovative methods. This energy can be very forceful and even explosive.

☉ Sunday

30

☽ VOC 9:18
☽→♉ 20:15

☿→♓ 2:18
☿☌♆ 2:46
☽□♂ 9:18
♆→♈ 11:59

☽ Monday

31

☽□♀ 1:53

♂ Tuesday

1 April

☽ VOC 17:42
☽→♊ 20:25

☽⚹♂ 10:14
☽⚹♄ 11:33
☽☌♅ 11:55
☽⚹♀ 15:54
☽⚹☿ 17:42
☽⚹♆ 20:34

GMT

April 2025

Mercury is retrograde from March 15th (☿℞ 9°35'♈) through April 7th (☿D 26°50'♓).

☿ Wednesday
2

☽△♇	2:16
☽✶☉	18:20
☽☌♃	23:25

♃ Thursday
3

☽VOC	18:26
☽→♋	22:50

☽☐♄	13:52
☽☐♀	16:36
☽☐☿	18:26
☽☐♆	23:07

♀ Friday
4

◐
First Quarter
15♋33

♄✶♅	16:25
♂✶♅	23:04

♄ Saturday
5

☽VOC	22:54

♂△♄	1:07
☽☐☉	2:14
☽✶♅	19:20
☽△♄	19:29
☽☌♂	19:49
☽△♀	20:36
☽△☿	22:54

Regulus 2025 Astrological Planner

♈ Aries

Venus is slowing down as she prepares to turn direct on the 13th of April. As she stations Venus gets locked into a conjunction with Saturn that will persist for the rest of this month. This speaks of a distance between lovers and friends and critical changes in personal relationships.

On Sunday Venus and Mars will form a trine aspect, so effectively during this time Mars is forming a trine to the longer term Venus-Saturn conjunction. There is passion and creative vitality, but it's disciplined, restricted and restrained.

Mercury turns direct at 26° Pisces on Monday, within a whisper of this Venus-Saturn conjunction. Difficult things need to be said in love and friendship, or a change occurs in the pattern of communication between lovers and friends.

☉ Sunday
6

☽→♌   4:34

☽ Monday
7

☽△♆   5:02
☉✶♃   9:44
☽☌♇   11:19
♀△♂   12:13

♀☌♄   11:01
☿ SD   11:07
☽✶♃   12:36
☽△☉   14:30

♂ Tuesday
8

☽ VOC   4:08
☽→♍   13:40

☽□♅   4:08
♀✶♅   4:48

80   GMT

April 2025

Mercury is retrograde from March 15th (☿ℝ 9°35'♈) through April 7th (☿D 26°50'♓).

☿ **Wednesday**

9

♃ **Thursday**   ☽ VOC   19:49

10

☽□♃	0:04
☽☌♀	14:39
☽△♅	15:36
☽☌♄	16:25
☽✶♂	19:19
☽☌☿	19:49

♀ **Friday**   ☽→♎   1:12

11

☽☌♆	2:03
☽△♇	8:37

♄ **Saturday**

12

☽△♃   13:20

Regulus 2025 Astrological Planner   81

♈ Aries

Congratulations Taureans!

This week starts with a Full Moon at 23° Libra on Sunday the 13th of April. The Sun-Moon opposition is forming a quincunx aspect to a stationary Venus, and so the prevailing theme of strains and adjustments to relationships is reinforced.

During this week Mars forms a trine to the Mercury-Neptune conjunction. Such a combination might favor very imaginative artistic expression, but it may also describe a cunningly persuasive argument, perhaps involving a measure of trickery or illusion.

☉ Sunday

13

○
Full Moon
23♎20

☽ VOC 10:00
☽→♏ 13:54

☽ Monday

14

☽☌☉ 0:22
♀ SD 1:02
☽□♂ 10:00
☽□♆ 21:26

♂ Tuesday

15

☽△♀ 16:03
☽☌♅ 17:31
☽△♄ 19:00

---

82   GMT

April 2025

☿ Wednesday
16

☽ VOC 2:23
☽→♐ 2:37

☽△♂ 0:51
☽△☿ 2:23
☽△♆ 3:50
☿→♈ 6:25
☽✶♇ 10:08

♃ Thursday
17

☿☌♆ 4:11
☽☍♃ 16:11

♀ Friday
18

☽ VOC 11:38
☽→♑ 14:12

♂→♌ 4:21
☽□♀ 4:40
☽□♄ 7:20
☽△☉ 11:38
☽□♆ 15:33
☽□☿ 17:50

♄ Saturday
19

☉→♉ 19:56
♂△♆ 22:52

Regulus 2025 Astrological Planner · 83

♉ Taurus

The week begins with Mercury forming a sextile to Pluto on Sunday. There's deep analysis and research, and penetrating and insightful discussions can occur.

There's a t-square forming this week involving the Sun, Mars and Pluto. The Sun will be in square aspect to Mars on Monday, then in square to Pluto on Wednesday, and then on Sunday Mars and Pluto arrive at their final exact opposition. The outcome could be dramatic and explosive. There's an uncompromising self-assertion. In the most ideal scenario it might produce feats of extraordinary courage and determination.

After weeks of austere entanglement, Venus forms her final conjunction with Saturn on Friday and gets to move on after a protracted period of distance between lovers and friends and critical changes in personal relationships.

☉ Sunday
20

☽ VOC 17:21
☽→♎ 23:21

● Last Quarter
01 ♒ 12

☽⚹♀ 15:23
☽△♅ 15:26
☽⚹♄ 17:21
♀⚹♅ 18:20
♀⚹♇ 21:39

☽ Monday
21

☽⚹♆ 0:47
☉□♂ 1:34
☽☌♂ 1:35
☽□☉ 1:35
☽☌♇ 6:19
☽⚹☿ 7:00

♂ Tuesday
22

☽ VOC 21:55

☽△♃ 11:04
☽□♅ 21:55

84 GMT

April 2025

☿ Wednesday

☽→♓ 5:06

23

☽✶☉ 11:14
☉□♇ 17:10

♃ Thursday

24

☽□♃ 15:10

♀ Friday

☽VOC 2:57
☽→♈ 7:24

25

♀☌♄ 0:02
☽✶♅ 0:50
☽☌♄ 2:53
☽☌♀ 2:57
☽☌♆ 8:53
☽△♂ 12:29
☽✶♇ 13:34
☽☌☿ 22:04

♄ Saturday

☽VOC 16:18

26

☽✶♃ 16:18

Regulus 2025 Astrological Planner — 85

♉ Taurus

The New Moon that occurs on Monday will be square both ends of the Mars-Pluto opposition, bringing it into sharper focus. The latter part of April 2025 is one of the flash points of this year, when simmering tensions and antagonisms can flare up and erupt. Please refer to the yearly overview in the introductory section of this planner for more on this.

Venus enters Aries on Wednesday and forms a conjunction to Neptune on Friday. Love and beauty is intoxicating but it can also be beguiling and confusing. Love is selfless and sacrificial. Art and beauty are mesmerising.

☉ Sunday
27

☽→♉   7:17

● New Moon
07♉47

♂☍♇   1:05
☽□♇   13:16
☽□♂   13:38
☽☌☉   19:31

☽ Monday
28

♂ Tuesday
29

☽ VOC   5:17
☽→♊   6:34

☽☌♅   0:33
☽⚹♄   2:51
☽⚹♀   5:17
☽⚹♆   8:14
☽△♇   12:39
☽⚹♂   14:28

---

86   GMT

May 2025

☿ Wednesday
30

☽✶☿	5:50
☽☌♃	16:58
♀→♈	17:16

♃ Thursday
1 May

☽VOC	3:48
☽→♋	7:22

☽□♄	3:48
☽□♀	7:57
☽□♆	9:14

♀ Friday
2

☽✶☉	3:45
☽□☿	13:37
♀☌♆	17:07

♄ Saturday
3

☽VOC	8:02
☽→♌	11:29

☽✶♅	5:06
☽△♄	8:02
☽△♆	13:36
☽△♀	14:32
☽☍♇	18:24

Regulus 2025 Astrological Planner

87

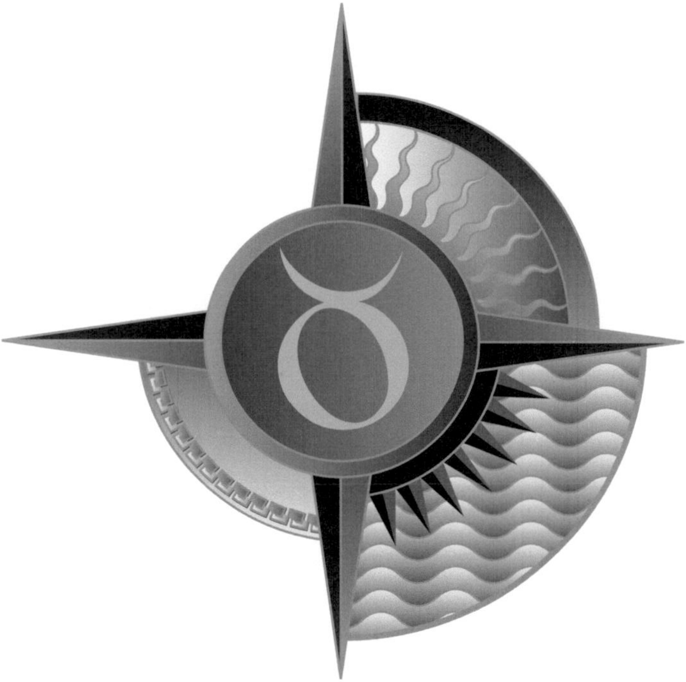

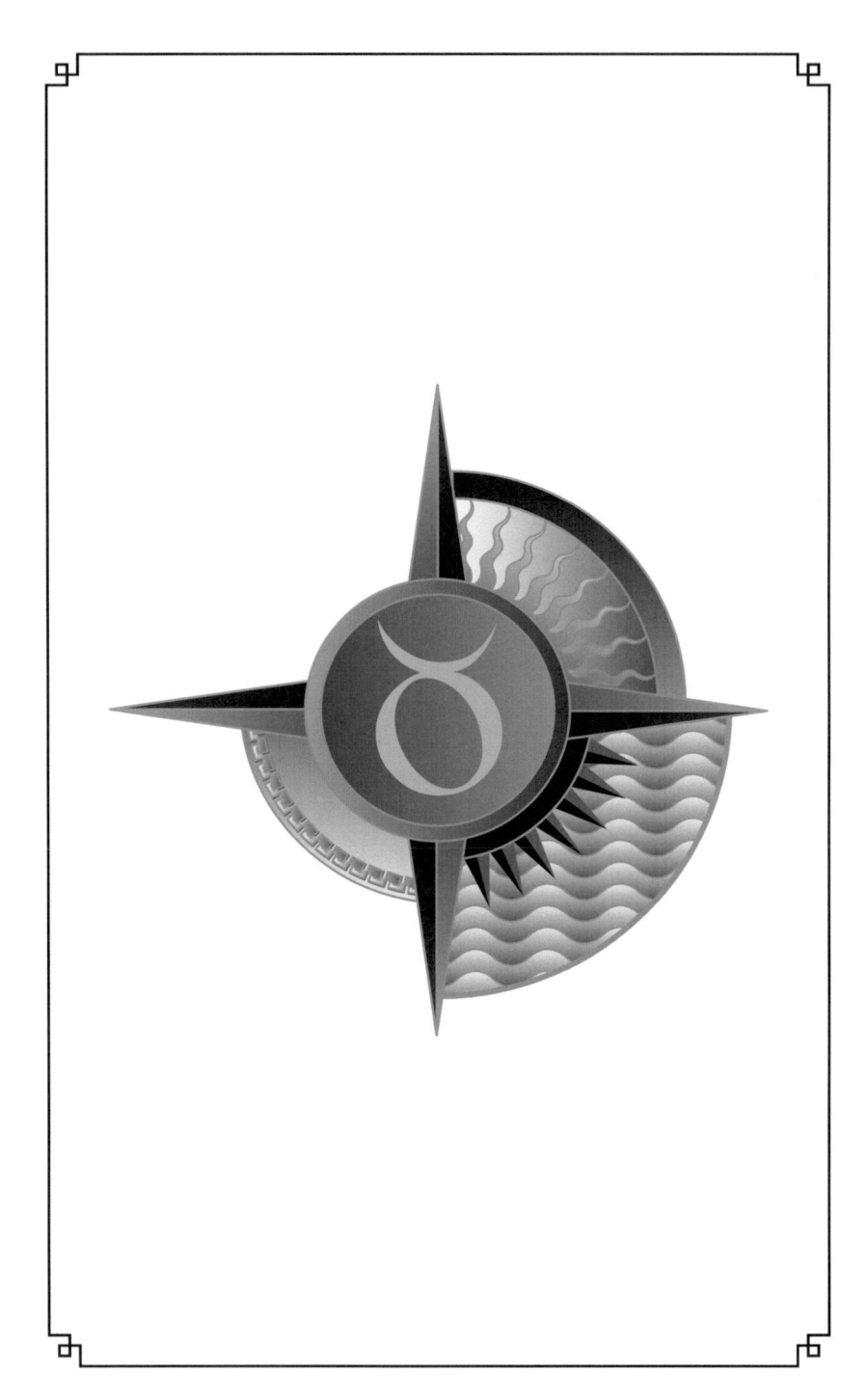

May 2025

Day	☉	☽	True ☊	☿	♀	♂	♃	♄	♅	♆	♇
01	10 ♉ 52 45	25 ♊ 34 24	26 ♓ 29 ℞	15 ♈ 31 D	00 ♈ 09 D	05 ♌ 36 D	21 ♊ 22 D	27 ♓ 51 D	26 ♉ 19 D	01 ♈ 06 D	03 ♒ 49 D
02	11 51 01	09 ♋ 49 10	26 23	16 54	00 44	06 03	21 34	27 57	26 22	01 08	03 49
03	12 49 14	23 35 01	26 20	18 18	01 19	06 31	21 46	28 03	26 26	01 09	03 49
04	13 47 26	06 ♌ 52 28	26 18	19 45	01 56	06 59	21 59	28 09	26 29	01 11	03 49
05	14 45 35	19 44 13	26 18 D	21 14	02 34	07 27	22 11	28 15	26 33	01 13	03 49 ℞
06	15 43 43	02 ♍ 14 19	26 19	22 45	03 13	07 55	22 23	28 21	26 36	01 15	03 49
07	16 41 48	14 27 27	26 20	24 18	03 53	08 24	22 35	28 26	26 40	01 16	03 49
08	17 39 52	26 28 22	26 21 ℞	25 53	04 34	08 53	22 48	28 32	26 43	01 18	03 49
09	18 37 53	08 ♎ 21 28	26 20	27 30	05 17	09 21	23 00	28 38	26 47	01 20	03 49
10	19 35 53	20 10 38	26 17	29 09	06 00	09 50	23 13	28 43	26 50	01 22	03 49
11	20 33 51	01 ♏ 59 05	26 12	00 ♉ 50	06 44	10 20	23 26	28 49	26 53	01 23	03 49
12	21 31 48	13 49 24	26 04	02 32	07 29	10 49	23 38	28 54	26 57	01 25	03 48
13	22 29 43	25 43 35	25 55	04 17	08 15	11 18	23 51	29 00	27 00	01 26	03 48
14	23 27 37	07 ♐ 43 13	25 44	06 04	09 02	11 48	24 04	29 05	27 04	01 28	03 48
15	24 25 29	19 49 42	25 33	07 53	09 49	12 18	24 16	29 10	27 07	01 30	03 48
16	25 23 20	02 ♑ 04 23	25 23	09 44	10 38	12 48	24 29	29 16	27 11	01 31	03 47
17	26 21 09	14 28 54	25 15	11 37	11 27	13 18	24 42	29 21	27 14	01 33	03 47
18	27 18 57	27 05 14	25 08	13 31	12 17	13 48	24 55	29 26	27 18	01 34	03 47
19	28 16 44	09 ♒ 55 45	25 05	15 28	13 07	14 18	25 08	29 31	27 21	01 36	03 46
20	29 14 30	23 03 12	25 03	17 27	13 58	14 48	25 21	29 36	27 25	01 37	03 46
21	00 ♊ 12 15	06 ♓ 30 19	25 03 D	19 27	14 50	15 19	25 34	29 41	27 28	01 38	03 45
22	01 09 59	20 19 21	25 03	21 29	15 43	15 50	25 47	29 45	27 32	01 40	03 45
23	02 07 42	04 ♈ 31 26	25 03 ℞	23 33	16 36	16 20	26 00	29 50	27 35	01 41	03 45
24	03 05 23	19 05 39	25 01	25 39	17 29	16 51	26 13	29 55	27 39	01 42	03 44
25	04 03 04	03 ♉ 58 27	24 57	27 46	18 23	17 23	26 27	29 59	27 42	01 44	03 43
26	05 00 44	19 03 16	24 50	29 55	19 18	17 54	26 40	00 ♈ 04	27 46	01 45	03 43
27	05 58 22	04 ♊ 11 08	24 41	02 ♊ 04	20 13	18 25	26 53	00 08	27 49	01 46	03 42
28	06 56 00	19 11 50	24 30	04 15	21 09	18 57	27 06	00 13	27 53	01 47	03 42
29	07 53 36	03 ♋ 55 47	24 20	06 26	22 05	19 28	27 20	00 17	27 56	01 49	03 41
30	08 51 11	18 15 38	24 11	08 38	23 01	20 00	27 33	00 21	28 00	01 50	03 40
31	09 48 45	02 ♌ 07 14	24 04	10 50	23 58	20 32	27 47	00 25	28 03	01 51	03 40

Declination

Day	☉	☽	True ☊	☿	♀	♂	♃	♄	♅	♆	♇
1	+15°14′	+28°32′	-01°25′	+03°43′	+01°06′	+20°44′	+22°56′	-02°40′	+19°08′	-00°44′	-22°44′
3	+15°50′	+24°17′	-01°28′	+04°49′	+01°17′	+20°28′	+22°57′	-02°36′	+19°09′	-00°42′	-22°45′
5	+16°24′	+15°18′	-01°28′	+06°00′	+01°31′	+20°11′	+22°59′	-02°32′	+19°11′	-00°41′	-22°45′
7	+16°58′	+04°16′	-01°27′	+07°15′	+01°47′	+19°54′	+23°01′	-02°27′	+19°12′	-00°40′	-22°45′
9	+17°30′	-07°05′	-01°28′	+08°33′	+02°06′	+19°37′	+23°02′	-02°23′	+19°14′	-00°38′	-22°46′
11	+18°01′	-17°21′	-01°32′	+09°53′	+02°27′	+19°19′	+23°04′	-02°19′	+19°16′	-00°37′	-22°46′
13	+18°31′	-25°02′	-01°40′	+11°16′	+02°51′	+19°01′	+23°05′	-02°15′	+19°17′	-00°36′	-22°47′
15	+19°00′	-28°26′	-01°49′	+12°41′	+03°16′	+18°42′	+23°07′	-02°11′	+19°19′	-00°35′	-22°47′
17	+19°27′	-26°22′	-01°55′	+14°07′	+03°43′	+18°23′	+23°08′	-02°08′	+19°20′	-00°34′	-22°48′
19	+19°53′	-18°56′	-01°57′	+15°33′	+04°12′	+18°03′	+23°09′	-02°04′	+19°22′	-00°33′	-22°48′
21	+20°18′	-07°30′	-01°57′	+16°58′	+04°42′	+17°43′	+23°10′	-02°01′	+19°24′	-00°32′	-22°49′
23	+20°41′	+05°59′	-01°57′	+18°20′	+05°13′	+17°23′	+23°11′	-01°57′	+19°25′	-00°31′	-22°49′
25	+21°03′	+18°45′	-02°01′	+19°40′	+05°46′	+17°02′	+23°12′	-01°54′	+19°27′	-00°30′	-22°50′
27	+21°23′	+27°03′	-02°08′	+20°54′	+06°20′	+16°41′	+23°13′	-01°51′	+19°28′	-00°29′	-22°51′
29	+21°42′	+27°46′	-02°16′	+22°01′	+06°55′	+16°19′	+23°14′	-01°48′	+19°30′	-00°28′	-22°51′
31	+21°59′	+21°30′	-02°22′	+23°00′	+07°30′	+15°57′	+23°15′	-01°45′	+19°32′	-00°27′	-22°52′

May, 2025

Degree of
Key Aspects

2 May 2025			
♀ ☌ ♆	1♈09	1♈09	
4 May 2025			
♇℞	3♒49		
5 May 2025			
☿ ⚹ ♃	22♈20	22♊20	
6 May 2025			
♀ ⚹ ♇℞	3♈49	3♒49	
12 May 2025			
☿ □ ♇℞	3♉48	3♒48	
17 May 2025			
☉ ☌ ♅	27♉18	27♉18	
18 May 2025			
☿ □ ♂	13♉53	13♌53	
20 May 2025			
☉ ⚹ ♄	29♉38	29♓38	
22 May 2025			
♀ △ ♂	16♈00	16♌00	
☉ ⚹ ♆	1♊40	1♈40	
24 May 2025			
☉ △ ♇℞	3♊44	3♒44	
☿ ☌ ♅	27♉42	27♉42	
26 May 2025			
☿ ⚹ ♄	0♊04	0♈04	
☿ ⚹ ♆	1♊46	1♈46	
27 May 2025			
☿ △ ♇℞	3♊42	3♒42	
30 May 2025			
☉ ☌ ☿	9♊01	9♊01	

Sunday	Monday	Tuesday
27	28 TAURUS	29
First Quarter 14♌21 ☽☌♂ 0:12 ☽□☉ 13:51 ♇ SR 16:00	5 ☽ voc 13:03 ☽→♍ 19:39 ☽△☿ 3:14 ☽⚹♃ 4:43 ☽□♅ 13:03 ☿⚹♃ 17:21	6 ♀⚹♇ 21:31
11 ☽□♇ 3:42 ☽□♂ 17:39	Full Moon 22♏13 ☽☍☉ 16:56 ☿□♇ 17:23	13 ☽ voc 6:37 ☽→♐ 8:34 ☽☍♅ 2:35 ☽△♄ 6:37 ☽△♆ 11:29 ☽⚹♇ 16:11
18 ☽ voc 4:27 ☽→♒ 5:29 ☽△♅ 0:24 ☽△☉ 0:28 ☽⚹♄ 4:27 ☿□♂ 4:35 ☽⚹♆ 8:27 ☽☌♇ 12:33	19 ☽⚹♀ 6:18 ☽☍♂ 8:23 ☽□☿ 12:00	☽ voc 11:59 ☽→♓ 12:28 Last Quarter 29♒43 ☽△♃ 4:13 ☽□♅ 7:53 ☉⚹♄ 9:38 ☽□☉ 11:59 ☉→♊ 18:54
25 ♄→♈ 3:33 ☽□♂ 22:06	26 ☽ voc 13:52 ☽→♊ 17:21 ☿→♊ 0:59 ☿⚹♄ 1:45 ☽☌♅ 13:52 ☽⚹♄ 17:32 ☽☌☿ 20:05 ☽⚹♆ 20:09 ☿⚹♆ 20:37 ☽△♇ 23:14	New Moon 06♊06 ☽☌☉ 3:02 ☿△♇ 17:56 ☽⚹♂ 23:34

Charts cast with Natural House System in GMT

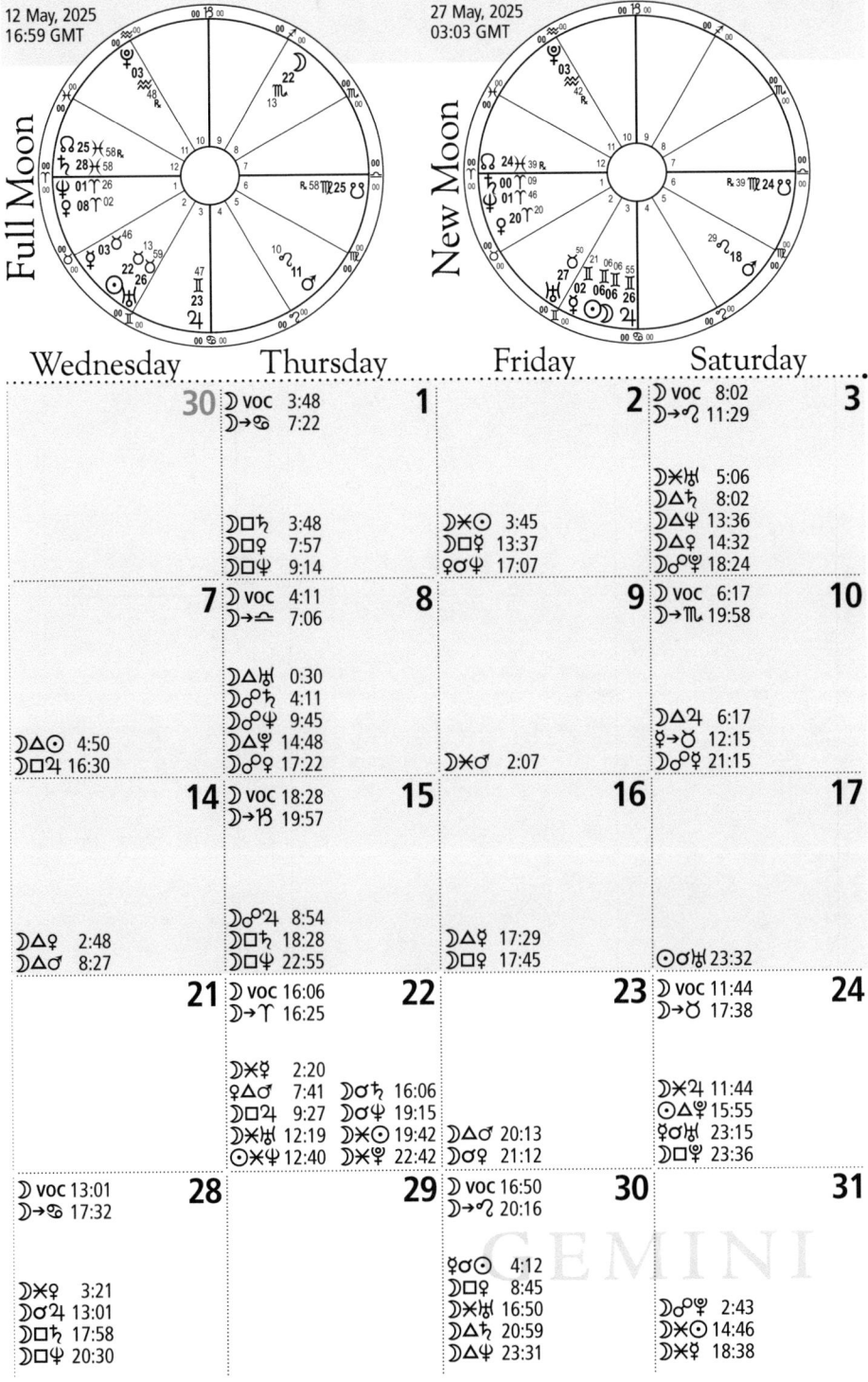

12 May, 2025
16:59 GMT

Full Moon

27 May, 2025
03:03 GMT

New Moon

Wednesday	Thursday	Friday	Saturday
30	**1** ☽ voc 3:48 ☽→♋ 7:22 ☽□♄ 3:48 ☽□♀ 7:57 ☽□♆ 9:14	**2** ☽✶☉ 3:45 ☽□☿ 13:37 ♀□♆ 17:07	**3** ☽ voc 8:02 ☽→♌ 11:29 ☽✶♅ 5:06 ☽△♄ 8:02 ☽△♆ 13:36 ☽△♀ 14:32 ☽☌♇ 18:24
7 ☽△☉ 4:50 ☽□♃ 16:30	**8** ☽ voc 4:11 ☽→♎ 7:06 ☽△♅ 0:30 ☽☍♄ 4:11 ☽☍♆ 9:45 ☽△♇ 14:48 ☽☍♀ 17:22	**9** ☽✶♂ 2:07	**10** ☽ voc 6:17 ☽→♏ 19:58 ☽△♃ 6:17 ♀☌♉ 12:15 ☽☍♀ 21:15
14 ☽△♀ 2:48 ☽△♂ 8:27	**15** ☽ voc 18:28 ☽→♑ 19:57 ☽☍♃ 8:54 ☽□♄ 18:28 ☽□♆ 22:55	**16** ☽△☿ 17:29 ☽□♀ 17:45	**17** ☉☌♅ 23:32
21	**22** ☽ voc 16:06 ☽→♈ 16:25 ☽✶☿ 2:20 ♀△♂ 7:41 ☽☌♄ 16:06 ☽□♃ 9:27 ☽☌♆ 19:15 ☽✶♅ 12:19 ☽✶♀ 19:42 ☉✶♆ 12:40 ☽✶☿ 22:42	**23** ☽△♂ 20:13 ☽☌♀ 21:12	**24** ☽ voc 11:44 ☽→♉ 17:38 ☽✶♃ 11:44 ☉△♇ 15:55 ☿☌♅ 23:15 ☽□♇ 23:36
28 ☽ voc 13:01 ☽→♋ 17:32 ☽✶☿ 3:21 ☽☌♃ 13:01 ☽□♄ 17:58 ☽□♆ 20:30	**29**	**30** ☽ voc 16:50 ☽→♌ 20:16 ☿☌☉ 4:12 ☽□♀ 8:45 ☽✶♅ 16:50 ☽△♄ 20:59 ☽△♆ 23:31	**31** ☽☍♇ 2:43 ☽✶☉ 14:46 ☽✶☿ 18:38

GEMINI

Regulus 2025 Astrological Planner   91

♉ Taurus

Pluto turns retrograde at 3° Aquarius on Sunday the 4th of May, and so some of the high voltage situations that have been developing in the past few weeks could reach a turning point now.

Mercury forms a sextile to Jupiter on Monday. This can be good news. There's a sound and proportionate evaluation of circumstances. Educational, cultural and literary gatherings. Truthful words are spoken and traveling is easy.

Venus forms a sextile to Pluto on Tuesday making social and romantic interaction deep and intense, but perhaps somewhat prone to expressions of jealousy.

☉ Sunday
4

◐ First Quarter
14♌21

☽☌♂ 0:12
☽□☉ 13:51
♇ SR 16:00

☽ Monday
5

☽ VOC 13:03
☽→♍ 19:39

☽△☿ 3:14
☽✶♃ 4:43
☽□♅ 13:03
☿✶♃ 17:21

♂ Tuesday
6

♀✶♇ 21:31

92 GMT

May 2025

☿ **Wednesday**

7

☽△☉	4:50
☽□♃	16:30

♃ **Thursday**

8

☽ VOC	4:11
☽→♎	7:06

☽△♅	0:30
☽☌♄	4:11
☽☌♆	9:45
☽△♇	14:48
☽☌♀	17:22

♀ **Friday**

9

☽✶♂	2:07

♄ **Saturday**

10

☽ VOC	6:17
☽→♏	19:58

☽△♃	6:17
☿→♉	12:15
☽☌☿	21:15

Regulus 2025 Astrological Planner   93

♉ Taurus

The week starts with a Full Moon at 22° Scorpio on Monday while Mercury and Pluto are in square aspect. Views and opinions are expressed with great forcefulness. There's intellectual or verbal domination, propaganda, explosive news and information. Research and investigation is zealously undertaken.

On Saturday the Sun and Uranus form a conjunction. There could be surprises and sudden twists in the plot. Wilful and impulsive actions can be disruptive, but there could also be an intense desire for freedom that is determined to shake off constraints.

Venus forms a semi-square to this Sun-Uranus conjunction, so love and friendship undergoes sudden disruption or a liberating awakening.

☉ Sunday

11

☽ Monday

12

☽□♀   3:42
☽□♂   17:39

○
Full Moon
22 ♏ 13

♂ Tuesday

13

☽☌♃☉   16:56
♀□♇   17:23
☽ VOC   6:37
☽→♐   8:34

☽☌♅   2:35
☽△♄   6:37
☽△♆   11:29
☽⚹♀   16:11

94

May 2025

☿ Wednesday

14

☽△♀ 2:48
☽△♂ 8:27

♃ Thursday

15

☽VOC 18:28
☽→♑ 19:57

☽☌♃ 8:54
☽□♄ 18:28
☽□♆ 22:55

♀ Friday

16

☽△☿ 17:29
☽□♀ 17:45

♄ Saturday

17

☉☌♅ 23:32

Regulus 2025 Astrological Planner

♊ Gemini

On Sunday Mercury forms a square to Mars and there are sharp, bold and forceful statements. Hasty speech and action easily lead to regret.

During this week the Sun forms a sextile to the forming Saturn-Neptune conjunction. The Sun is sextile Saturn on Tuesday and then sextile Neptune on Thursday. This can describe a gathering or fellowship of the woebegone. Selfless work and sacrifices for the benefit of the community.

Congratulations Geminis!

Venus forms a trine to Mars on Thursday. Romantic attraction, social interactions and engagements. Creativity and a zest for life.

On Saturday the 24th of May the Sun forms a trine to Pluto while Mercury is conjunct Uranus. There is a strong purposeful focus. Sudden surprising news and information pounces in from unexpected corners. New and novel knowledge.

☉ Sunday
18

☽ VOC 4:27
☽→♒ 5:29

☽ Monday
19

☽△♅ 0:24
☽△☉ 0:28
☽✶♄ 4:27
☿□♂ 4:35
☽✶♆ 8:27
☽☌♇ 12:33

♂ Tuesday
20

☽✶♀ 6:18
☽☍♂ 8:23
☽□☿ 12:00

☽ VOC 11:59
☽→♓ 12:28

◐ Last Quarter
29♒43

☽△♃ 4:13
☽□♅ 7:53
☉✶♄ 9:38
☽□☉ 11:59
☉→♊ 18:54

May 2025

☿ Wednesday
21

♃ Thursday
22

☽ VOC	16:06
☽→♈	16:25
☽✶☿	2:20
♀△♂	7:41
☽□♃	9:27
☽✶♅	12:19
☉✶♆	12:40
☽☌♄	16:06
☽☌♆	19:15
☽✶☉	19:42
☽✶♇	22:42

♀ Friday
23

☽△♂	20:13
☽☌♀	21:12

♄ Saturday
24

☽ VOC	11:44
☽→♉	17:38
☽✶♃	11:44
☉△♇	15:55
☿☌♅	23:15
☽□♆	23:36

Regulus 2025 Astrological Planner

♊ Gemini

Saturn ingresses into Aries on Sunday the 25th of May. Not much to celebrate.

Mercury enters Gemini and forms a sextile to the forming Saturn-Neptune conjunction, which speaks of subdued deep and thoughtful conversations.

The next day a New Moon occurs at 6° Gemini conjunct Mercury and trine Pluto. Communication is focused, resolute and purposeful. Analysis is insightful and ideas are communicated with depth, gravitas and thoroughness.

Messenger Mercury is clearly busy this week as it goes on to form a conjunction with the Sun on Friday the 30th of May, indicating important announcements and official authoritative statements. Official letters are dispatched and received.

☉ Sunday
25

♄→♈	3:33
☽□♂	22:06

☽ Monday
26

☽ VOC	13:52
☽→♊	17:21

☿→♊	0:59
☿⚹♄	1:45
☽☌♅	13:52
☽⚹♄	17:32
☽☌☿	20:05
☽⚹♆	20:09
☿⚹♆	20:37
☽△♇	23:14

♂ Tuesday
27

New Moon
06♊06

☽☌☉	3:02
☿△♇	17:56
☽⚹♂	23:34

GMT

May 2025

☿ Wednesday
28

☽VOC 13:01
☽→♋ 17:32

☽⚹♀ 3:21
☽☌♃ 13:01
☽□♄ 17:58
☽□♆ 20:30

♃ Thursday
29

♀ Friday
30

☽VOC 16:50
☽→♌ 20:16

☿☌☉ 4:12
☽□♀ 8:45
☽⚹♅ 16:50
☽△♄ 20:59
☽△♆ 23:31

♄ Saturday
31

☽☍♇ 2:43
☽⚹☉ 14:46
☽⚹☿ 18:38

Regulus 2025 Astrological Planner

99

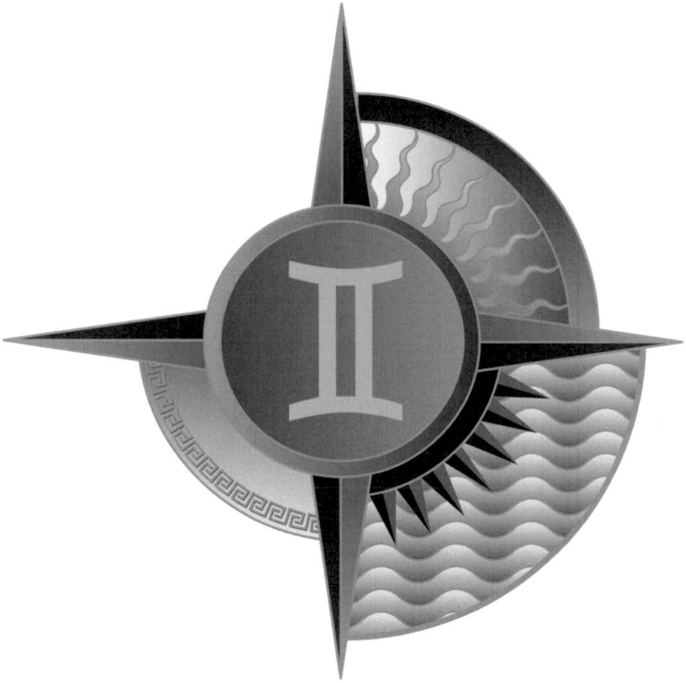

Ephemeris for June 2025, set at Midnight GMT.

June 2025

Day	☉	☽	True ☊	☿	♀	♂	♃	♄	♅	♆	♇
01	10♊46 17	15♌29 42	23♓59 R	13♊02 D	24♈56 D	21♌04 D	28♊00 D	00♈29 D	28♉07 D	01♈52 D	03♒39 R
02	11 43 48	28 24 55	23 57	15 14	25 53	21 36	28 13	00 33	28 10	01 53	03 38
03	12 41 18	10♍56 38	23 57	17 25	26 52	22 08	28 27	00 37	28 13	01 54	03 38
04	13 38 46	23 09 46	23 57 D	19 35	27 50	22 40	28 40	00 41	28 17	01 55	03 37
05	14 36 13	05♎09 37	23 56 R	21 44	28 49	23 12	28 54	00 44	28 20	01 56	03 36
06	15 33 39	17 01 24	23 54	23 52	29 48	23 45	29 07	00 48	28 24	01 57	03 35
07	16 31 04	28 49 55	23 50	25 58	00♉48	24 17	29 21	00 52	28 27	01 58	03 34
08	17 28 27	10♏39 19	23 44	28 03	01 48	24 50	29 35	00 55	28 30	01 59	03 33
09	18 25 50	22 32 58	23 34	00♋05	02 48	25 23	29 48	00 58	28 34	02 00	03 33
10	19 23 12	04♐33 24	23 22	02 06	03 49	25 55	00♋02	01 02	28 37	02 00	03 32
11	20 20 33	16 42 20	23 09	04 04	04 50	26 28	00 15	01 05	28 40	02 01	03 31
12	21 17 53	29 00 48	22 56	06 01	05 51	27 01	00 29	01 08	28 44	02 02	03 30
13	22 15 13	11♑29 23	22 43	07 55	06 52	27 35	00 43	01 11	28 47	02 03	03 29
14	23 12 32	24 08 28	22 32	09 46	07 54	28 08	00 56	01 14	28 50	02 04	03 28
15	24 09 50	06♒58 34	22 24	11 36	08 56	28 41	01 10	01 17	28 53	02 04	03 27
16	25 07 08	20 00 28	22 19	13 22	09 58	29 15	01 24	01 19	28 57	02 05	03 26
17	26 04 26	03♓15 22	22 16	15 07	11 01	29 48	01 37	01 22	29 00	02 05	03 25
18	27 01 43	16 44 48	22 16	16 49	12 04	00♍22	01 51	01 24	29 03	02 06	03 24
19	27 59 00	00♈30 17	22 16	18 29	13 07	00 55	02 05	01 27	29 06	02 06	03 23
20	28 56 17	14 32 48	22 15	20 06	14 10	01 29	02 18	01 29	29 09	02 07	03 22
21	29 53 33	28 52 10	22 13	21 41	15 14	02 03	02 32	01 31	29 12	02 07	03 20
22	00♋50 50	13♉26 18	22 08	23 13	16 17	02 37	02 46	01 34	29 16	02 08	03 19
23	01 48 06	28 10 52	22 01	24 43	17 21	03 11	02 59	01 36	29 19	02 08	03 18
24	02 45 22	12♊59 17	21 52	26 10	18 26	03 45	03 13	01 38	29 22	02 09	03 17
25	03 42 38	27 43 30	21 41	27 34	19 30	04 19	03 27	01 39	29 25	02 09	03 16
26	04 39 54	12♋15 18	21 30	28 56	20 35	04 53	03 41	01 41	29 28	02 09	03 15
27	05 37 09	26 27 37	21 20	00♋16	21 39	05 28	03 54	01 43	29 31	02 10	03 13
28	06 34 24	10♌15 45	21 12	01 33	22 44	06 02	04 08	01 44	29 34	02 10	03 12
29	07 31 39	23 37 43	21 07	02 47	23 49	06 37	04 22	01 46	29 37	02 10	03 11
30	08 28 53	06♍34 09	21 05	03 58	24 55	07 11	04 35	01 47	29 40	02 10	03 10

Declination

Day	☉	☽	True ☊	☿	♀	♂	♃	♄	♅	♆	♇
1	+22°08'	+16°43'	-02°24'	+23°26'	+07°48'	+15°46'	+23°15'	-01°44'	+19°32'	-00°27'	-22°52'
3	+22°23'	+05°40'	-02°24'	+24°10'	+08°24'	+15°23'	+23°15'	-01°41'	+19°34'	-00°26'	-22°53'
5	+22°36'	-05°45'	-02°24'	+24°43'	+09°01'	+15°00'	+23°16'	-01°39'	+19°35'	-00°25'	-22°54'
7	+22°48'	-16°12'	-02°28'	+25°06'	+09°38'	+14°37'	+23°16'	-01°36'	+19°37'	-00°25'	-22°54'
9	+22°59'	-24°15'	-02°35'	+25°17'	+10°16'	+14°13'	+23°16'	-01°34'	+19°38'	-00°24'	-22°55'
11	+23°07'	-28°13'	-02°46'	+25°18'	+10°53'	+13°49'	+23°17'	-01°32'	+19°40'	-00°24'	-22°56'
13	+23°14'	-26°44'	-02°56'	+25°09'	+11°31'	+13°24'	+23°17'	-01°30'	+19°41'	-00°23'	-22°57'
15	+23°20'	-19°48'	-03°02'	+24°52'	+12°08'	+12°59'	+23°17'	-01°28'	+19°43'	-00°23'	-22°57'
17	+23°24'	-08°50'	-03°03'	+24°27'	+12°46'	+12°34'	+23°17'	-01°27'	+19°44'	-00°22'	-22°58'
19	+23°26'	+04°11'	-03°03'	+23°56'	+13°22'	+12°09'	+23°16'	-01°25'	+19°45'	-00°22'	-22°59'
21	+23°26'	+16°51'	-03°05'	+23°19'	+13°59'	+11°43'	+23°16'	-01°24'	+19°47'	-00°22'	-23°00'
23	+23°25'	+25°58'	-03°11'	+22°37'	+14°35'	+11°17'	+23°16'	-01°23'	+19°48'	-00°21'	-23°01'
25	+23°22'	+28°13'	-03°19'	+21°51'	+15°10'	+10°50'	+23°15'	-01°22'	+19°49'	-00°21'	-23°01'
27	+23°18'	+23°01'	-03°27'	+21°02'	+15°44'	+10°23'	+23°15'	-01°21'	+19°51'	-00°21'	-23°02'
29	+23°12'	+13°07'	-03°32'	+20°12'	+16°18'	+09°56'	+23°14'	-01°20'	+19°52'	-00°21'	-23°03'

June, 2025

Degree of
Key Aspects

5 Jun 2025			
♀ ⚹ ♃		28♈55	28♊55
☿ ⚹ ♂		23♊42	23♌42
8 Jun 2025			
☿ ☌ ♃		29♊46	29♊46
9 Jun 2025			
☿ □ ♄		1♋00	1♈00
♀ □ ♇℞		3♉32	3♒32
☿ □ ♆		2♋00	2♈00
11 Jun 2025			
☿ ⚹ ♀		5♋40	5♉40
15 Jun 2025			
♂ □ ♅		28♌55	28♉55
♃ □ ♄		1♋18	1♈18
19 Jun 2025			
♃ □ ♆		2♋06	2♈06
22 Jun 2025			
♂ ⚹ ♃		2♍52	2♋52
☉ □ ♄		1♋35	1♈35
23 Jun 2025			
☉ □ ♆		2♋08	2♈08
24 Jun 2025			
☉ ☌ ♃		3♋22	3♋22
26 Jun 2025			
☿ ⚹ ♅		29♋29	29♉29
☉ ⚹ ♂		5♋14	5♍14
28 Jun 2025			
☿ △ ♄		1♌45	1♈45
☿ △ ♆		2♌10	2♈10
29 Jun 2025			
☿ ☍ ♇℞		3♌11	3♒11

GEMINI

Sunday	Monday	Tuesday
1 ☽ voc 23:38 ☽☌♂ 10:41 ☽△♀ 18:52 ☽□♅ 23:32 ☽⚹♃ 23:38	☽→♍ 3:00 First Quarter 12♍50	**3** ☽□☉ 3:41 ☽□☿ 15:23
8 ☿☌♃ 20:12 ☿→♋ 22:58	**9** ☽ voc 12:06 ☽→♐ 14:55 ☽□♂ 5:57 ☿□♄ 10:48 ☽☍♅ 12:06 ☽△♄ 16:56 ♀□♇ 17:20 ☽△♆ 18:55 ♃→♋ 21:03 ☽⚹♇ 21:57 ☿□♆ 22:54	**10**
15 ☽□♀ 3:57 ♂□♅ 9:47 ♃□♄ 14:35	**16** ☽ voc 17:30 ☽→♓ 18:08 ☽△☉ 10:02 ☽□♅ 16:18 ☽☍♂ 17:30 ☽△♃ 21:00	**17** ♂→♍ 8:35 ☽⚹♀ 15:01
22 ☽☌♀ 5:01 ♂⚹♃ 10:30 ☽⚹☿ 17:44 ☉□♄ 18:35	**23** ☽ voc 1:50 ☽→♊ 2:57 ☽ voc 8:26 ☽☌♅ 1:50 ☽⚹♄ 5:33 ☽⚹♆ 6:25 ☽△♇ 8:17 ☽□♂ 8:26 ☉□♆ 8:29	**24** ☉☌♃ 15:17
29 ☽ voc 11:02 ☽→♍ 11:43 ☽□♀ 0:23 ☿☍♇ 7:57 ☽□♅ 11:02 ☽⚹♃ 20:13	**30** ☽☌♂ 1:14 ☽⚹☉ 3:54	**1**

Charts cast with Natural House System in GMT

Full Moon

11 June, 2025
7:44 GMT

New Moon

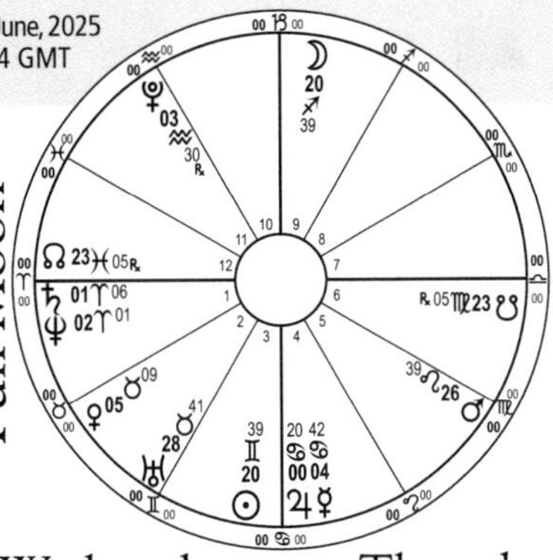

25 June, 2025
10:31 GMT

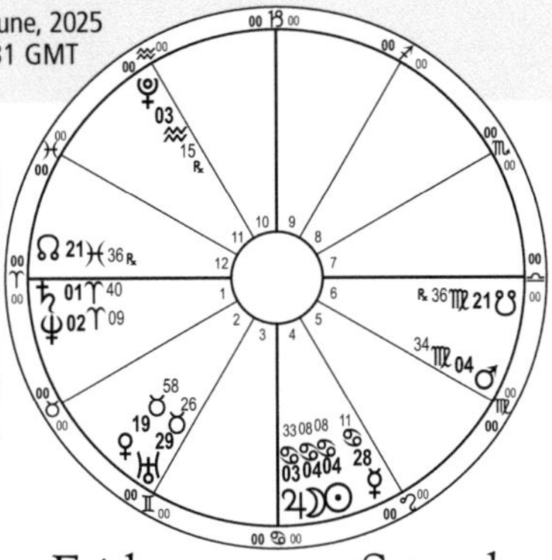

Wednesday	Thursday	Friday	Saturday
4 ☽ voc 11:11 ☽→♎ 13:38 ☽△♅ 10:14 ☽□♃ 11:11 ☽☍♄ 15:04 ☽☍♆ 17:30 ☽△♇ 20:52	**5** ☿⚹♃ 2:32 ☽△☉ 20:46 ☿⚹♂ 22:09	**6** ♀→♉ 4:42 ☽⚹♂ 14:19 ☽△☿ 16:55	**7** ☽ voc 1:04 ☽→♏ 2:22 ☽△♃ 1:04 ☽☍♀ 4:22 ☽□♆ 9:37
11 ☽ voc 19:58 ☽☍☉ 7:44 ☿⚹♀ 19:41 ☽△♂ 19:58	○ Full Moon 20♐39	**12** ☽→♑ 1:55 ☽☍♃ 2:54 ☽□♄ 4:07 ☽□♆ 5:51 ☽△♀ 14:22 ☽☍♇ 15:56	**13**	**14** ☽ voc 8:51 ☽→♒ 11:00 ☽△♅ 8:51 ☽⚹♄ 13:21 ☽⚹♆ 14:51 ☽☌♇ 17:27
18 ☽ voc 21:34 ☽→♈ 23:08 ☽△☿ 0:09 ☽□☉ 19:19 ☽⚹♅ 21:34	☾ Last Quarter 27♓48 ☽☌♄ 1:38 ☽□♃ 2:45 ☽☌♆ 2:46 ♃□♆ 3:13 ☽⚹♇ 4:57	**19** ☽□☿ 10:32	**20**	Summer Solstice **21** ☽ voc 1:49 ☽→♉ 1:53 ☽⚹☉ 1:49 ☽⚹♃ 6:10 ☉→♋ 2:42 ☽□♀ 7:24 ☽△♂ 5:29
25 ☽→♋ 3:44 ☽□♄ 6:28 ☽□♆ 7:16 ☽☌♃ 9:33 ☽☌☉ 10:31 ☽⚹♂ 11:17	● New Moon 04♋08	**26** ☿⚹♅ 9:45 ☉☌♂ 14:11 ☽⚹♀ 15:08 ☿→♌ 19:09	**27** ☽ voc 5:16 ☽→♌ 6:05 ☽⚹♅ 5:16 ☽☌☿ 7:13 ☽△♄ 9:04 ☽△♆ 9:49 ☽☍♇ 11:39	**28** ☿△♄ 3:52 ☿△♆ 11:58

CANCER

Regulus 2025 Astrological Planner

103

♊ Gemini

On Thursday the 5th of June Venus forms a sextile aspect to Jupiter, promising friendship, benevolence and joyous social interactions. In fact, around now Uranus is very close to the midpoint of this Venus-Jupiter sextile, which makes it all the more exciting and electric. Mercury and Mars also happen to be forming a sextile this day, so messengers, thieves, merchants and tricksters are plying their trade with skill and efficiency. Clever, cunning and mobile.

On Saturday the 7th of June Mercury is semi-sextile Uranus and speeding towards a conjunction with Jupiter the following day. Advances in science and human knowledge can take place, while righteous and noble agreements are made. True words are spoken.

In the coming days Mercury and Jupiter will both be entering the sign of Cancer, touching one of the Cardinal degrees of the tropical zodiac. This suggests that new plans and noble initiatives are launched and important new information becomes public.

☉ Sunday ☽ VOC 23:38

1

☽ Monday

☽☌♂ 10:41
☽△♀ 18:52
☽□♅ 23:32
☽⚹♃ 23:38

☽→♍ 03:00

2

♂ Tuesday

◐
First Quarter
12 ♍ 50

3

☽□☉ 3:41
☽□☿ 15:23

104 GMT

June 2025

☿ Wednesday
4

☽ VOC 11:11
☽→♎ 13:38

☽△♅ 10:14
☽□♃ 11:11
☽☍♄ 15:04
☽☍♆ 17:30
☽△♇ 20:52

♃ Thursday
5

♀⚹♃ 2:32
☽△☉ 20:46
☿⚹♂ 22:09

♀ Friday
6

♀→♉ 4:42
☽⚹♂ 14:19
☽△☿ 16:55

♄ Saturday
7

☽ VOC 1:04
☽→♏ 2:22

☽△♃ 1:04
☽☍♀ 4:22
☽□♇ 9:37

Regulus 2025 Astrological Planner

♊ Gemini

On Tuesday the 9th of June Venus squares Pluto, implying that personal relationships are undergoing cathartic changes. Also occurring at this time is a conjunction of Mercury and Jupiter that is square a conjunction of Saturn and Neptune. Good bold ideas have to face up against a spirit of gloom. There are words of truth, hope and inspiration in times of uncertainty and disillusionment. Practical plans can be developed for improvement of disintegrated systems.

The Full Moon on Wednesday occurs at 20° Sagittarius while Mercury and Venus happen to be forming a sextile aspect. This is convivial, cordial and sociable. Love letters and sweet talk.

☉ Sunday
8

☽ Monday
9

☿☌♃	20:12
☿→♋	22:58
☽VOC	12:06
☽→♐	14:55
☽□♂	5:57
♀□♄	10:48
☽☍♅	12:06
☽△♄	16:56
♀□♇	17:20
☽△♆	18:55
♃→♋	21:03
☽✶♇	21:57
☿□♆	22:54

♂ Tuesday
10

GMT

June 2025

☿ Wednesday
11

☽VOC 19:58

○
Full Moon
20♐39

☽☌☉ 7:44
☿⚹♀ 19:41
☽△♂ 19:58

♃ Thursday
12

☽→♑ 1:55

☽☌♃ 2:54
☽□♄ 4:07
☽□♆ 5:51
☽△♀ 14:22
☽☌☿ 15:56

♀ Friday
13

♄ Saturday
14

☽VOC 8:51
☽→♒ 11:00

☽△♅ 8:51
☽⚹♄ 13:21
☽⚹♆ 14:51
☽☌♇ 17:27

Regulus 2025 Astrological Planner

Ⅱ Gemini

Mars and Uranus form a square on Sunday the 15th, though this square might be brought into sharper focus the following day when the Moon squares Uranus and opposes Mars. This is very volatile live-wire energy. Events happen suddenly and abruptly. There's high speed activity, impulsiveness and impatience.

Jupiter reaches a square aspect to Saturn this week, the third and final in a series of three Jupiter-Saturn squares going back to August 2024. It implies that there is a major change of gear in the global economic and political landscape. Some big projects and endeavours will surge forward while others may collapse.

On Thursday we have a square between Jupiter and Neptune which describes spiritual devotion and altruism, utopian visions, dreams and ideals. There's charitable good-will, but also some susceptibility to waste and careless extravagance.

Congratulations Cancerians!

☉ Sunday

15

☽□♀ 3:57
♂□♅ 9:47
♃□♄ 14:35

☽ Monday

16

☽VOC 17:30
☽→♓ 18:08

☽△☉ 10:02
☽□♅ 16:18
☽☌♂ 17:30
☽△♃ 21:00

♂ Tuesday

17

♂→♍ 8:35
☽✶♀ 15:01

GMT

June 2025

☿ Wednesday
18

☽VOC 21:34
☽→♈ 23:08

◐
Last Quarter
27♓48

☽△☿ 0:09
☽□☉ 19:19
☽✶♅ 21:34

♃ Thursday
19

☽☌♄ 1:38
☽□♃ 2:45
☽☌♆ 2:46
♃□♇ 3:13
☽✶♇ 4:57

♀ Friday
20

☽□☿ 10:32

♄ Saturday
21

☽VOC 1:49
☽→♉ 1:53

☽✶☉ 1:49
☉→♋ 2:42
☽△♂ 5:29
☽✶♃ 6:10
☽□♆ 7:24

Summer Solstice

Regulus 2025 Astrological Planner

♋ Cancer

The solstice occurs on the 21st of June marking the Sun's ingress into Cancer. Soon thereafter the Sun forms a series of potent aspects to Jupiter, Saturn and Neptune. Then we have the New Moon at 4° of Cancer, occurring very close to Jupiter, signalling an orientation towards wisdom and benevolence and noble plans and projects.

Mercury forms a sextile to Uranus on Thursday the 26th of June, accelerating the pace and tempo of events and bringing novel and unexpected news and information. There's quick and innovative thinking and exciting conversation.

Towards the end of the week Mercury enters Leo and soon after forms a trine to Saturn and Neptune in early Aries. This looks like communication of very deep ideas or words of gravity and austerity. Then just before the new week dawns, Mercury forms an opposition to Pluto and spoken and written words become loaded and laden with intensity. Firm and emphatic opinions are expressed.

☉ Sunday
22

☽☌♀	5:01
♂✶♃	10:30
☽✶♀	17:44
☉□♄	18:35
☽☌♅	1:50

☽ Monday
23

☽ VOC	1:50
☽→♊	2:57
☽ VOC	8:26

☽✶♄	5:33
☽✶♆	6:25
☽△♇	8:17
☽□♂	8:26
☉□♆	8:29

♂ Tuesday
24

☉☌♃	15:17

GMT

June 2025

☿ **Wednesday**

25

☽→♋ 3:44

●
New Moon
04♋08

☽□♄ 6:28
☽□♆ 7:16
☽☌♃ 9:33
☽☌☉ 10:31
☽⚹♂ 11:17

♃ **Thursday**

26

☿⚹♅ 9:45
☉⚹♂ 14:11
☽⚹♀ 15:08
☿→♌ 19:09

♀ **Friday**

27

☽ VOC 5:16
☽→♌ 6:05

☽⚹♅ 5:16
☽☌☿ 7:13
☽△♄ 9:04
☽△♆ 9:49
☽☍♇ 11:39

♄ **Saturday**

28

☿△♄ 3:52
☿△♆ 11:58

Regulus 2025 Astrological Planner

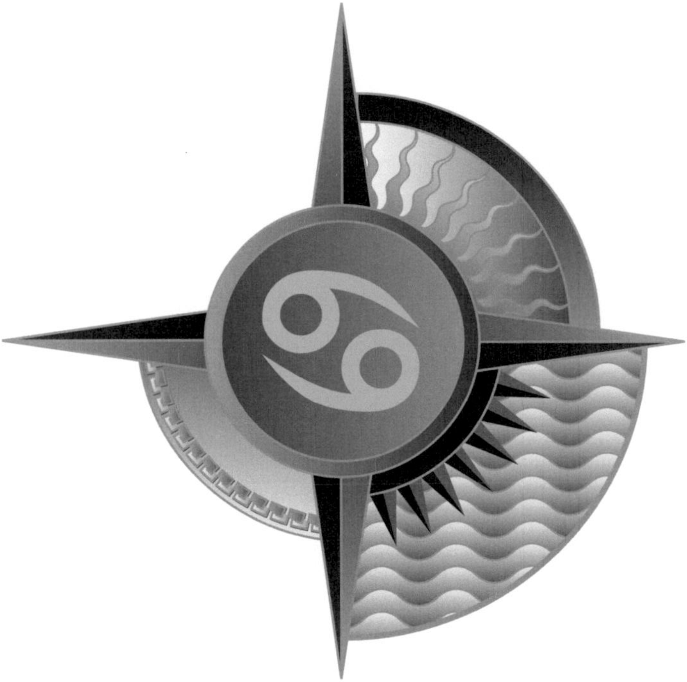

Ephemeris for July 2025, set at Midnight GMT.

July 2025

Day	☉	☽	True ☊	☿	♀	♂	♃	♄	♅	♆	♇
01	09 ♋ 26 06	19 ♍ 07 48	21 ♓ 04 R	05 ♌ 06 D	26 ♉ 00 D	07 ♍ 46 D	04 ♋ 49 D	01 ♈ 49 D	29 ♉ 42 D	02 ♈ 10 D	03 ♒ 08 R
02	10 23 19	01 ♎ 22 51	21 04 D	06 12	27 06	08 21	05 03	01 50	29 45	02 10	03 07
03	11 20 32	13 24 18	21 04 R	07 14	28 11	08 56	05 16	01 51	29 48	02 10	03 06
04	12 17 45	25 17 28	21 03	08 14	29 17	09 31	05 30	01 52	29 51	02 11	03 05
05	13 14 57	07 ♏ 07 34	21 01	09 10	00 ♊ 23	10 06	05 44	01 53	29 54	02 11 R	03 03
06	14 12 09	18 59 24	20 56	10 03	01 30	10 41	05 57	01 53	29 56	02 11	03 02
07	15 09 21	00 ♐ 57 08	20 48	10 52	02 36	11 16	06 11	01 54	29 59	02 10	03 01
08	16 06 32	13 04 05	20 39	11 38	03 43	11 51	06 24	01 55	00 ♊ 02	02 10	02 59
09	17 03 44	25 22 36	20 28	12 21	04 49	12 26	06 38	01 55	00 04	02 10	02 58
10	18 00 56	07 ♑ 54 04	20 17	12 59	05 56	13 02	06 51	01 56	00 07	02 10	02 57
11	18 58 08	20 38 54	20 07	13 34	07 03	13 37	07 05	01 56	00 10	02 10	02 55
12	19 55 20	03 ♒ 36 48	19 58	14 04	08 10	14 13	07 19	01 56	00 12	02 10	02 54
13	20 52 32	16 47 00	19 51	14 31	09 17	14 48	07 32	01 56	00 15	02 09	02 53
14	21 49 45	00 ♓ 08 37	19 47	14 52	10 25	15 24	07 45	01 56 R	00 17	02 09	02 51
15	22 46 58	13 40 55	19 46	15 10	11 32	16 00	07 59	01 56	00 20	02 09	02 50
16	23 44 11	27 23 26	19 46 D	15 23	12 40	16 36	08 12	01 56	00 22	02 09	02 48
17	24 41 25	11 ♈ 15 56	19 47	15 31	13 48	17 11	08 26	01 55	00 24	02 08	02 47
18	25 38 40	25 18 08	19 47	15 34	14 56	17 47	08 39	01 55	00 27	02 08	02 46
19	26 35 56	09 ♉ 29 18	19 46 R	15 33 R	16 04	18 23	08 52	01 54	00 29	02 07	02 44
20	27 33 12	23 47 50	19 44	15 27	17 12	18 59	09 06	01 54	00 31	02 07	02 43
21	28 30 30	08 ♊ 10 53	19 39	15 15	18 20	19 36	09 19	01 53	00 34	02 06	02 41
22	29 27 48	22 34 15	19 33	14 59	19 28	20 12	09 32	01 52	00 36	02 06	02 40
23	00 ♌ 25 06	06 ♋ 52 49	19 25	14 39	20 37	20 48	09 46	01 51	00 38	02 05	02 39
24	01 22 26	21 01 05	19 17	14 14	21 46	21 25	09 59	01 50	00 40	02 05	02 37
25	02 19 46	04 ♌ 54 00	19 11	13 44	22 54	22 01	10 12	01 49	00 42	02 04	02 36
26	03 17 07	18 27 49	19 05	13 11	24 03	22 38	10 25	01 48	00 44	02 03	02 34
27	04 14 28	01 ♍ 40 30	19 02	12 34	25 12	23 14	10 38	01 46	00 46	02 03	02 33
28	05 11 49	14 31 54	19 00	11 55	26 21	23 51	10 51	01 45	00 48	02 02	02 32
29	06 09 12	27 03 37	19 01 D	11 13	27 30	24 27	11 04	01 43	00 50	02 01	02 30
30	07 06 34	09 ♎ 18 40	19 02	10 29	28 39	25 04	11 17	01 42	00 52	02 01	02 29
31	08 03 57	21 21 06	19 03	09 45	29 49	25 41	11 30	01 40	00 54	02 00	02 27

Declination

Day	☉	☽	True ☊	☿	♀	♂	♃	♄	♅	♆	♇
1	+23°04'	+01°32'	-03°33'	+19°20'	+16°50'	+09°29'	+23°13'	-01°20'	+19°53'	-00°21'	-23°04'
3	+22°55'	-09°48'	-03°33'	+18°27'	+17°21'	+09°01'	+23°12'	-01°19'	+19°54'	-00°21'	-23°05'
5	+22°44'	-19°33'	-03°34'	+17°35'	+17°52'	+08°33'	+23°11'	-01°19'	+19°56'	-00°21'	-23°06'
7	+22°31'	-26°18'	-03°40'	+16°44'	+18°20'	+08°05'	+23°10'	-01°19'	+19°57'	-00°21'	-23°07'
9	+22°17'	-28°22'	-03°49'	+15°55'	+18°48'	+07°37'	+23°09'	-01°19'	+19°58'	-00°22'	-23°07'
11	+22°02'	-24°42'	-03°57'	+15°09'	+19°14'	+07°08'	+23°08'	-01°20'	+19°59'	-00°22'	-23°08'
13	+21°45'	-15°50'	-04°02'	+14°26'	+19°38'	+06°39'	+23°06'	-01°20'	+20°00'	-00°22'	-23°09'
15	+21°26'	-03°42'	-04°03'	+13°49'	+20°01'	+06°10'	+23°05'	-01°21'	+20°01'	-00°22'	-23°10'
17	+21°06'	+09°25'	-04°02'	+13°17'	+20°22'	+05°41'	+23°04'	-01°21'	+20°02'	-00°23'	-23°11'
19	+20°45'	+20°55'	-04°03'	+12°51'	+20°41'	+05°11'	+23°02'	-01°22'	+20°03'	-00°23'	-23°12'
21	+20°22'	+27°42'	-04°06'	+12°33'	+20°59'	+04°41'	+23°00'	-01°23'	+20°04'	-00°24'	-23°12'
23	+19°57'	+27°20'	-04°12'	+12°23'	+21°14'	+04°11'	+22°59'	-01°25'	+20°05'	-00°24'	-23°13'
25	+19°32'	+20°16'	-04°18'	+12°22'	+21°27'	+03°41'	+22°57'	-01°26'	+20°06'	-00°25'	-23°14'
27	+19°05'	+09°25'	-04°21'	+12°29'	+21°38'	+03°11'	+22°55'	-01°28'	+20°07'	-00°25'	-23°15'
29	+18°37'	-02°27'	-04°21'	+12°45'	+21°47'	+02°40'	+22°53'	-01°29'	+20°07'	-00°26'	-23°16'
31	+18°08'	-13°31'	-04°20'	+13°08'	+21°54'	+02°10'	+22°51'	-01°31'	+20°08'	-00°27'	-23°17'

Regulus 2025 Astrological Planner

July, 2025

Degree of
Key Aspects

4 Jul 2025
♀ ☌ ♅ 29♉52 29♉52
♆℞ 2♈11

6 Jul 2025
♀ ⚹ ♄ 1♊54 1♈54
♀ ⚹ ♆℞ 2♊10 2♈10

7 Jul 2025
♀ △ ♇℞ 3♊00 3♒00

13 Jul 2025
♄℞ 1♈56

18 Jul 2025
☿℞ 15♌35
☿℞ ⚹ ♀ 15♌34 15♊34

23 Jul 2025
☉ ⚹ ♅ 0♌38 0♊38
♀ □ ♂ 21♊01 21♍01

24 Jul 2025
☉ △ ♄℞ 1♌50 1♈50
☉ △ ♆℞ 2♌04 2♈04

25 Jul 2025
☉ ☍ ♇℞ 2♌35 2♒35

31 Jul 2025
☉ ☌ ☿℞ 9♌01 9♌01

CANCER

Sunday	Monday	Tuesday
29	30	1 ☽ voc 20:46 ☽→♎ 21:16 ☽△♀ 14:42 ☽△♅ 20:46
6 ☽ voc 22:04 ☽→♐ 22:06 ♀⚹♄ 8:43 ♀⚹♆ 14:46 ☽☍♅ 22:04	7 ☽ voc 21:29 ☽△♄ 1:54 ☽△♆ 2:26 ☽☍♀ 3:37 ☽⚹♇ 4:06 ♅→♊ 7:41 ♀△♇ 8:44 ☽△☿ 21:00 ☽□♂ 21:29	8
13 ☽→♓ 23:45 ♄ SR 3:42	14 ☽□♅ 0:15 ☽△♃ 13:46 ☽□♀ 19:53	15 ☽ voc 17:09 ☽☍♂ 4:15 ☽△☉ 17:09
20 ☽ voc 6:43 ☽→♊ 10:21 ☽⚹☉ 6:43 ☽☌♅ 11:15 ☽⚹♄ 13:30 ☽⚹♆ 13:53 ☽△♇ 14:52	21 ☽ voc 19:52 ☽⚹☿ 11:36 ☽☌♀ 18:23 ☽□♂ 19:52	22 ☽→♋ 12:26 ☉→♌ 13:29 ☽□♄ 15:33 ☽□♆ 15:57
27 ☽⚹♃ 16:57	28 ☽☌♂ 18:42	29 ☽ voc 0:57 ☽→♎ 5:43 ☽□♀ 0:57 ☽△♅ 7:21 ☽☍♄ 9:04 ☽☍♆ 9:39 ☽△♇ 10:35 ☽⚹☉ 19:17

Charts cast with Natural House System in GMT

10 July, 2025
20:36 GMT

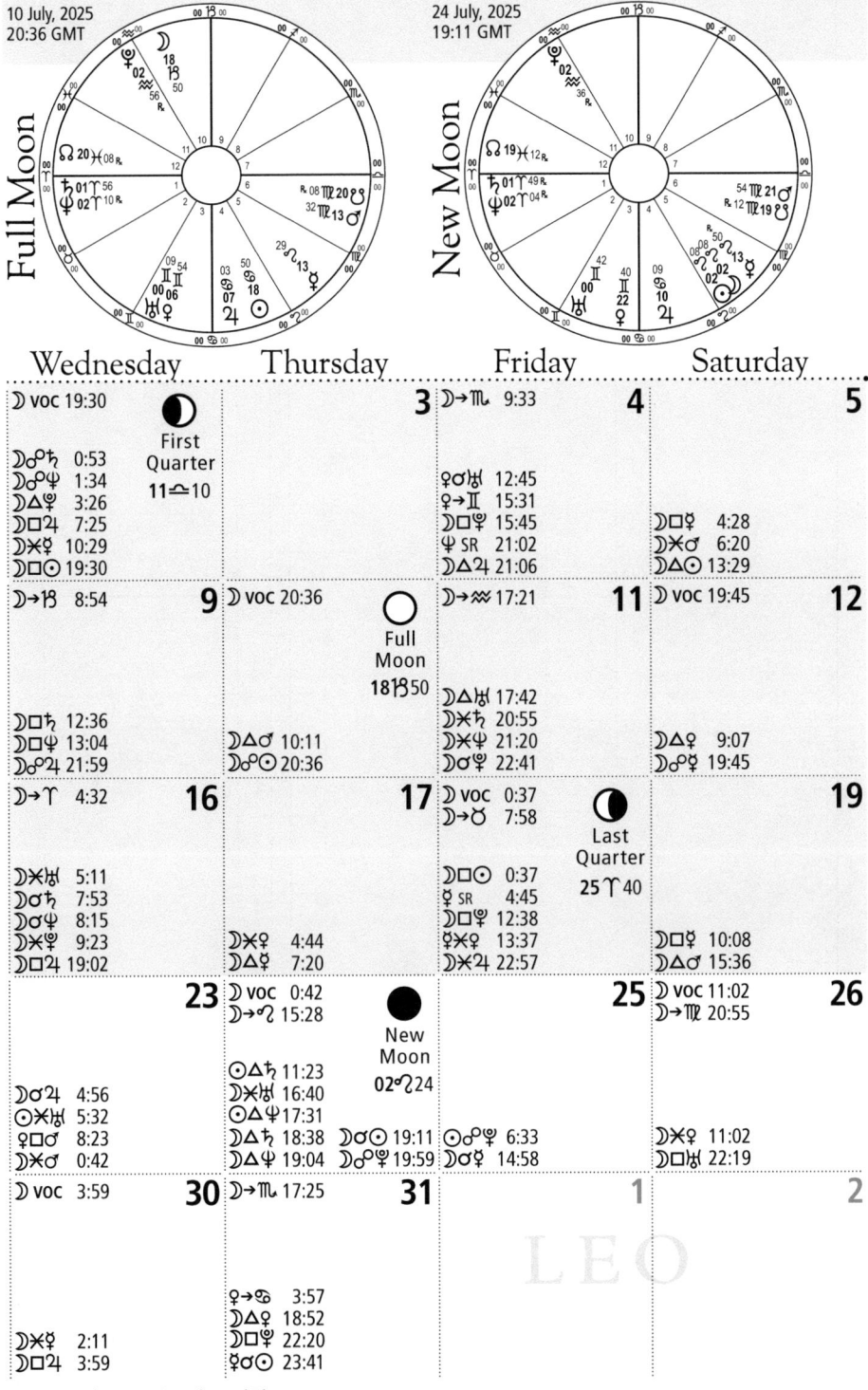

Full Moon

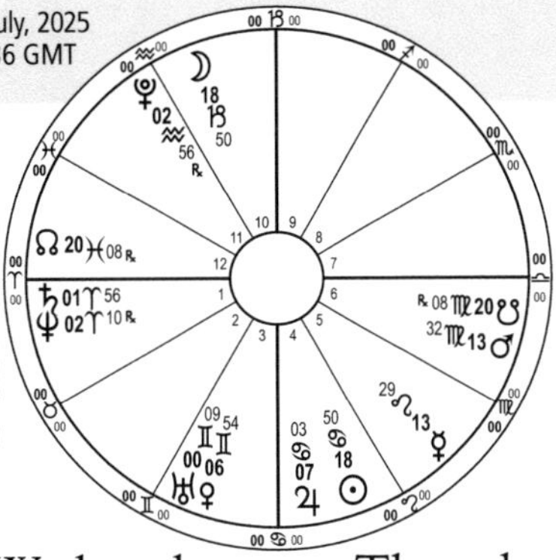

24 July, 2025
19:11 GMT

New Moon

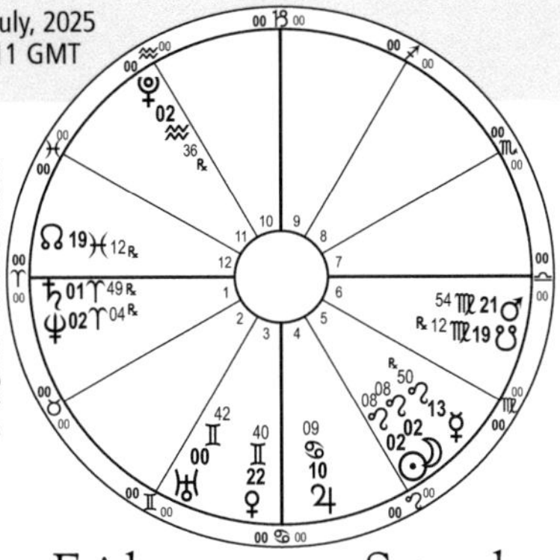

Wednesday	Thursday	Friday	Saturday
☽ voc 19:30 First Quarter 11♎10 ☽☍♄ 0:53 ☽☍♆ 1:34 ☽△♇ 3:26 ☽□♃ 7:25 ☽⚹☿ 10:29 ☽□☉ 19:30	3	4 ☽→♏ 9:33 ♀☌♅ 12:45 ♀→♊ 15:31 ☽□♇ 15:45 ♆ SR 21:02 ☽△♃ 21:06	5 ☽□☿ 4:28 ☽⚹♂ 6:20 ☽△☉ 13:29
9 ☽→♑ 8:54 ☽□♄ 12:36 ☽□♆ 13:04 ☽☍♃ 21:59	☽ voc 20:36 Full Moon 18♑50 ☽△♂ 10:11 ☽☍☉ 20:36	11 ☽→♒ 17:21 ☽△♅ 17:42 ☽⚹♄ 20:55 ☽⚹♆ 21:20 ☽☌♇ 22:41	12 ☽ voc 19:45 ☽△♀ 9:07 ☽☍☿ 19:45
16 ☽→♈ 4:32 ☽⚹♅ 5:11 ☽☌♄ 7:53 ☽☌♆ 8:15 ☽⚹♇ 9:23 ☽□♃ 19:02	17 ☽⚹♀ 4:44 ☽△☿ 7:20	☽ voc 0:37 ☽→♉ 7:58 Last Quarter 25♈40 ☽□☉ 0:37 ☿ SR 4:45 ☽□♇ 12:38 ☿⚹♀ 13:37 ☽⚹♃ 22:57	19 ☽□☿ 10:08 ☽△♂ 15:36
23 ☽☌♃ 4:56 ☉⚹♅ 5:32 ♀□♂ 8:23 ☽⚹♂ 0:42	☽ voc 0:42 ☽→♌ 15:28 New Moon 02♌24 ☉△♄ 11:23 ☽⚹♅ 16:40 ☉△♆ 17:31 ☽△♄ 18:38 ☽△♆ 19:04 ☽☌☉ 19:11 ☽☍♇ 19:59	25 ☉☍♇ 6:33 ☽☌☿ 14:58	26 ☽ voc 11:02 ☽→♍ 20:55 ☽⚹♀ 11:02 ☽□♅ 22:19
30 ☽ voc 3:59 ☽⚹☿ 2:11 ☽□♃ 3:59	31 ☽→♏ 17:25 ♀→♋ 3:57 ☽△♀ 18:52 ☽□♇ 22:20 ☿☌☉ 23:41	1 LEO	2

♋ Cancer

Venus forms a conjunction with Uranus on Friday the 4th of July, and hours later enters the sign of Gemini. This speaks of exotic art, fashion and unusual tastes in love and romance. Impulsive and experimental relationships.

Neptune turns retrograde on this same day as Saturn and Neptune reach the closest they'll get in 2025 to an exact conjunction. This looks like an important turning of the tide's direction in relation to the major global narratives of the time.

☉ Sunday

29

☽ VOC 11:02
☽→♍ 11:43

☽ Monday

30

☽□♀ 0:23
☿☌♆ 7:57
☽□♅ 11:02
☽⚹♃ 20:13

♂ Tuesday

I July

☽☌♂ 1:14
☽⚹☉ 3:54
☽ VOC 20:46
☽→♎ 21:16

☽△♀ 14:42
☽△♅ 20:46

GMT

July 2025

☿ Wednesday

2

☽ VOC 19:30

🌓
First Quarter
11 ♎ 10

☽ ☌ ♄	0:53
☽ ☍ ♆	1:34
☽ △ ♇	3:26
☽ □ ♃	7:25
☽ ✶ ☿	10:29
☽ □ ☉	19:30

♃ Thursday

3

♀ Friday

4

☽ → ♏ 9:33

♀ ☌ ♅	12:45
♀ → ♊	15:31
☽ □ ♀	15:45
♆ SR	21:02
☽ △ ♃	21:06

♄ Saturday

5

☽ □ ☿	4:28
☽ ✶ ♂	6:20
☽ △ ☉	13:29

Regulus 2025 Astrological Planner

♋ Cancer

Venus, after having formed a jolting conjunction to Uranus some days ago, now forms a sextile to the Saturn-Neptune conjunction, and then a trine to Pluto. Friendships and personal relationships may experience some form of constraint or there is a need for self-sacrifice in relationships, and yet there is also the potential here for a profound depth of feeling and kinship. Deep commitments and seriousness in relationships.

Uranus enters Gemini on Monday the 7th of July. This might herald new and novel approaches in Gemini related areas such as language, communication and education in the years ahead.

The Full Moon occurs on Thursday the 10th of July coinciding with a semi-sextile aspect between Venus and Jupiter, as well as a semi-sextile aspect between Mercury and Mars. The Venus-Jupiter combination could speak of luxuries and indulging in social and sensual pleasures, while Mercury semi-sextile Mars is almost deviously cunning and efficient in achieving its ends.

☉ Sunday
6

☽ VOC   22:04
☽→♐   22:06

♀⚹♄   8:43
♀⚹♆   14:46
☽☌♅   22:04

☽ Monday
7

☽ VOC   21:29

☽△♄   1:54
☽△♆   2:26
☽☍♀   3:37
☽⚹♇   4:06
♅→♊   7:41
♀△♇   8:44
☽△☿   21:00
☽□♂   21:29

♂ Tuesday
8

GMT

July 2025

☿ Wednesday

9

☽→♑ 8:54

☽□♄ 12:36
☽□♆ 13:04
☽☍♃ 21:59

♃ Thursday

10

☽VOC 20:36

○
Full Moon
18♑50

☽△♂ 10:11
☽☍☉ 20:36

♀ Friday

11

☽→♒ 17:21

☽△♅ 17:42
☽⚹♄ 20:55
☽⚹♆ 21:20
☽☌♇ 22:41

♄ Saturday

12

☽VOC 19:45

☽△♀ 9:07
☽☍☿ 19:45

Regulus 2025 Astrological Planner

119

♋ Cancer

Mars forms a sesquiquadrate to Pluto on Thursday the 17th of July which makes for indomitable determination and a capacity for vigorous physical exertion. This is a raw vigorous energy that can achieve a great deal when channeled into hard work and industriousness.

Mercury turns retrograde on Friday the 18th of July and remains retrograde until the 11th of August. During this period keep reviewing ongoing plans and dedicate your attention to unfinished business. There could be delays in matters pertaining to Mercury.

Mercury and Venus form a sextile aspect on the 18th of July, making for light-hearted conversation and friendly social interactions.

☉ Sunday   ☽→♓ 23:45

13

♄ SR   3:42

☽ Monday

14

☽□♅   0:15
☽△♃   13:46
☽□♀   19:53

♂ Tuesday   ☽ VOC 17:09

15

☽☍♂   4:15
☽△☉   17:09

---

120   GMT

July 2025

Mercury is retrograde from the 18th of Jul (15°35'♌) through the 11th of Aug (4°15'♌).

☿ Wednesday
16

☽→♈ 4:32

☽⚹♅ 5:11
☽☌♄ 7:53
☽☌♆ 8:15
☽⚹♇ 9:23
☽□♃ 19:02

♃ Thursday
17

◐
Last Quarter
25♈40

☽⚹♀ 4:44
☽△☿ 7:20

♀ Friday
18

☽ VOC 0:37
☽→♉ 7:58

☽□☉ 0:37
☿ SR 4:45
☽□♆ 12:38
☿⚹♀ 13:37
☽⚹♃ 22:57

♄ Saturday
19

☽□☿ 10:08
☽△♂ 15:36

Regulus 2025 Astrological Planner   121

♌ Leo

Congratulations Leos!

The New Moon occurs on Thursday at 2° Leo, very tightly opposite Pluto, and at the same time sextile Uranus and trine the Saturn-Neptune conjunction. This is a very potent and complex astrological pattern that speaks of highly charged interactions in which power is wielded or resisted intensively. Innovative new technologies could be applied to this end.

Venus forms a square to Mars on Wednesday the 23rd and social interactions are energetic and lively. Passions run high and lovers are boisterous and unruly, either revelling or arguing.

☉ Sunday

20

☽ VOC   6:43
☽→♊   10:21

☽✶☉   6:43
☽☌♅   11:15
☽✶♄   13:30
☽✶♆   13:53
☽△♇   14:52

☽ Monday

21

☽ VOC   19:52

☽✶♀   11:36
☽☌♀   18:23
☽□♂   19:52

♂ Tuesday

22

☽→♋   12:26

☉→♌   13:29
☽□♄   15:33
☽□♆   15:57

July 2025

Mercury is retrograde from the 18th of Jul (15°35'♌) through the 11th of Aug (4°15'♌).

☿ Wednesday
23

☽☌♃	4:56
☉✶♅	5:32
♀□♂	8:23
☽✶♂	0:42

♃ Thursday
24

New Moon
02♌24

☽VOC	0:42
☽→♌	15:28
☉△♄	11:23
☽✶♅	16:40
☉△♆	17:31
☽△♄	18:38
☽△♆	19:04
☽☌☉	19:11
☽☌♆	19:59

♀ Friday
25

☉☍♆	6:33
☽☌☿	14:58

♄ Saturday
26

☽VOC	11:02
☽→♍	20:55
☽✶♀	11:02
☽□♅	22:19

Regulus 2025 Astrological Planner

♌ Leo

Venus enters Cancer on Thursday the 31st of July heading towards a conjunction to Jupiter, but first she has to honor an appointment with Saturn and Neptune through square aspects on Friday. Love can be experienced through sacrifice. There's a stoical acceptance of the real world limitations of romantic ideals and dreams. The coming Venus-Jupiter conjunction should help to revive some hope, faith and joyousness.

Retrograde Mercury arrives at a conjunction with the Sun at 9° of Leo. Official announcements and authoritative statements are made. An intentional and purposeful articulation of ideas, views and opinions. This will be especially significant if you have important planets located around 9° of the fixed signs (Taurus, Leo, Scorpio or Aquarius).

☉ Sunday
27

☽✶♃ 16:57

☽ Monday
28

☽☌♂ 18:42

♂ Tuesday
29

☽ VOC 0:57
☽→♎ 5:43

☽□♀ 0:57
☽△♅ 7:21
☽☍♄ 9:04
☽☍♆ 9:39
☽△♇ 10:35
☽✶☉ 19:17

124   GMT

July 2025

Mercury is retrograde from the 18th of Jul (15°35'♌) through the 11th of Aug (4°15'♌).

☿ Wednesday   ☽ VOC   3:59

30

☽✶☿   2:11
☽□♃   3:59

♃ Thursday   ☽→♏ 17:25

31

♀→♋   3:57
☽△♀   18:52
☽□♇   22:20
☿☌☉   23:41

♀ Friday

1 August

First Quarter
09♏32

☽□☿   10:56
☽□☉   12:41
♀□♄   13:34
☽△♃   17:25
♀□♆   20:48

♄ Saturday

2

Regulus 2025 Astrological Planner

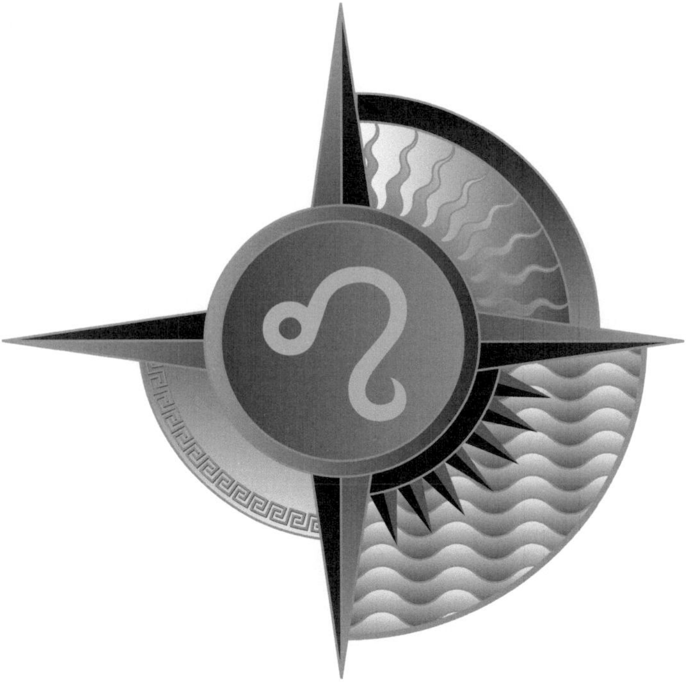

August 2025

Day	☉	☽	True ☊	☿	♀	♂	♃	♄	♅	♆	♇
01	09♌01 21	03♏15 35	19♓04 D	09♌00 ℞	00♋58 D	26♍18 D	11♋43 D	01♈38 ℞	00♊55 D	01♈59 ℞	02♒26 ℞
02	09 58 46	15 07 06	19 04 ℞	08 16	02 07	26 55	11 56	01 36	00 57	01 58	02 25
03	10 56 11	27 00 36	19 03	07 34	03 17	27 32	12 08	01 34	00 59	01 57	02 23
04	11 53 37	09♐00 48	19 00	06 53	04 27	28 09	12 21	01 32	01 00	01 56	02 22
05	12 51 03	21 11 47	18 56	06 16	05 37	28 46	12 34	01 30	01 02	01 55	02 20
06	13 48 30	03♑36 54	18 50	05 43	06 46	29 24	12 46	01 28	01 03	01 54	02 19
07	14 45 59	16 18 24	18 44	05 14	07 56	00♎01	12 59	01 26	01 05	01 53	02 18
08	15 43 27	29 17 24	18 39	04 51	09 06	00 38	13 11	01 23	01 06	01 52	02 16
09	16 40 57	12♒33 43	18 35	04 33	10 17	01 16	13 24	01 21	01 08	01 51	02 15
10	17 38 28	26 06 04	18 31	04 21	11 27	01 53	13 36	01 18	01 09	01 50	02 13
11	18 36 00	09♓52 13	18 30	04 15	12 37	02 31	13 49	01 15	01 11	01 49	02 12
12	19 33 33	23 49 24	18 30 D	04 17 D	13 48	03 08	14 01	01 12	01 12	01 48	02 11
13	20 31 08	07♈54 40	18 31	04 25	14 58	03 46	14 13	01 10	01 13	01 47	02 09
14	21 28 44	22 05 11	18 32	04 40	16 09	04 24	14 25	01 07	01 14	01 46	02 08
15	22 26 21	06♉18 19	18 33	05 03	17 19	05 02	14 37	01 04	01 15	01 45	02 07
16	23 24 00	20 31 45	18 34	05 32	18 30	05 40	14 49	01 00	01 16	01 44	02 06
17	24 21 41	04♊43 17	18 34 ℞	06 09	19 41	06 18	15 01	00 57	01 18	01 42	02 04
18	25 19 23	18 50 42	18 32	06 53	20 52	06 56	15 13	00 54	01 19	01 41	02 03
19	26 17 07	02♋51 42	18 30	07 44	22 03	07 34	15 25	00 51	01 19	01 40	02 02
20	27 14 52	16 43 49	18 27	08 42	23 14	08 12	15 37	00 47	01 20	01 39	02 00
21	28 12 39	00♌24 38	18 24	09 46	24 25	08 50	15 49	00 44	01 21	01 37	01 59
22	29 10 28	13 51 57	18 22	10 56	25 37	09 28	16 00	00 40	01 22	01 36	01 58
23	00♍08 17	27 04 03	18 20	12 13	26 48	10 07	16 12	00 37	01 23	01 35	01 57
24	01 06 09	10♍00 01	18 19	13 35	27 59	10 45	16 23	00 33	01 23	01 33	01 56
25	02 04 01	22 39 48	18 19 D	15 02	29 11	11 24	16 35	00 29	01 24	01 32	01 54
26	03 01 55	05♎04 23	18 19	16 34	00♌23	12 02	16 46	00 25	01 25	01 30	01 53
27	03 59 50	17 15 44	18 20	18 11	01 34	12 41	16 57	00 22	01 25	01 29	01 52
28	04 57 47	29 16 42	18 22	19 51	02 46	13 19	17 09	00 18	01 26	01 28	01 51
29	05 55 45	11♏10 50	18 23	21 35	03 58	13 58	17 20	00 14	01 26	01 26	01 50
30	06 53 45	23 02 19	18 24	23 22	05 10	14 37	17 31	00 10	01 27	01 25	01 49
31	07 51 46	04♐55 39	18 24	25 11	06 22	15 16	17 42	00 06	01 27	01 23	01 48

Declination

Day	☉	☽	True ☊	☿	♀	♂	♃	♄	♅	♆	♇
1	+17°52′	-18°20′	-04°20′	+13°21′	+21°56′	+01°54′	+22°50′	-01°32′	+20°08′	-00°27′	-23°17′
3	+17°21′	-25°39′	-04°20′	+13°53′	+22°00′	+01°24′	+22°48′	-01°34′	+20°09′	-00°28′	-23°18′
5	+16°49′	-28°32′	-04°24′	+14°27′	+22°01′	+00°53′	+22°46′	-01°36′	+20°10′	-00°29′	-23°19′
7	+16°16′	-25°46′	-04°28′	+15°03′	+21°59′	+00°22′	+22°43′	-01°39′	+20°10′	-00°30′	-23°19′
9	+15°41′	-17°27′	-04°31′	+15°39′	+21°56′	-00°09′	+22°41′	-01°41′	+20°11′	-00°30′	-23°20′
11	+15°06′	-05°21′	-04°32′	+16°12′	+21°49′	-00°41′	+22°39′	-01°44′	+20°12′	-00°31′	-23°21′
13	+14°30′	+08°03′	-04°32′	+16°40′	+21°41′	-01°12′	+22°36′	-01°46′	+20°12′	-00°32′	-23°21′
15	+13°53′	+19°57′	-04°31′	+17°03′	+21°30′	-01°43′	+22°34′	-01°49′	+20°12′	-00°33′	-23°22′
17	+13°14′	+27°22′	-04°31′	+17°18′	+21°17′	-02°14′	+22°32′	-01°52′	+20°13′	-00°34′	-23°23′
19	+12°35′	+27°57′	-04°33′	+17°24′	+21°01′	-02°46′	+22°29′	-01°55′	+20°13′	-00°36′	-23°23′
21	+11°56′	+21°50′	-04°36′	+17°20′	+20°43′	-03°17′	+22°26′	-01°58′	+20°14′	-00°37′	-23°24′
23	+11°15′	+11°27′	-04°38′	+17°05′	+20°22′	-03°49′	+22°24′	-02°01′	+20°14′	-00°38′	-23°25′
25	+10°34′	-00°27′	-04°38′	+16°39′	+19°59′	-04°20′	+22°21′	-02°05′	+20°14′	-00°39′	-23°25′
27	+09°52′	-11°51′	-04°37′	+16°01′	+19°34′	-04°51′	+22°19′	-02°08′	+20°14′	-00°40′	-23°26′
29	+09°10′	-21°16′	-04°36′	+15°11′	+19°07′	-05°23′	+22°16′	-02°11′	+20°15′	-00°41′	-23°26′
31	+08°26′	-27°15′	-04°36′	+14°11′	+18°38′	-05°54′	+22°13′	-02°15′	+20°15′	-00°42′	-23°27′

August, 2025

Degree of
Key Aspects

1 Aug 2025
♀ □ ♄℞ 1♋37 1♈37
♀ □ ♆℞ 1♋58 1♈58

8 Aug 2025
♂ △ ♅ 1♎08 1♊08

9 Aug 2025
♂ ☍ ♄℞ 1♎20 1♈20
♂ ☍ ♆℞ 1♎50 1♈50

10 Aug 2025
♂ △ ♇℞ 2♎13 2♒13

11 Aug 2025
☿D 4♌15

12 Aug 2025
♄℞ ⚹ ♅ 1♈12 1♊12
♀ ☌ ♃ 14♋04 14♋04

15 Aug 2025
☿ ⚹ ♂ 5♌05 5♎05

18 Aug 2025
☿ ⚹ ♂ 7♌04 7♎04

24 Aug 2025
☉ □ ♅ 1♍24 1♊24

26 Aug 2025
♀ △ ♄℞ 0♌25 0♈25
♀ ⚹ ♅ 1♌25 1♊25
♀ △ ♆℞ 1♌29 1♈29

27 Aug 2025
♀ ☍ ♇℞ 1♌52 1♒52

29 Aug 2025
♅ ⚹ ♆℞ 1♊26 1♈26

Sunday	Monday	Tuesday
27	28 LEO	29
3 ☽ voc 1:07 ☽→♐ 6:00 ☽⚹♂ 1:07 ☽☍♅ 7:59 ☽△♄ 9:08 ☽△♆ 9:54 ☽⚹♇ 10:46 ☽△☿ 20:00	4 ☽△☉ 6:12	5 ☽ voc 15:28 ☽→♑ 17:04 ☽□♂ 15:28 ☽□♄ 19:54 ☽□♆ 20:44
10 ☽→♓ 6:50 ☽□♅ 8:52 ♂△♇ 12:29	11 ☽ voc 6:54 ☽△♀ 5:11 ☽△♃ 6:54 ☿ SD 7:30	12 ☽→♈ 10:33 ♄⚹♅ 3:31 ♀☌♃ 5:30 ☽☌♄ 12:34 ☽⚹♅ 12:36 ☽☌♆ 13:36 ☽⚹♇ 14:14 ☽☍♂ 16:38 ☽△☿ 17:59
17 ☽⚹☿ 2:33 ☽△♂ 2:47	18 ☽ voc 11:53 ☽→♋ 19:05 ☿⚹♂ 5:33 ☽⚹☉ 11:53 ☽□♄ 20:33 ☽□♆ 21:57	19 ☽□♂ 8:29 ☽☌♃ 22:02
24 ☉□♅ 7:15 ☽⚹♃ 12:14	25 ☽ voc 13:53 ☽→♎ 14:08 ☽⚹♀ 13:53 ☽☍♄ 15:00 ♀→♌ 16:27 ☽△♅ 16:52 ☽☍♆ 17:04 ☽△♇ 17:48	26 ♀△♄ 0:55 ☽☌♂ 14:25 ♀⚹♅ 20:58 ♀△♆ 22:18 ☽□♃ 23:23

Charts cast with Natural House System in GMT

Full Moon
9 August, 2025
7:55 GMT

New Moon 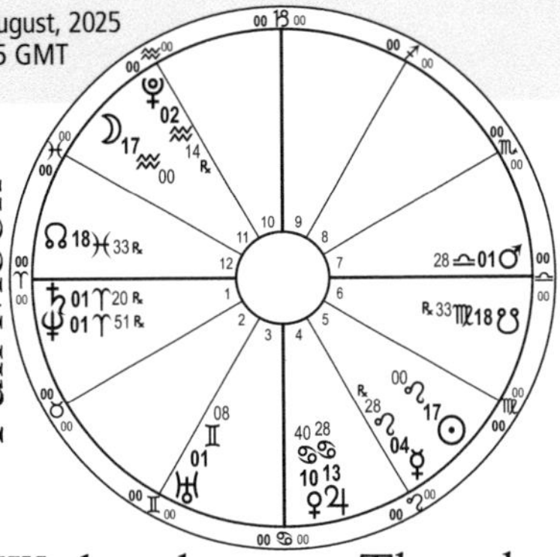
23 August, 2025
6:07 GMT

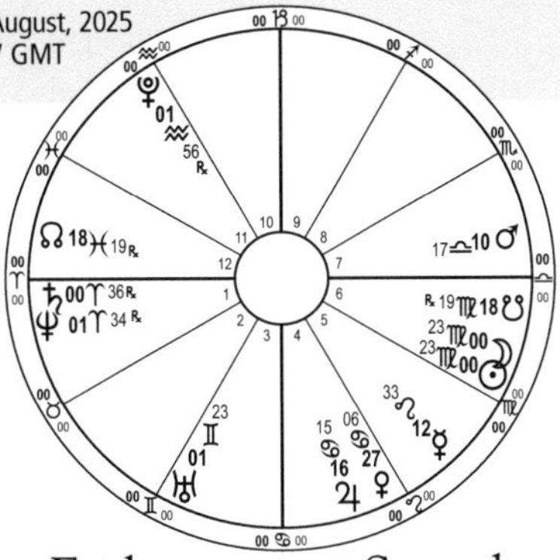

Wednesday	Thursday	Friday	Saturday
30	31	☽ First Quarter 09♏32	2 ☽□☿ 10:56 ☽□☉ 12:41 ♀□♄ 13:34 ☽△♃ 17:25 ♀△♆ 20:48
6 ☽ voc 17:40 ☽☌♀ 6:38 ☽☌♃ 17:40 ♂→♎ 23:23	7	8 ☽→♒ 1:18 ☽△♂ 2:35 ☽△♅ 3:19 ☽✶♄ 3:49 ☽✶♆ 4:42 ☽☌♇ 5:25 ☽☌☿ 9:52 ♂△♒ 18:45	9 ☽ voc 7:55 ♂☍♄ 2:52 ☽☌☉ 7:55 ♂☍♆ 22:13 ○ Full Moon 17♒00
13 ☽ voc 22:54 ☽□♃ 10:51 ☽□♀ 13:03 ☽△☉ 22:54	14 ☽→♉ 13:22 ☽□♇ 16:56 ☽□☿ 21:48	15 ☿✶♂ 2:05 ☽✶♃ 14:14 ☽✶♀ 20:16	16 ☽ voc 5:12 ☽→♊ 16:00 ☽□☉ 5:12 ☽✶♄ 17:39 ☽△♅ 18:11 ☽✶♆ 18:54 ☽△♇ 19:31 ☽ Last Quarter 23♉36
20 ☽ voc 12:27 ☽→♌ 23:16	21 ☽ voc 18:13 ☽△♄ 0:34 ☽✶♅ 1:40 ☽△♆ 2:08 ☽☌♇ 2:47 ☽✶♂ 15:43 ☽☌♀ 18:13	22 ☉→♍ 20:34	23 ☽→♍ 5:24 ● New Moon 00♍23 ☽☌☉ 6:06 ☽□♅ 7:57
27 ☽ voc 2:06 ☽✶☿ 2:06 ♀☍♇ 5:54	28 ☽→♏ 1:27 ☽□☿ 5:10 ☽☌♀ 7:48 ☽✶☉ 12:27	29 ♅✶♆ 0:12 ☽△♃ 12:38	30 ☽ voc 0:47 ☽→♐ 14:04 ☽☌☿ 0:47 ☽△♄ 14:19 ☽△♆ 16:53 ☽☌♇ 16:59 ☽✶♀ 17:42

VIRGO

Regulus 2025 Astrological Planner

129

♌ Leo

At the time of the Full Moon on the 9th of August the Sun and Moon will both be forming 45 degree multiple aspects to the Saturn-Neptune conjunction, once again bringing that important longer term process into sharper focus. This is further emphasised by the fact that Mars gets involved on the weekend of 9-10 August, forming a potent opposition to the Saturn-Neptune conjunction. This looks like an intense effort that is somehow bogged down by circumstances or factors that are difficult to discern and identify. Initiatives may lack follow through.

☉ Sunday

3

☽ VOC   1:07
☽→♐   6:00

☽ Monday

4

☽✶♂   1:07
☽☍♅   7:59
☽△♄   9:08
☽△♆   9:54
☽✶♇   10:46
☽△☿   20:00

♂ Tuesday

5

☽△☉   6:12
☽ VOC   15:28
☽→♑   17:04

☽□♂   15:28
☽□♄   19:54
☽□♆   20:44

GMT

August 2025

Mercury is retrograde from the 18th of Jul (15°35'♌) through the 11th of Aug (4°15'♌).

☿ **Wednesday**

6

☽VOC 17:40

☽☌°♀ 6:38
☽☌°♃ 17:40
♂→♎ 23:23

♃ **Thursday**

7

♀ **Friday**

8

☽→♒ 1:18

☽△♂ 2:35
☽△♅ 3:19
☽⚹♄ 3:49
☽⚹♆ 4:42
☽☌♇ 5:25
☽☌°☿ 9:52
♂△♅ 18:45

♄ **Saturday**

9

☽VOC 7:55

○
Full Moon
17♒00

☿☌°♄ 2:52
☽☌°☉ 7:55
♂☌°♆ 22:13

♌ Leo

Mars is all over the show during the weekend of 9-10 August. Not only is there the conspicuous opposition of Mars to Saturn and Neptune, Mars is also trine both Uranus and Pluto! This is very impatient and lively energy that wants to break out and break free.

Mercury turns Direct on the 11th of August while at 4 degrees Leo.

Mars reaches a sextile aspect to this stationing Mercury during the second half of the week and this aspect will remain in place till around the 20th of August, making for vigorous mental energy and frank and forthright communication. The energy is sharp, alert and efficient.

☉ Sunday

10

☽→♓ 6:50

☽ Monday

11

☽□♅ 8:52
♂△♇ 12:29
☽ VOC 6:54

♂ Tuesday

12

☽△♀ 5:11
☽△♃ 6:54
☿ SD 7:30
☽→♈ 10:33

♄✶♅ 3:31
♀♂♃ 5:30
☽☌♄ 12:34
☽✶♅ 12:36
☽☌♆ 13:36
☽✶♇ 14:14
☽☍♂ 16:38
☽△☿ 17:59

GMT

August 2025

Mercury is retrograde from the 18th of Jul (15°35'♌) through the 11th of Aug (4°15'♌).

☿ Wednesday
13

☽VOC 22:54

☽□♃ 10:51
☽□♀ 13:03
☽△☉ 22:54

♃ Thursday
14

☽→♉ 13:22

☽□♇ 16:56
☽□☿ 21:48

♀ Friday
15

☿⚹♂ 2:05
☽⚹♃ 14:14
☽⚹♀ 20:16

♄ Saturday
16

☽VOC 5:12
☽→♊ 16:00

◐
Last Quarter
23♉36

☽□☉ 5:12
☽⚹♄ 17:39
☽☌♅ 18:11
☽⚹♆ 18:54
☽△♇ 19:31

♌ Leo

As mentioned in the previous week, Mercury and Mars remain locked in a sextile aspect during the first half of this week indicating general busyness and rapid and skillful execution of plans.

The New Moon on Saturday the 23rd of August occurs at 0 degrees Virgo and forms a tight square to Uranus at 1 degree Gemini. This is another restless and high energy configuration that suggests events occur very suddenly and take people by surprise. The status quo is emphatically defied or resisted. In fact Jupiter at this time is about 45 degrees from both ends of this square between Sun-Moon and Uranus; so Jupiter is close to the midpoint of this square. This could be "lucky" and it hints at an optimistic and adventurous energy, enthusiastic about new novel ideas and concepts. There's a desire to break free from rigid social patterns and explore new vistas, physically, mentally and spiritually.

☉ Sunday
17

☽⚹☿	2:33
☽△♂	2:47

☽ Monday
18

☽ VOC	11:53
☽→♋	19:05

☿⚹♂	5:33
☽⚹☉	11:53
☽□♄	20:33
☽□♆	21:57

♂ Tuesday
19

☽□♂	8:29
☽☌♃	22:02

GMT

August 2025

☿ Wednesday

20

☽VOC 12:27
☽→♌ 23:16

♃ Thursday

21

☽☌♀ 12:27
☽VOC 18:13

♀ Friday

22

☽△♄ 0:34
☽✶♅ 1:40
☽△♆ 2:08
☽☍♇ 2:47
☽✶♂ 15:43
☽☌☿ 18:13

♄ Saturday

23

☉→♍ 20:34
☽→♍ 5:24

●
New Moon
00 ♍ 23

☽☌☉ 6:06
☽□♅ 7:57

Regulus 2025 Astrological Planner

♍ Virgo

Early in the week Venus forms a series of notable aspects: a trine to Saturn and Neptune, a sextile to Uranus, and an opposition to Pluto. Friendships and personal relationships undergo a phase of deepened intensity. Boundaries, obligations and expectations in relationships become a matter that needs clarifying and adjusting.

On Monday the 25th of August Mercury will be sesquiquadrate the Saturn-Neptune conjunction, so the tone of discussion is somewhat serious and deep, or there may even be avoidance and evasion of communication. The fact that Mercury at this time is also semi-sextile Jupiter does hint that there is some element of sincerity and authentic goodwill in discussions and agreements that are entered into, but thoroughness could be lacking. Fine-print may be ignored or overlooked.

☉ Sunday
24

☽ Monday
25

☉□♅ 7:15
☽⚹♃ 12:14
☽VOC 13:53
☽→♎ 14:08

♂ Tuesday
26

☽⚹♀ 13:53
☽☍♄ 15:00
♀→♌ 16:27
☽△♅ 16:52
☽☌♆ 17:04
☽△♆ 17:48

♀△♄ 0:55
☽☌♂ 14:25
♀⚹♅ 20:58
♀△♆ 22:18
☽□♃ 23:23

136   GMT

August 2025

☿ Wednesday   ☽ VOC   2:06

27

☽✶☿   2:06
♀☍♆   5:54

♃ Thursday   ☽→♏   1:27

28

☽□♇   5:10
☽□♀   7:48
☽✶☉   12:27

♀ Friday

29

♅✶♆   0:12
☽△♃   12:38

♄ Saturday   ☽ VOC   0:47
                      ☽→♐   14:04

30

☽□☿   0:47
☽△♄   14:19
☽△♆   16:53
☽☍♅   16:59
☽✶♇   17:42

Regulus 2025 Astrological Planner

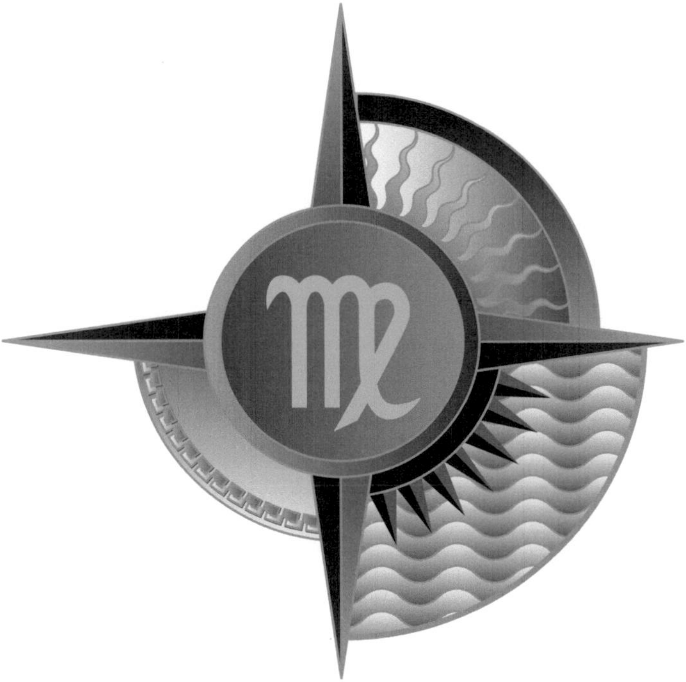

Ephemeris for September 2025, set at Midnight GMT.

September 2025

Day	☉	☽	True ☊	☿	♀	♂	♃	♄	♅	♆	♇
01	08 ♍ 49 48	16 ♐ 55 31	18 ♓ 24 ℞	27 ♌ 03 D	07 ♌ 34 D	15 ♎ 55 D	17 ♋ 52 D	00 ♈ 01 ℞	01 ♊ 27 D	01 ♈ 22 ℞	01 ♒ 47 ℞
02	09 47 51	29 06 28	18 23	28 56	08 46	16 34	18 03	29 ♓ 57	01 27	01 20	01 46
03	10 45 56	11 ♑ 32 44	18 23	00 ♍ 51	09 58	17 13	18 14	29 53	01 28	01 19	01 44
04	11 44 03	24 17 47	18 22	02 46	11 10	17 52	18 24	29 49	01 28	01 17	01 43
05	12 42 10	07 ♒ 24 01	18 21	04 42	12 22	18 31	18 35	29 44	01 28	01 16	01 42
06	13 40 20	20 52 27	18 20	06 39	13 35	19 10	18 45	29 40	01 28	01 14	01 41
07	14 38 31	04 ♓ 42 20	18 20	08 35	14 47	19 50	18 55	29 36	01 28 ℞	01 12	01 41
08	15 36 43	18 51 09	18 20 D	10 31	16 00	20 29	19 05	29 31	01 28	01 11	01 40
09	16 34 57	03 ♈ 14 45	18 20	12 27	17 12	21 08	19 16	29 27	01 28	01 09	01 39
10	17 33 13	17 47 44	18 20	14 22	18 25	21 48	19 25	29 22	01 27	01 08	01 38
11	18 31 32	02 ♉ 24 09	18 20 ℞	16 17	19 37	22 27	19 35	29 18	01 27	01 06	01 37
12	19 29 52	16 58 13	18 20	18 11	20 50	23 07	19 45	29 13	01 27	01 04	01 36
13	20 28 14	01 ♊ 24 57	18 20	20 04	22 03	23 47	19 55	29 09	01 27	01 03	01 35
14	21 26 39	15 40 34	18 20	21 56	23 16	24 26	20 04	29 04	01 26	01 01	01 34
15	22 25 05	29 42 35	18 20 D	23 47	24 29	25 06	20 14	29 00	01 26	01 00	01 34
16	23 23 34	13 ♋ 29 46	18 20	25 37	25 42	25 46	20 23	28 55	01 25	00 58	01 33
17	24 22 05	27 01 46	18 21	27 27	26 55	26 26	20 32	28 50	01 25	00 56	01 32
18	25 20 38	10 ♌ 18 50	18 21	29 15	28 08	27 06	20 41	28 46	01 24	00 55	01 31
19	26 19 14	23 21 33	18 22	01 ♎ 02	29 21	27 46	20 50	28 41	01 24	00 53	01 31
20	27 17 51	06 ♍ 10 41	18 22	02 48	00 ♍ 35	28 26	20 59	28 36	01 23	00 51	01 30
21	28 16 30	18 47 03	18 23 ℞	04 33	01 48	29 06	21 08	28 32	01 22	00 50	01 29
22	29 15 11	01 ♎ 11 36	18 22	06 17	03 01	29 47	21 16	28 27	01 22	00 48	01 29
23	00 ♎ 13 54	13 25 30	18 21	08 00	04 15	00 ♏ 27	21 25	28 22	01 21	00 46	01 28
24	01 12 39	25 30 11	18 20	09 43	05 28	01 07	21 33	28 18	01 20	00 45	01 28
25	02 11 26	07 ♏ 27 34	18 18	11 24	06 42	01 48	21 41	28 13	01 19	00 43	01 27
26	03 10 15	19 20 03	18 16	13 04	07 55	02 28	21 49	28 08	01 18	00 41	01 27
27	04 09 05	01 ♐ 10 39	18 13	14 43	09 09	03 09	21 57	28 04	01 17	00 40	01 26
28	05 07 58	13 02 53	18 12	16 22	10 23	03 50	22 05	27 59	01 16	00 38	01 26
29	06 06 52	25 00 48	18 10	17 59	11 37	04 30	22 13	27 55	01 15	00 36	01 25
30	07 05 48	07 ♑ 08 48	18 10 D	19 36	12 50	05 11	22 20	27 50	01 14	00 35	01 25
01	08 04 46	19 31 25	18 10	21 11	14 04	05 52	22 28	27 45	01 13	00 33	01 24

Declination

Day	☉	☽	True ☊	☿	♀	♂	♃	♄	♅	♆	♇
1	+08°05′	-28°30′	-04°36′	+13°38′	+18°22′	-06°10′	+22°12′	-02°17′	+20°15′	-00°43′	-23°27′
3	+07°21′	-26°48′	-04°36′	+12°25′	+17°50′	-06°41′	+22°09′	-02°20′	+20°15′	-00°44′	-23°28′
5	+06°36′	-19°28′	-04°36′	+11°04′	+17°15′	-07°12′	+22°07′	-02°24′	+20°15′	-00°46′	-23°28′
7	+05°52′	-07°44′	-04°36′	+09°39′	+16°38′	-07°43′	+22°04′	-02°28′	+20°15′	-00°47′	-23°29′
9	+05°06′	+05°59′	-04°36′	+08°09′	+16°00′	-08°14′	+22°02′	-02°31′	+20°15′	-00°48′	-23°29′
11	+04°21′	+18°37′	-04°36′	+06°37′	+15°20′	-08°44′	+21°59′	-02°35′	+20°15′	-00°50′	-23°30′
13	+03°35′	+26°52′	-04°37′	+05°03′	+14°38′	-09°15′	+21°56′	-02°39′	+20°15′	-00°51′	-23°30′
15	+02°49′	+28°18′	-04°37′	+03°28′	+13°54′	-09°45′	+21°54′	-02°43′	+20°14′	-00°52′	-23°30′
17	+02°03′	+22°57′	-04°37′	+01°52′	+13°08′	-10°15′	+21°51′	-02°47′	+20°14′	-00°54′	-23°31′
19	+01°16′	+13°08′	-04°37′	+00°17′	+12°22′	-10°45′	+21°49′	-02°50′	+20°14′	-00°55′	-23°31′
21	+00°30′	+01°26′	-04°36′	-01°17′	+11°33′	-11°15′	+21°46′	-02°54′	+20°14′	-00°56′	-23°31′
23	-00°17′	-10°08′	-04°37′	-02°49′	+10°44′	-11°45′	+21°44′	-02°58′	+20°13′	-00°58′	-23°31′
25	-01°04′	-19°58′	-04°39′	-04°21′	+09°53′	-12°14′	+21°41′	-03°02′	+20°13′	-00°59′	-23°32′
27	-01°51′	-26°34′	-04°41′	-05°50′	+09°01′	-12°43′	+21°39′	-03°05′	+20°13′	-01°00′	-23°32′
29	-02°37′	-28°33′	-04°41′	-07°18′	+08°08′	-13°12′	+21°37′	-03°09′	+20°12′	-01°02′	-23°32′

Regulus 2025 Astrological Planner

September, 2025

Degree of
Key Aspects

3 Sep 2025
☿ □ ♅ 1♍28 1♊28

5 Sep 2025
♂ □ ♃ 18♎36 18♋36

6 Sep 2025
♅℞ 1♊28

12 Sep 2025
☉ ⚹ ♃ 19♍48 19♋48
☿ ⚹ ♃ 19♍54 19♋54

13 Sep 2025
☉ ☌ ☿ 20♍55 20♍55

16 Sep 2025
♀ ⚹ ♂ 25♌51 25♎51

17 Sep 2025
☿ ☍ ♄℞ 28♍47 28♓47

18 Sep 2025
☿ ☍ ♆℞ 0♎53 0♈53

19 Sep 2025
☿ △ ♅℞ 1♎24 1♊24
☿ △ ♇℞ 1♎31 1♒31

20 Sep 2025
♀ □ ♅℞ 1♍23 1♊23

21 Sep 2025
☉ ☍ ♄℞ 28♍31 28♓31

23 Sep 2025
☉ ☍ ♆℞ 0♎45 0♈45

24 Sep 2025
☉ △ ♅℞ 1♎20 1♊20
☉ △ ♇℞ 1♎28 1♒28
♂ □ ♇℞ 1♏27 1♒27

VIRGO

Sunday	Monday	Tuesday
First Quarter 08♐07 ☽△♀ 0:12 ☽□☉ 3:25 ☽⚹♂ 18:52	**1** ♄→♈ 8:06 ☽△☿ 23:36	**2** ☽ voc 1:38 ☽→♑ 1:44 ☽□♄ 1:38 ☽□♆ 4:20 ☿→♍ 13:23 ☽△☉ 22:23
Lunar Eclipse 15♓24 ☽☍☿ 7:41 ☽●☉ 18:12	**8** ☽ voc 17:44 ☽→♈ 18:37 ☽△♃ 0:24 ☽☌♄ 17:44 ☽☌♆ 20:32 ☽⚹♅ 21:02 ☽⚹♇ 21:21	**9**
☽ voc 22:46 Last Quarter 21♊52 ☽□☉ 10:33 ☽□☿ 12:16 ☽⚹♀ 14:09 ☽△♂ 15:41 ☽□♄ 22:46	**15** ☽→♏ 0:30 ☽□♆ 2:13	**16** ♀⚹♂ 3:04 ☽☌♃ 12:18 ☽⚹☉ 18:52 ☽□♂ 22:53
☽ voc 19:42 ☽→♎ 21:41 New Moon 28♍59 ☽⚹♃ 4:34 ☉☍♄ 5:45 ☽☍♄ 18:42 ☽●☉ 19:42 ☽☍♆ 23:14	**22** ☽△♅ 0:19 ☽△♇ 0:34 ♂→♏ 7:54 ☽☌☿ 11:35 ☉→♎ 18:19	**23** ☽ voc 16:02 ☉☍♆ 12:53 ☽□♃ 16:02
28 ☽⚹☿ 7:43	☽ voc 5:44 ☽→♑ 9:55 First Quarter 07♑06 ☽□♄ 5:44 ☽□♆ 11:05 ☽⚹♂ 19:55 ☽□☉ 23:54	**30** ☽△♀ 12:20

Charts cast with Natural House System in GMT

7 September, 2025
18:12 GMT

Lunar Eclipse

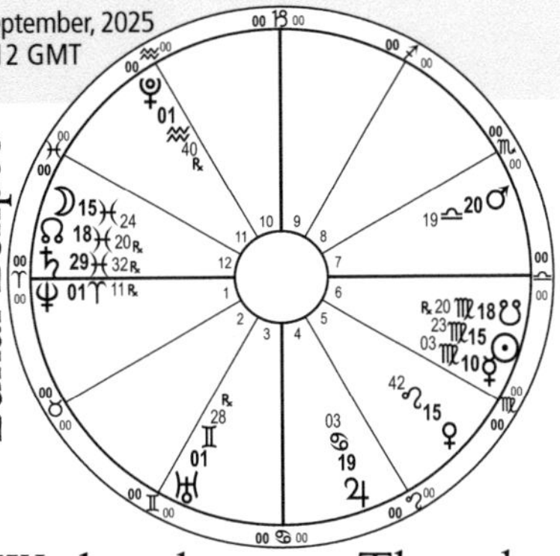

21 September, 2025
19:42 GMT

Solar Eclipse

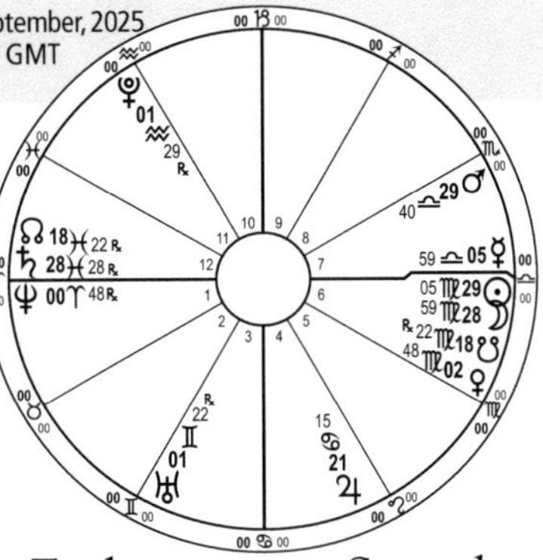

Wednesday	Thursday	Friday	Saturday
3 ☿□♅ 7:40 ☽□♂ 11:20 ☽☍♃ 12:50	**4** ☽ voc 10:08 ☽→♒ 10:32 ☽⚹♄ 10:08 ☽⚹♆ 12:51 ☽△♅ 13:12 ☽☌♇ 13:40	**5** ☽ voc 20:51 ♂□♃ 2:59 ☽☍♀ 9:49 ☽△♂ 20:51	**6** ☽→♓ 15:54 ♅ SR 5:24 ☽□♅ 18:26
10 ☽ voc 6:53 ☽→♉ 20:03 ☽△♀ 1:06 ☽□♃ 2:42 ☽☍♂ 6:53 ☽□♇ 22:42	**11**	**12** ☽ voc 20:14 ☽→♊ 21:38 ☽△☿ 2:18 ☽△☉ 4:29 ☽⚹♃ 4:39 ☽□♀ 6:59 ☉⚹♃ 7:30 ☽⚹♄ 20:14 ☿⚹♃ 21:53 ☽⚹♆ 23:23	**13** ☽☌♅ 0:03 ☽△♇ 0:17 ☿☌☉ 10:51
17 ☽ voc 3:13 ☽→♌ 5:20 ☽⚹☿ 0:51 ☽△♄ 3:13 ☽△♆ 7:00 ☽⚹♅ 7:52 ☽☍♇ 8:05 ☿☍♄ 17:47	**18** ☿→♎ 10:06 ☿☍♆ 22:01	**19** ☽ voc 12:21 ☽→♍ 12:23 ☿△♅ 4:52 ☿△♇ 6:27 ☽⚹♂ 8:40 ☽☌♀ 12:21 ♀→♍ 12:39 ☽□♅ 14:59	**20** ♀□♅ 15:41
24 ☽→♏ 9:00 ☉△♅ 2:55 ☉△♇ 6:05 ♂□♇ 11:52 ☽□♇ 11:55 ☽☌♂ 11:56 ☽⚹♀ 22:17	**25**	**26** ☽ voc 17:44 ☽→♐ 21:37 ☽△♃ 5:06 ☽△♄ 17:44 ☽△♆ 22:57	**27** ☽☍♅ 0:13 ☽⚹♇ 0:31 ☽⚹☉ 6:34 ☽□♀ 18:00
1	2	3	4

LIBRA

♍ Virgo

A retrograde Saturn re-enters Pisces on the 1st of September and will only return to the first degree of Aries on the 14th of February 2026.

Mars reaches a square to Jupiter on the 5th of September which means "go big or go home". It's about bold opportunism and a strong feeling of entitlement. It can cause people to bite off more than they can chew, but this is definitely better than being inert, fearful or apathetic. Go for it!

Mercury forms a square to Uranus on the 3rd of September which suggests there's an almost frenetic tempo in information being delivered or received. Pace yourself and keep track. There will be unexpected news or messages that cause surprise. On Tuesday the 4th of September Mercury is located at the midpoint of the forming Mars-Jupiter square which in itself makes for bold and forthright words, discussions and messages. Views and opinions are expressed emphatically.

☉ Sunday
31

First Quarter
08 ♐ 07

☽△♀	3:12
☽☐☉	6:25
☽✶♂	21:52

☽ Monday
1 September

♄→♈	8:06
☽△♀	23:36

♂ Tuesday
2

☽ VOC	1:38
☽→♑	1:44

☽☐♄	1:38
☽☐♆	4:20
☿→♍	13:23
☽△☉	22:23

GMT

September 2025

☿ Wednesday
3

☿□♅ 7:40
☽□♂ 11:20
☽☍♃ 12:50

♃ Thursday
4

☽ VOC 10:08
☽→♒ 10:32

☽⚹♄ 10:08
☽⚹♆ 12:51
☽△♅ 13:12
☽☌♇ 13:40

♀ Friday
5

☽ VOC 20:51

♂□♃ 2:59
☽☍♀ 9:49
☽△♂ 20:51

♄ Saturday
6

☽→♓ 15:54

♅ SR 5:24
☽□♅ 18:26

Regulus 2025 Astrological Planner

♍ Virgo

A Lunar Eclipse occurs on Sunday the 7th of September at 15 degrees Pisces, just over a degree from semi-square Pluto.

The Sun and Mercury together form a sextile aspect to Jupiter on Friday the 12th of September, and so scholars and teachers meet and cultivate knowledge together, honest and noble words are spoken, and honorable agreements are made. Friendship and cooperation is supported; there is fraternity and a sharing of knowledge among people.

☉ Sunday

7

🌘 Lunar Eclipse
15 ♓ 24

☽ Monday

8

☽☍☿ 7:41
☽●☉ 18:12

☽ VOC 17:44
☽→♈ 18:37

♂ Tuesday

9

☽△♃ 0:24
☽☌♄ 17:44
☽☌♆ 20:32
☽⚹♅ 21:02
☽⚹♇ 21:21

---

144   GMT

September 2025

☿ Wednesday

10

☽VOC 6:53
☽→♉ 20:03

☽△♀ 1:06
☽□♃ 2:42
☽☌♂ 6:53
☽□☿ 22:42

♃ Thursday

11

♀ Friday

12

☽VOC 20:14
☽→♊ 21:38

☽△☿ 2:18
☽△☉ 4:29
☽✶♃ 4:39
☽□♀ 6:59
☉✶♃ 7:30
☽✶♄ 20:14
☿✶♃ 21:53
☽✶♆ 23:23

♄ Saturday

13

☽☌♅ 0:03
☽△♆ 0:17
☿☌☉ 10:51

Regulus 2025 Astrological Planner 145

♍ Virgo

Venus and Mars form a sextile aspect this week which reaches its peak around Tuesday the 16th of September, at 25 degrees Leo and Libra respectively. This looks like gregarious self expression and lively social interactions. Highly interactive group activities. Taking the initiative and sparking up a connection and pleasant banter.

On the 17th of September Mercury is precisely opposite Saturn and there's some gravitas in communication and very thorough and painstaking analysis. There's practical thinking and practical plans can be clarified and agreed upon. As the Venus-Mars sextile loosens after the 17th of September both Venus and Mars in turn form quincunx aspects to Saturn in the days that follow. Obligations and duties constrain social connections and there is a need to work rather than play. Loving sacrifices are made for others and hard work saves the day.

On the 18th and 19th of September Mercury forms an opposition to Neptune and a trine to both Uranus and Pluto, creating a "kite" formation. This could indicate some sort of explosive and extraordinary investigation, perhaps of supernatural phenomenon. Very unusual information comes to light.

☉ Sunday
14

☽ VOC 22:46

◐ Last Quarter
21 ♊ 52

☽□☉ 10:33
☽□☿ 12:16
☽⚹♀ 14:09
☽△♂ 15:41
☽□♄ 22:46

☽ Monday
15

☽→♋ 0:30

☽□♆ 2:13

♂ Tuesday
16

♀⚹♂ 3:04
☽☌♃ 12:18
☽⚹☉ 18:52
☽□♂ 22:53

GMT

September 2025

☿ Wednesday

17

☽VOC 3:13
☽→♌ 5:20

☽✶♀ 0:51
☽△♄ 3:13
☽△♆ 7:00
☽✶♅ 7:52
☽☌♇ 8:05
☿☍♄ 17:47

♃ Thursday

18

☿→♎ 10:06
☿☌♆ 22:01

♀ Friday

19

☽VOC 12:21
☽→♍ 12:23

☿△♅ 4:52
☿△♆ 6:27
☽✶♂ 8:40
☽☌♀ 12:21
♀→♍ 12:39
☽□♅ 14:59

♄ Saturday

20

♀□♅ 15:41

Regulus 2025 Astrological Planner   147

♎ Libra

This is an important week. There's a Solar Eclipse on the 21st of September at 29 degrees Virgo, on the eve of the equinox, which occurs the next day. Both of these solar events occur in the face of an opposition with Saturn and Neptune, and it could be that this will be one of the most potent triggers of the longer term Saturn-Neptune conjunction process during 2025.

It is likely to be a test of the resilience of some of the systems and structures that keep society functional. It could bring altruistic projects into sharp focus. There's some sort of need for selfless work here.

On the 24th of September the Sun will be trine both Uranus and Pluto creating an impressive grand trine picture. It looks revolutionary. There's a determined and defiant attitude. Sudden radical decisions are made and drastic changes are accelerated.

☉ Sunday 21

☽ VOC 19:42
☽ → ♎ 21:41

Solar Eclipse
28 ♍ 59

☽ ⚹ ♃ 4:34
☉ ☍ ♄ 5:45
☽ ☌ ♄ 18:42
☽ ☌ ☉ 19:42
☽ ☌ ♆ 23:14

☽ Monday 22

Autumn Equinox

☽ △ ♅ 0:19
☽ △ ♆ 0:34
♂ → ♏ 7:54
☽ ☌ ☿ 11:35
☉ → ♎ 18:19

♂ Tuesday 23

☽ VOC 16:02

☉ ☌ ♆ 12:53
☽ □ ♃ 16:02

September 2025

☿ Wednesday

24

☽→♏ 9:00

☉△♅ 2:55
☉△♆ 6:05
♂□♇ 11:52
☽□♇ 11:55
☽☌♂ 11:56
☽⚹♀ 22:17

♃ Thursday

25

♀ Friday

26

☽ VOC 17:44
☽→♐ 21:37

☽△♃ 5:06
☽△♄ 17:44
☽△♆ 22:57

♄ Saturday

27

☽☍♅ 0:13
☽⚹♇ 0:31
☽⚹☉ 6:34
☽□♀ 18:00

Regulus 2025 Astrological Planner

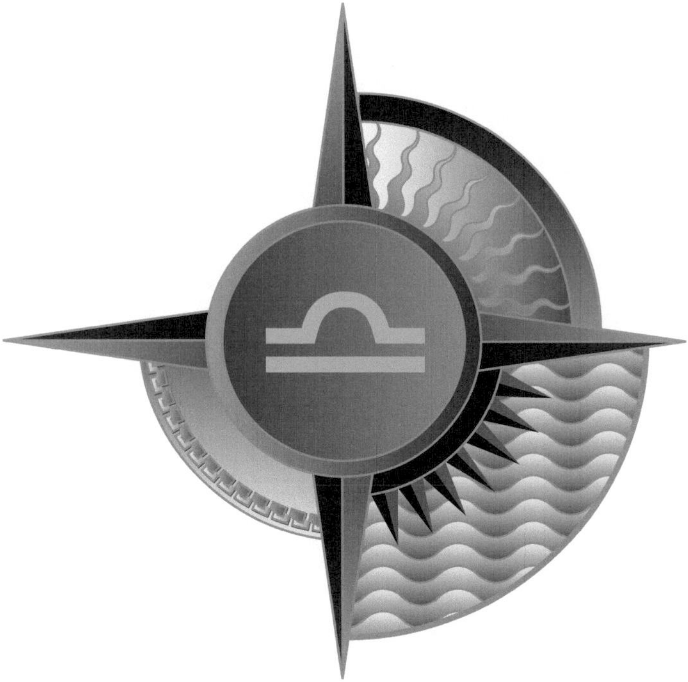

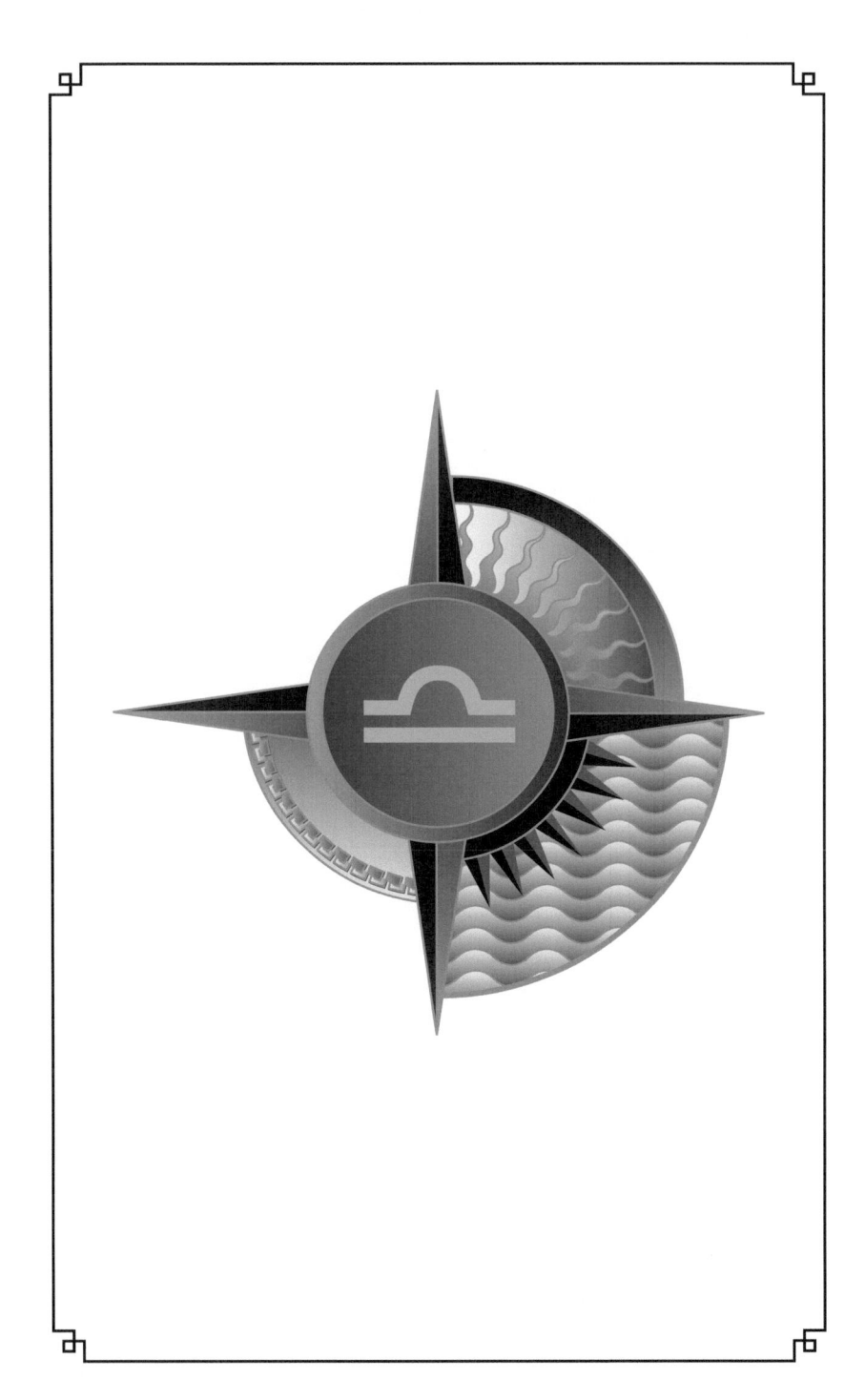

Ephemeris for October 2025, set at Midnight GMT.

October 2025

Day	☉	☽	True ☊	☿	♀	♂	♃	♄	♅	♆	♇
01	08♎04 46	19♑31 25	18♓10 D	21♎11 D	14♍04 D	05♏52 D	22♋28 D	27♓45 R	01♊13 R	00♈33 R	01♒24 R
02	09 03 45	02♒13 02	18 12	22 46	15 18	06 33	22 35	27 41	01 11	00 31	01 24
03	10 02 46	15 17 28	18 13	24 20	16 32	07 14	22 42	27 36	01 10	00 30	01 24
04	11 01 49	28 47 23	18 14	25 53	17 46	07 55	22 49	27 32	01 09	00 28	01 23
05	12 00 54	12♓43 45	18 15	27 25	19 00	08 36	22 56	27 28	01 07	00 27	01 23
06	13 00 00	27 05 11	18 15 R	28 57	20 14	09 17	23 03	27 23	01 06	00 25	01 23
07	13 59 08	11♈47 37	18 14	00♏28	21 28	09 58	23 09	27 19	01 05	00 23	01 23
08	14 58 19	26 44 27	18 11	01 57	22 42	10 39	23 15	27 14	01 03	00 22	01 23
09	15 57 32	11♉47 09	18 07	03 27	23 57	11 21	23 22	27 10	01 02	00 20	01 22
10	16 56 46	26 46 33	18 03	04 55	25 11	12 02	23 28	27 06	01 00	00 19	01 22
11	17 56 04	11♊34 19	18 00	06 22	26 25	12 43	23 34	27 02	00 58	00 17	01 22
12	18 55 23	26 04 02	17 57	07 49	27 40	13 25	23 39	26 58	00 57	00 15	01 22
13	19 54 45	10♋11 56	17 55	09 15	28 54	14 06	23 45	26 53	00 55	00 14	01 22
14	20 54 09	23 56 47	17 54 D	10 39	00♎08	14 48	23 50	26 49	00 53	00 12	01 22
15	21 53 36	07♌19 22	17 55	12 03	01 23	15 30	23 56	26 45	00 52	00 11	01 22 D
16	22 53 04	20 21 49	17 57	13 27	02 37	16 12	24 01	26 41	00 50	00 09	01 22
17	23 52 35	03♍06 59	17 58	14 49	03 52	16 53	24 06	26 38	00 48	00 08	01 22
18	24 52 08	15 37 48	17 59	16 10	05 06	17 35	24 10	26 34	00 46	00 06	01 22
19	25 51 44	27 57 05	17 59 R	17 30	06 21	18 17	24 15	26 30	00 44	00 05	01 22
20	26 51 21	10♎07 11	17 56	18 49	07 36	18 59	24 19	26 26	00 42	00 03	01 23
21	27 51 01	22 10 08	17 52	20 07	08 50	19 41	24 24	26 23	00 40	00 02	01 23
22	28 50 42	04♏07 36	17 46	21 23	10 05	20 23	24 28	26 19	00 38	00 01	01 23
23	29 50 26	16 01 08	17 38	22 38	11 20	21 06	24 31	26 16	00 36	29♓59	01 23
24	00♏50 11	27 52 22	17 30	23 52	12 35	21 48	24 35	26 12	00 34	29 58	01 23
25	01 49 59	09♐43 10	17 21	25 04	13 49	22 30	24 39	26 09	00 32	29 56	01 24
26	02 49 48	21 35 54	17 14	26 14	15 04	23 13	24 42	26 06	00 30	29 55	01 24
27	03 49 39	03♑33 29	17 07	27 22	16 19	23 55	24 45	26 02	00 28	29 54	01 24
28	04 49 32	15 39 29	17 03	28 28	17 34	24 38	24 48	25 59	00 26	29 52	01 25
29	05 49 26	27 57 57	17 01	29 32	18 49	25 20	24 51	25 56	00 23	29 51	01 25
30	06 49 22	10♒33 22	17 01 D	00♐33	20 04	26 03	24 53	25 53	00 21	29 50	01 26
31	07 49 20	23 30 11	17 01	01 31	21 19	26 45	24 56	25 51	00 19	29 49	01 26

Declination

Day	☉	☽	True ☊	☿	♀	♂	♃	♄	♅	♆	♇
1	-03°24'	-25°04'	-04°41'	-08°43'	+07°14'	-13°40'	+21°35'	-03°13'	+20°12'	-01°03'	-23°32'
3	-04°10'	-16°23'	-04°39'	-10°06'	+06°19'	-14°08'	+21°33'	-03°16'	+20°11'	-01°04'	-23°32'
5	-04°56'	-03°54'	-04°38'	-11°26'	+05°23'	-14°36'	+21°31'	-03°20'	+20°11'	-01°05'	-23°32'
7	-05°42'	+10°01'	-04°39'	-12°43'	+04°27'	-15°03'	+21°29'	-03°23'	+20°10'	-01°07'	-23°32'
9	-06°28'	+21°56'	-04°42'	-13°58'	+03°30'	-15°30'	+21°27'	-03°26'	+20°09'	-01°08'	-23°32'
11	-07°13'	+28°09'	-04°45'	-15°09'	+02°32'	-15°56'	+21°25'	-03°30'	+20°09'	-01°09'	-23°32'
13	-07°58'	+26°51'	-04°47'	-16°17'	+01°34'	-16°22'	+21°23'	-03°33'	+20°08'	-01°10'	-23°32'
15	-08°43'	+19°27'	-04°47'	-17°22'	+00°36'	-16°48'	+21°22'	-03°36'	+20°07'	-01°12'	-23°32'
17	-09°27'	+08°46'	-04°46'	-18°23'	-00°23'	-17°13'	+21°20'	-03°39'	+20°06'	-01°13'	-23°32'
19	-10°10'	-02°56'	-04°46'	-19°20'	-01°22'	-17°38'	+21°19'	-03°41'	+20°06'	-01°14'	-23°32'
21	-10°53'	-13°56'	-04°49'	-20°13'	-02°20'	-18°02'	+21°18'	-03°44'	+20°05'	-01°15'	-23°32'
23	-11°35'	-22°43'	-04°55'	-21°01'	-03°19'	-18°25'	+21°17'	-03°47'	+20°04'	-01°16'	-23°32'
25	-12°17'	-27°45'	-05°02'	-21°45'	-04°17'	-18°48'	+21°16'	-03°49'	+20°03'	-01°17'	-23°32'
27	-12°58'	-27°49'	-05°06'	-22°24'	-05°15'	-19°11'	+21°15'	-03°51'	+20°02'	-01°18'	-23°31'
29	-13°38'	-22°35'	-05°08'	-22°56'	-06°13'	-19°32'	+21°14'	-03°53'	+20°01'	-01°19'	-23°31'
31	-14°17'	-12°49'	-05°07'	-23°23'	-07°10'	-19°53'	+21°13'	-03°55'	+20°00'	-01°20'	-23°31'

Regulus 2025 Astrological Planner 151

October, 2025

Degree of
Key Aspects

1 Oct 2025
☿ □ ♃ 22♎34 22♋34

7 Oct 2025
☿ □ ♇℞ 1♏23 1♒23

8 Oct 2025
♀ ⚹ ♃ 23♍19 23♋19

11 Oct 2025
♀ ☍ ♄℞ 27♍00 27♓00

14 Oct 2025
♀ ☍ ♆℞ 0♎12 0♈12
♇D 1♒22
♀ △ ♅℞ 0♎52 0♊52
♀ △ ♇ 1♎22 1♒22

17 Oct 2025
☉ □ ♃ 24♎07 24♋07

20 Oct 2025
☿ ☌ ♂ 19♏11 19♏11

24 Oct 2025
☉ □ ♇ 1♏24 1♒24
☿ △ ♃ 24♏37 24♋37

25 Oct 2025
☿ △ ♄℞ 26♏06 26♓06

28 Oct 2025
♂ △ ♃ 24♏49 24♋49

29 Oct 2025
☿ △ ♆℞ 29♏51 29♓51
♂ △ ♄℞ 25♏54 25♓54
☿ ☍ ♅℞ 0♐22 0♊22

30 Oct 2025
☿ ⚹ ♇ 1♐26 1♒26

Sunday	Monday	Tuesday
28	29 LIBRA	30
5 ☽☍♀ 11:34 ☽△♃ 17:15 ☽☌♄ 0:29	6 ☽ voc 0:29 ☽→♈ 4:48 ☽☌♆ 5:28 ☽⚹♅ 6:35 ☽⚹♇ 7:04 ☿→♏ 16:40	☽ voc 18:23 Full Moon 14♈08 ☽☍☉ 3:47 ☿□♇ 14:40 ☽□♃ 18:23
12 ☽ voc 2:55 ☽→♋ 6:37 ☽□♄ 1:29 ☽□♀ 2:55 ☽□♆ 7:02 ☽△☿ 22:10	Last Quarter 20♋40 ☽△♂ 7:07 ☽□☉ 18:12 ♀→♎ 21:19 ☽☌♃ 23:49	14 ☽ voc 5:05 ☽→♌ 10:47 ♀☍♆ 1:16 ♇ SD 4:48 ☽△♄ 5:05 ☽△♆ 11:08 ☽⚹♀ 12:10 ☽⚹♅ 12:21 ☽☍♇ 13:14 ♀△♅ 14:10 ♀△♇ 23:45
19 ☽→♎ 4:01 ☽☍♆ 4:10 ☽△♅ 5:27 ☽△♇ 6:43 ☽☌♀ 18:26	20 ☿☌♂ 6:51	☽ voc 12:25 ☽→♏ 15:42 New Moon 28♎22 ☽□♃ 4:28 ☽☌☉ 12:25 ☽□♇ 18:28
26 ☽ voc 16:41 ☽→♑ 16:53 ☽□♄ 9:00 ☽□♆ 16:41	27 ☽⚹☉ 0:35	28 ☽□♀ 4:11 ♂△♃ 6:19 ☽☍♃ 17:56 ☽⚹♂ 18:36 ☽⚹♄ 20:06

Charts cast with Natural House System in GMT

7 October, 2025
03:48 GMT

Full Moon

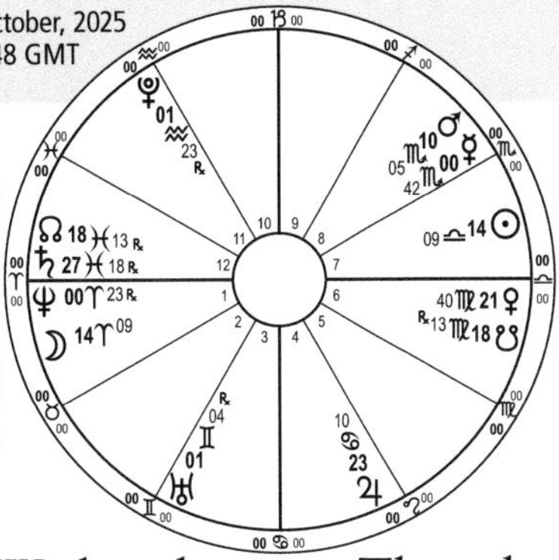

21 October, 2025
12:25 GMT

New Moon

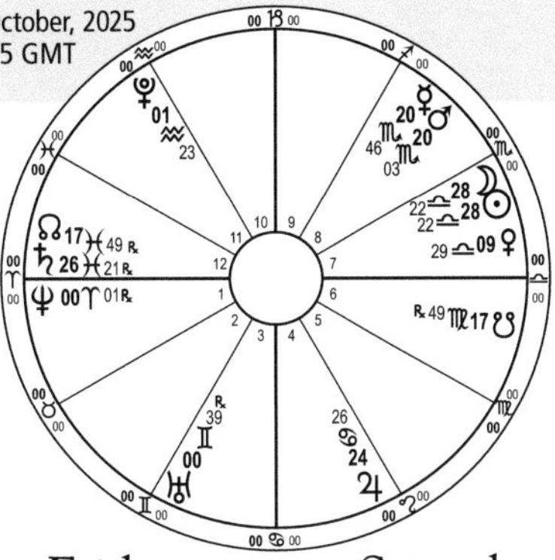

Wednesday	Thursday	Friday	Saturday
1 ☽ voc 15:33 ☽→♒ 19:51 ☽□☿ 3:38 ☽☍♃ 5:40 ☽⚹♄ 15:33 ☽⚹♆ 20:51 ☿□♃ 20:59 ☽△♅ 22:05 ☽☌♇ 22:29	**2** ☽□♂ 8:28 ☽△☉ 13:41	**3** ☽ voc 18:15 ☽△☿ 18:15	**4** ☽→♓ 2:07 ☽□♅ 4:06 ☽△♂ 16:36
8 ☽→♉ 5:12 ☽□♇ 7:24 ☽☍☿ 9:14 ♀⚹♃ 11:41 ☽☍♂ 23:16	**9** ☽⚹♃ 18:38 ☽△♀ 21:12	**10** ☽ voc 0:31 ☽→♊ 5:12 ☽⚹♄ 0:31 ☽⚹♆ 5:41 ☽☌♅ 6:48 ☽△♇ 7:25	**11** ♀☍♄ 11:10 ☽△☉ 11:14
15 ☽□☿ 9:41 ☽□♂ 15:49	**16** ☽ voc 5:06 ☽→♍ 18:05 ☽⚹☉ 5:06 ☽□♅ 19:37	**17** ☉□♃ 5:43	**18** ☽ voc 21:10 ☽⚹☿ 1:10 ☽⚹♂ 4:01 ☽⚹♃ 16:42 ☽☍♄ 21:10
22 ♆→♓ 9:51	**23** ☉→♏ 3:51 ☽☌♂ 10:55 ☽☌☿ 14:57 ☽△♃ 17:18 ☽△♄ 20:38	**24** ☽ voc 4:14 ☽→♐ 4:19 ☽△♆ 4:14 ☽☍♅ 5:27 ☽⚹♇ 7:08 ☉□♇ 13:24 ☿△♃ 15:08	**25** ☽⚹♀ 9:17 ☿△♄ 21:17
◐ First Quarter 06♒30 ☽ voc 3:38 ☽→♒ 3:55 ☽⚹☿ 3:17 ☽⚹♆ 3:38 ☽△♅ 4:39 ☽☌♇ 6:39 ☿△♆ 7:26 ☿→♐ 11:02 ☽□☉ 16:21 ♂△♄ 19:05 ☿☍♅ 19:36	**30** ☽△♀ 19:34 ☿⚹♇ 22:06	**31** ☽ voc 6:15 ☽→♓ 11:46 ☽□♂ 6:15 ☽□♅ 12:18 ☽□☿ 15:32	**1**

SCORPIO

♎ Libra

Mercury is square Jupiter on Wednesday the 1st of October, so there's an attempt to understand complex ideas and plans, and keeping a clear and balanced sense of proportion can be challenging. It's a time to expand and broaden knowledge, but there's also a need for some caution and circumspection when it comes to drawing final conclusions. Don't get lost in detail or be too content with the broadest of generalizations.

On the 2nd of October Venus forms a sesquiquadrate aspect to Pluto, so personal relationships contend with a greater intensity than usual. This may either deepen the experience of the connection or it may manifest as an element of controlling behaviour within the relationship.

☉ Sunday
28

☽ Monday
29

☽⚹☿ 7:43

☽ VOC 5:44
☽→♑ 9:55

◐
First Quarter
07♑06

☽☐♄ 5:44
☽☐♆ 11:05
☽⚹♂ 19:55
☽☐☉ 23:54

♂ Tuesday
30

☽△♀ 12:20

154   GMT

October 2025

☿ Wednesday   ☽ VOC   15:33
                                                ☽→♒   19:51

1 October

☽□☿   3:38
☽☍♃   5:40
☽⚹♄   15:33
☽⚹♆   20:51
♀□♃   20:59
☽△♅   22:05
☽☌♇   22:29

♃ Thursday

2

☽□♂   8:28
☽△☉   13:41

♀ Friday   ☽ VOC   18:15

3

☽△☿   18:15

♄ Saturday   ☽→♓   2:07

4

☽□♅   4:06
☽△♂   16:36

♎ Libra

Mercury forms a quincunx aspect to Saturn on Sunday the 5th of October. There's some restraint and inhibition in communication here. Practical painstaking mental work and clarifying the details of mutual duties and obligations.

The full moon on the 7th of October occurs at 14 degrees Aries. On the same day Mercury is square Pluto and quincunx both Uranus and Neptune. This seems to speak of extraordinary news and information and a deep delving or research into unusual topics.

On Wednesday the 8th of October Venus forms a sextile to Jupiter describing friendships, fellowship and celebrations. There's tolerance and generosity in personal relationships.

Then Venus arrives at an opposition to Saturn on Saturday the 11th of October, and this paints a picture of obstacles, restrictions or inhibitions in personal relationships.

☉ Sunday
5

☽☌♀ 11:34
☽△♃ 17:15
☽☌♄ 0:29

☽ Monday
6

☽VOC 0:29
☽→♈ 4:48

☽☌♆ 5:28
☽✶♅ 6:35
☽✶♇ 7:04
☿→♏ 16:40

♂ Tuesday
7

☽VOC 18:23

○
Full Moon
14♈08

☽☌☉ 3:47
☿□♇ 14:40
☽□♃ 18:23

October 2025

☿ Wednesday
8

☽→♉ 5:12

☽□♆ 7:24
☽☌♀ 9:14
♀⚹♃ 11:41
☽☌♂ 23:16

♃ Thursday
9

☽⚹♃ 18:38
☽△♀ 21:12

♀ Friday
10

☽ VOC 0:31
☽→♊ 5:12

☽⚹♄ 0:31
☽⚹♆ 5:41
☽☌♅ 6:48
☽△♇ 7:25

♄ Saturday
11

♀☌♄ 11:10
☽△☉ 11:14

Regulus 2025 Astrological Planner 157

♎ Libra

On the 14th of September Venus reaches an opposition aspect to Neptune along with trine aspects to both Uranus and Pluto. Romantic and other personal relationships are mystical or beguiling, and also prone to sudden and intense shifts.

On Friday the 17th of September the Sun is square Jupiter which makes for grand gestures and bold optimistic actions.

☉ Sunday
12

☽ VOC 2:55
☽→♍ 6:37

☽ Monday
13

☽□♄ 1:29
☽□♀ 2:55
☽□♆ 7:02
☽△☿ 22:10

◐
Last Quarter
20♋40

☽△♂ 7:07
☽□☉ 18:12
♀→♎ 21:19
☽☌♃ 23:49

♂ Tuesday
14

☽ VOC 5:05
☽→♌ 10:47

♀☍♆ 1:16
♀ SD 4:48
☽△♄ 5:05
☽△♆ 11:08
☽⚹♀ 12:10
☽⚹♅ 12:21
☽☌♇ 13:14
♀△♅ 14:10
♀△♆ 23:45

October 2025

☿ Wednesday
15

☽□☿	9:41
☽□♂	15:49

♃ Thursday
16

☽ VOC	5:06
☽→♍	18:05

☽✶☉	5:06
☽□♅	19:37

♀ Friday
17

☉□♃	5:43
☽ VOC	21:10

♄ Saturday
18

☽✶☿	1:10
☽✶♂	4:01
☽✶♃	16:42
☽☍♄	21:10

Regulus 2025 Astrological Planner

♎ Libra

On Sunday the 19th of September the Sun is quincunx Saturn, which is somewhat duty-bound. Work related obligations can limit freedom and feel tedious and onerous. In fact the New Moon of 21 October at 28 degrees Libra arguably reiterates this theme, since the Sun and Moon will then both be quincunx Saturn.

Mercury forms a trine to Jupiter on Friday the 24th of September, and then a trine to Saturn on Saturday the 25th, so there's a Mercury-Jupiter-Saturn grand trine towards the end of the week. Discussions are serious and practical, but also expansive and visionary. Meticulous planning of big projects. Important agreements and decisions are made.

The Sun is also square Pluto (and opposite the Uranus-Neptune midpoint) on the 24th of September which shows intensely focussed and purposeful exertion of energy. Challenges are confronted head-on, but there may be some elements in the situation that are veiled or obscured.

⊙ Sunday   ☽→♎   4:01

19

                                            ☽☍♆   4:10
                                            ☽△♅   5:27
                                            ☽△♀   6:43
                                            ☽☌♀ 18:26

☽ Monday

20

                                            ☿☌♂   6:51

♂ Tuesday   ☽VOC 12:25
                                            ☽→♏ 15:42

21

              ●
         New Moon
          28♎22

                                            ☽□♃   4:28
                                            ☽☌⊙ 12:25
                                            ☽□♇ 18:28

160   GMT

October 2025

☿ Wednesday
22

♆→♓ 9:51

♃ Thursday
23

☉→♏ 3:51
☽☌♂ 10:55
☽☌☿ 14:57
☽△♃ 17:18
☽△♄ 20:38

♀ Friday
24

☽VOC 4:14
☽→♐ 4:19

☽△♆ 4:14
☽☍♅ 5:27
☽✶♇ 7:08
☉□♆ 13:24
☿△♃ 15:08

♄ Saturday
25

☽✶♀ 9:17
☿△♄ 21:17

Regulus 2025 Astrological Planner

♏ Scorpio

Mars forms a trine to Jupiter on Tuesday the 28th of September, and this gives almost boundless creative energy and vitality. There's a can-do spirit and an enthusiastic pursuit of goals. All of this is conducive to "luck" and success. Righteous causes are espoused and defended.

Mercury is trine Neptune on Wednesday the 29th of September, communication is subtle and nuanced, elusive ideas are eloquently articulated, thinking is abstract and intuitive. Spiritual or poetic literature.

Then Mercury forms an opposition to Uranus and sextile to Pluto on the following day. Sudden and surprising news pops up, novel subjects and highly technical information become fascinating. A very rapid pace and tempo in communication, so it may be hard to keep track of everything.

☉ Sunday
26

☽ VOC   16:41
☽→♑   16:53

☽ Monday
27

☽☐♄   9:00
☽☐♆   16:41

♂ Tuesday
28

☽✶☉   0:35

☽☐♀   4:11
♂△♃   6:19
☽☍♃   17:56
☽✶♂   18:36
☽✶♄   20:06

GMT

October 2025

☿ Wednesday

29

☽ VOC 3:38
☽→♒ 3:55

◐ First Quarter
06 ♒ 30

☽⚹⚷ 3:17
☽⚹♆ 3:38
☽△♅ 4:39
☽☌♆ 6:39
☿△♆ 7:26
☿→♐ 11:02
☽□☉ 16:21
♂△♄ 19:05
☿☍♅ 19:36

♃ Thursday

30

☽△♀ 19:34
☿⚹♇ 22:06

♀ Friday

31

☽ VOC 6:15
☽→♓ 11:46

☽□♂ 6:15
☽□♅ 12:18
☽□☿ 15:32

♄ Saturday

1 November

Regulus 2025 Astrological Planner 163

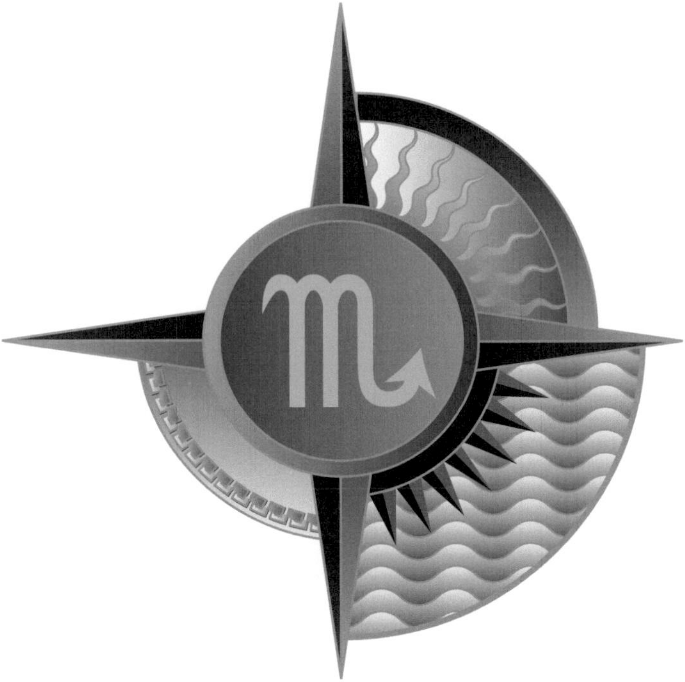

Ephemeris for November 2025, set at Midnight GMT.

November 2025

Day	☉	☽	True ☊	☿	♀	♂	♃	♄	♅	♆	♇
01	08 ♏ 49 19	06 ♓ 52 24	17 ♓ 03 D	02 ♐ 25 D	22 ♎ 34 D	27 ♏ 28 D	24 ♋ 58 D	25 ♓ 48 R	00 ♊ 17 R	29 ♓ 48 R	01 ♒ 27 D
02	09 49 20	20 42 47	17 03 R	03 16	23 49	28 11	25 00	25 45	00 14	29 46	01 27
03	10 49 22	05 ♈ 02 00	17 01	04 03	25 04	28 54	25 02	25 42	00 12	29 45	01 28
04	11 49 26	19 47 43	16 58	04 46	26 19	29 37	25 03	25 40	00 10	29 44	01 28
05	12 49 32	04 ♉ 54 10	16 52	05 23	27 34	00 ♐ 20	25 05	25 38	00 07	29 43	01 29
06	13 49 39	20 12 16	16 44	05 54	28 49	01 03	25 06	25 35	00 05	29 42	01 30
07	14 49 49	05 ♊ 30 54	16 35	06 20	00 ♏ 04	01 46	25 07	25 33	00 03	29 41	01 30
08	15 50 00	20 38 47	16 26	06 38	01 19	02 29	25 08	25 31	00 00	29 40	01 31
09	16 50 14	05 ♋ 26 32	16 18	06 49	02 35	03 12	25 08	25 29	29 ♉ 58	29 39	01 32
10	17 50 29	19 48 02	16 13	06 52 R	03 50	03 55	25 09	25 27	29 55	29 38	01 32
11	18 50 46	03 ♌ 40 45	16 09	06 45	05 05	04 39	25 09	25 25	29 53	29 37	01 33
12	19 51 06	17 05 18	16 08	06 29	06 20	05 22	25 09 R	25 23	29 50	29 36	01 34
13	20 51 27	00 ♍ 04 29	16 08 D	06 03	07 35	06 06	25 09	25 22	29 48	29 35	01 35
14	21 51 50	12 42 22	16 09	05 27	08 51	06 49	25 09	25 20	29 46	29 34	01 36
15	22 52 15	25 03 29	16 09 R	04 41	10 06	07 33	25 08	25 19	29 43	29 33	01 37
16	23 52 42	07 ♎ 12 11	16 06	03 45	11 21	08 16	25 07	25 17	29 41	29 32	01 37
17	24 53 11	19 12 23	16 02	02 41	12 36	09 00	25 06	25 16	29 38	29 32	01 38
18	25 53 41	01 ♏ 07 18	15 54	01 29	13 52	09 44	25 05	25 15	29 36	29 31	01 39
19	26 54 13	12 59 28	15 43	00 11	15 07	10 28	25 04	25 14	29 33	29 30	01 40
20	27 54 47	24 50 47	15 30	28 ♏ 50	16 22	11 11	25 02	25 13	29 31	29 29	01 41
21	28 55 22	06 ♐ 42 44	15 16	27 29	17 38	11 55	25 00	25 12	29 28	29 29	01 42
22	29 55 59	18 36 36	15 02	26 10	18 53	12 39	24 58	25 11	29 26	29 28	01 43
23	00 ♐ 56 37	00 ♑ 33 46	14 49	24 55	20 09	13 23	24 56	25 11	29 23	29 28	01 45
24	01 57 17	12 35 56	14 37	23 48	21 24	14 08	24 54	25 10	29 21	29 27	01 46
25	02 57 58	24 45 22	14 29	22 49	22 39	14 52	24 51	25 10	29 18	29 26	01 47
26	03 58 39	07 ♒ 05 01	14 24	22 01	23 55	15 36	24 49	25 10	29 15	29 26	01 48
27	04 59 22	19 38 26	14 21	21 24	25 10	16 20	24 46	25 10	29 13	29 25	01 49
28	06 00 06	02 ♓ 29 39	14 20	20 59	26 26	17 04	24 43	25 09	29 11	29 25	01 50
29	07 00 51	15 42 47	14 20	20 45	27 41	17 49	24 39	25 09 D	29 08	29 25	01 52
30	08 01 37	29 21 22	14 20	20 43 D	28 56	18 33	24 36	25 10	29 06	29 24	01 53

Declination

Day	☉	☽	True ☊	☿	♀	♂	♃	♄	♅	♆	♇
1	-14°36'	-06°41'	-05°06'	-23°34'	-07°39'	-20°04'	+21°13'	-03°56'	+20°00'	-01°21'	-23°31'
3	-15°14'	+06°54'	-05°08'	-23°51'	-08°35'	-20°24'	+21°13'	-03°58'	+19°59'	-01°21'	-23°30'
5	-15°50'	+19°36'	-05°12'	-24°00'	-09°31'	-20°43'	+21°13'	-04°00'	+19°58'	-01°22'	-23°30'
7	-16°26'	+27°23'	-05°19'	-23°59'	-10°26'	-21°02'	+21°12'	-04°01'	+19°57'	-01°23'	-23°30'
9	-17°00'	+27°21'	-05°25'	-23°49'	-11°20'	-21°20'	+21°12'	-04°03'	+19°56'	-01°24'	-23°29'
11	-17°34'	+20°29'	-05°28'	-23°27'	-12°12'	-21°37'	+21°13'	-04°04'	+19°55'	-01°24'	-23°29'
13	-18°06'	+09°57'	-05°29'	-22°52'	-13°04'	-21°53'	+21°13'	-04°05'	+19°54'	-01°25'	-23°29'
15	-18°37'	-01°40'	-05°29'	-22°03'	-13°54'	-22°09'	+21°14'	-04°05'	+19°53'	-01°26'	-23°28'
17	-19°07'	-12°43'	-05°33'	-21°01'	-14°43'	-22°24'	+21°14'	-04°06'	+19°52'	-01°26'	-23°28'
19	-19°35'	-21°45'	-05°41'	-19°49'	-15°31'	-22°38'	+21°15'	-04°06'	+19°51'	-01°27'	-23°27'
21	-20°02'	-27°16'	-05°51'	-18°34'	-16°17'	-22°51'	+21°16'	-04°07'	+19°50'	-01°27'	-23°27'
23	-20°27'	-27°55'	-06°01'	-17°24'	-17°01'	-23°03'	+21°17'	-04°07'	+19°49'	-01°28'	-23°26'
25	-20°51'	-23°20'	-06°07'	-16°27'	-17°44'	-23°14'	+21°18'	-04°07'	+19°48'	-01°28'	-23°26'
27	-21°13'	-14°20'	-06°09'	-15°48'	-18°24'	-23°24'	+21°20'	-04°07'	+19°47'	-01°28'	-23°25'
29	-21°34'	-02°20'	-06°09'	-15°29'	-19°03'	-23°34'	+21°21'	-04°06'	+19°46'	-01°29'	-23°24'

Regulus 2025 Astrological Planner

November, 2025

Degree of
Key Aspects

2 Nov 2025		
♀ □ ♃	25♎02	25♋02
4 Nov 2025		
♂ △ ♆R	29♏44	29♓44
♂ ☍ ♅R	0♐08	0♊08
6 Nov 2025		
♂ ⚹ ♇	1♐30	1♒30
8 Nov 2025		
♀ □ ♇	1♏31	1♒31
9 Nov 2025		
☿R	6♐52	
11 Nov 2025		
♃R	25♋09	
12 Nov 2025		
☿R ☌ ♂	6♐04	6♐04
17 Nov 2025		
☉ △ ♃R	25♏06	25♋06
☉ △ ♄R	25♏16	25♓16
☿R ⚹ ♇	1♐39	1♒39
19 Nov 2025		
☿R ☍ ♅R	29♏32	29♉32
☿R △ ♆R	29♏30	29♓30
20 Nov 2025		
☉ ☌ ☿R	28♏18	28♏18
♅R ⚹ ♆R	29♉29	29♓29
21 Nov 2025		
☉ ☍ ♅R	29♏27	29♉27
☉ △ ♆R	29♏28	29♓28
22 Nov 2025		
☿R △ ♄R	25♏11	25♓11
☿R △ ♃R	24♏56	24♋56
23 Nov 2025		
☉ ⚹ ♇	1♐45	1♒45
25 Nov 2025		
☿R ☌ ♀	22♏45	22♏45
26 Nov 2025		
♀ △ ♃R	24♏47	24♋47
♀ △ ♄R	25♏10	25♓10
28 Nov 2025		
♄D	25♓09	
29 Nov 2025		
☿D	20♏42	
30 Nov 2025		
♀ ☍ ♅R	29♏05	29♉05
♀ △ ♆R	29♏24	29♓24

Sunday	Monday	Tuesday
26	**27**	**28**
S C O	R	P I O
2 ☽ voc 15:15 ☽→♈ 15:39 ☽△☉ 3:42 ☽△♃ 7:17 ☽☌♄ 8:30 ☽△♂ 13:17 ☽☌♆ 15:15 ☽⚹♅ 16:01 ☽⚹♇ 18:05 ☽△☿ 22:18 ♀□♃ 23:16	**3**	**4** ☽ voc 11:21 ☽→♉ 16:15 ♂△♆ 3:59 ☽□♃ 8:25 ☽☍♀ 11:21 ♂→♐ 13:01 ♂☍♅ 17:30 ☽□♇ 18:36
9 ☿ SR 19:01 ☽△☉ 20:25	**10** ☽ voc 17:22 ☽→♌ 17:33 ☽☌♃ 9:09 ☽△♄ 9:39 ☽△♆ 16:53 ☽⚹♅ 17:22 ☽☍♇ 20:16	**11** ☽△♂ 1:48 ☽□♀ 2:43 ☽△☿ 5:21 ♃ SR 15:50
16 ☽⚹♂ 2:16	**17** ☽ voc 11:51 ☽→♏ 21:44 ☉△♃ 5:07 ☉△♄ 8:56 ☽□♃ 11:51 ☿⚹♇ 20:35	**18** ☽□♇ 1:05
23 ☉⚹♇ 19:19	**24** ☽⚹♀ 19:24 ☽⚹☿ 20:28	**25** ☽ voc 9:09 ☽→♒ 10:15 ☽☍♃ 0:12 ☽⚹♄ 0:48 ☿☌♀ 1:51 ☽△♅ 8:52 ☽⚹♆ 9:09 ☽☌♇ 13:45 ☽⚹☉ 17:27

Charts cast with Natural House System in GMT

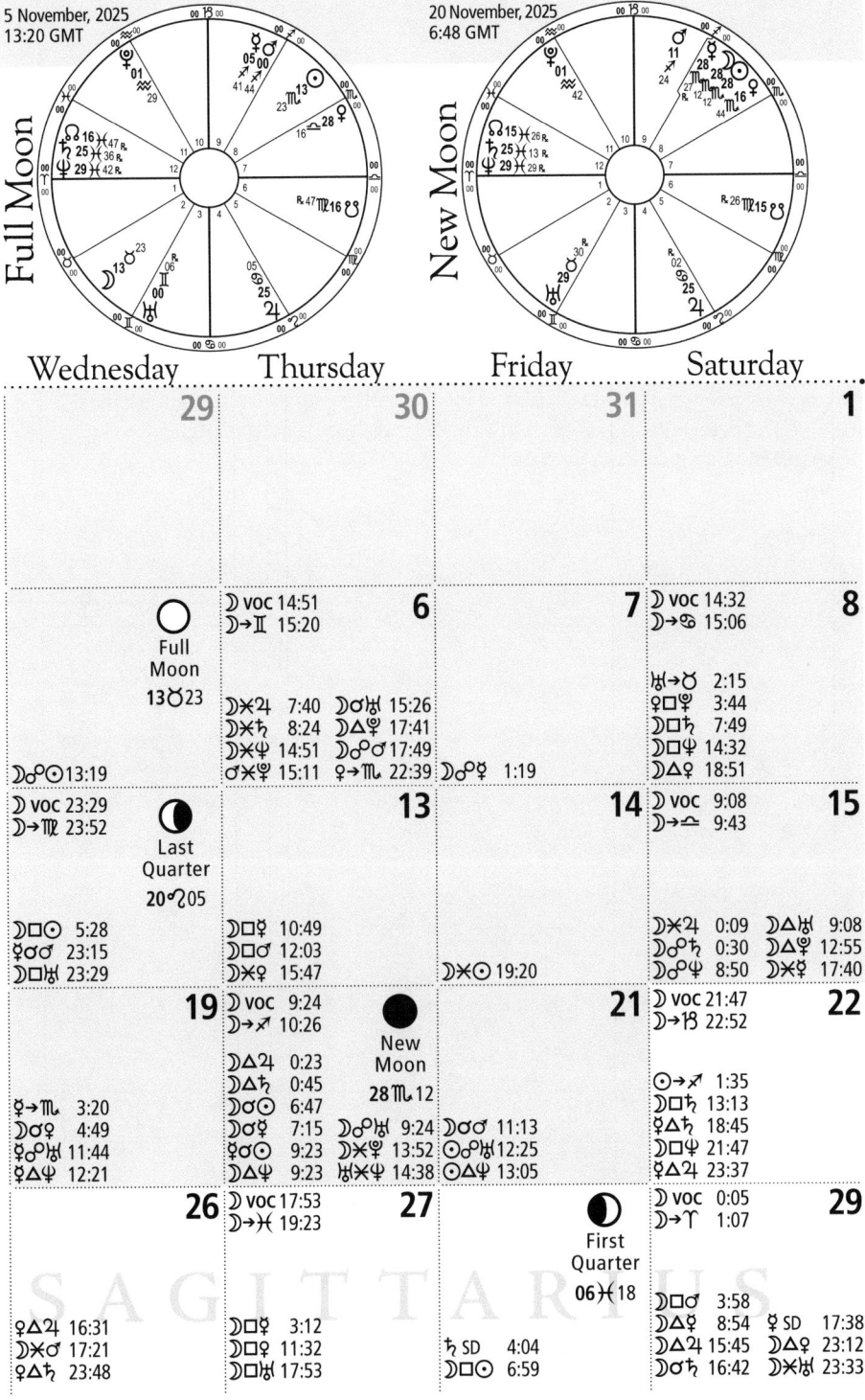

5 November, 2025
13:20 GMT

Full Moon

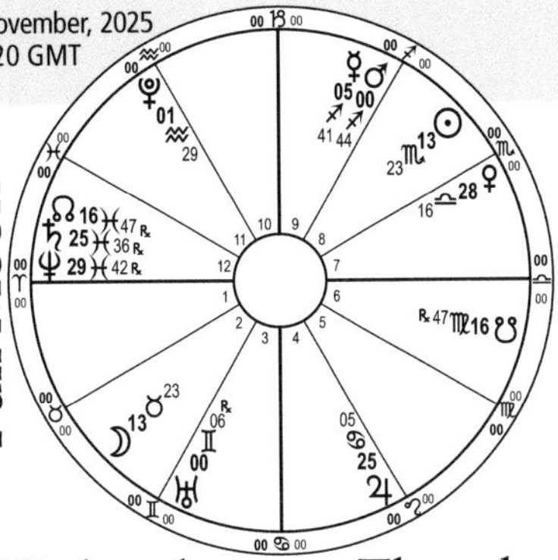

20 November, 2025
6:48 GMT

New Moon

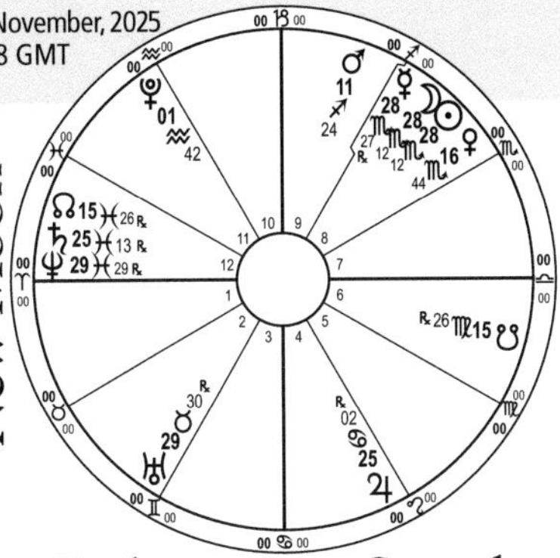

Wednesday	Thursday	Friday	Saturday
29	30	31	1
Full Moon 13♉23 ☽☍☉ 13:19	6 ☽ voc 14:51 ☽→♊ 15:20 ☽⚹♃ 7:40 ☽⚹♄ 8:24 ☽⚹♆ 14:51 ♂⚹♇ 15:11 ☽☌♅ 15:26 ☽△♇ 17:41 ☽☍♂ 17:49 ♀→♏ 22:39	7 ☽☍☿ 1:19	8 ☽ voc 14:32 ☽→♋ 15:06 ♅→♉ 2:15 ♀□♇ 3:44 ☽□♄ 7:49 ☽□♆ 14:32 ☽△♀ 18:51
☽ voc 23:29 ☽→♍ 23:52 Last Quarter 20♌05 ☽□☉ 5:28 ☿☌♂ 23:15 ☽□♅ 23:29	13 ☽□☿ 10:49 ☽□♂ 12:03 ☽⚹♀ 15:47	14 ☽⚹☉ 19:20	15 ☽ voc 9:08 ☽→♎ 9:43 ☽⚹♃ 0:09 ☽☍♄ 0:30 ☽☍♆ 8:50 ☽△♅ 9:08 ☽△♇ 12:55 ☽⚹☿ 17:40
19 ☿→♏ 3:20 ☽☌♀ 4:49 ☿☍♅ 11:44 ☿△♆ 12:21	☽ voc 9:24 ☽→♐ 10:26 New Moon 28♏12 ☽△♃ 0:23 ☽△♄ 0:45 ☽☌☉ 6:47 ☽☌☿ 7:15 ☿☌☉ 9:23 ☽△♆ 9:23 ☽☍♅ 9:24 ☽⚹♇ 13:52 ♅⚹♆ 14:38	21 ☽☌♂ 11:13 ☉☍♅ 12:25 ☉△♆ 13:05	22 ☽ voc 21:47 ☽→♑ 22:52 ☉→♐ 1:35 ☽□♄ 13:13 ☿△♄ 18:45 ☽□♆ 21:47 ☿△♃ 23:37
26 ♀△♃ 16:31 ☽⚹♂ 17:21 ♀△♄ 23:48	27 ☽ voc 17:53 ☽→♓ 19:23 ☽□☿ 3:12 ☽□♀ 11:32 ☽□♅ 17:53	First Quarter 06♓18 ♄ SD 4:04 ☽□☉ 6:59	29 ☽ voc 0:05 ☽→♈ 1:07 ☽□♂ 3:58 ☽△☿ 8:54 ☽△♃ 15:45 ☽☌♄ 16:42 ☿ SD 17:38 ☽△♀ 23:12 ☽⚹♅ 23:33

SAGITTARIUS

♏ Scorpio

On Sunday the 2nd of November Venus forms a square to Jupiter and a quincunx to Saturn. Personal relationships are required to adjust to social obligations of the parties concerned, which may not be convenient. There's a warm and generous social impulse here. Luxury and extravagance, but with some limits and constraints.

The Full Moon on the 5th of November occurs at 13 degrees Taurus shortly after Mars and Uranus reach an exact opposition. This is a restless live wire energy. There's a spirit of bold daring and even defiance. Mars in opposition to Uranus could describe feats of extraordinary physical prowess and courage.

Mars goes on to form a sextile aspect to Pluto the following day, reinforcing the assertive and determined quality of this time. There's a strong pushing and a concerted effort to get things over the line.

☉ Sunday 2

☽ VOC 15:15
☽→♈ 15:39

☽△☉ 3:42
☽△♃ 7:17
☽☌♄ 8:30
☽△♂ 13:17
☽☌♆ 15:15
☽✶♅ 16:01
☽✶♀ 18:05
☽△☿ 22:18
♀□♃ 23:16

☽ Monday 3

♂ Tuesday 4

☽ VOC 11:21
☽→♉ 16:15

♂△♆ 3:59
☽□♃ 8:25
☽☍♀ 11:21
♂→♐ 13:01
♂☍♅ 17:30
☽□♆ 18:36

168   GMT

November 2025

☿ Wednesday
5

○
Full Moon
13♉23

☽☍☉ 13:19

♃ Thursday
6

☽VOC 14:51
☽→♊ 15:20

☽⚹♃ 7:40
☽⚹♄ 8:24
☽⚹♆ 14:51
♂⚹♇ 15:11
☽☌♅ 15:26
☽△♇ 17:41
☽☍♂ 17:49
♀→♏ 22:39

♀ Friday
7

☽☍☿ 1:19

♄ Saturday
8

☽VOC 14:32
☽→♋ 15:06

♅ᴿ→♉ 2:15
♀□♆ 3:44
☽□♄ 7:49
☽□♆ 14:32
☽△♀ 18:51

Regulus 2025 Astrological Planner

♏ Scorpio

Mercury and Jupiter both turn retrograde this week. There's a shift in the rhythm of the social discourse. Perhaps a more reflective period has begun.

Even more conspicuous is the trine of Jupiter and Saturn this week that very nearly reaches exactitude. This looks like sensible new social initiatives, good projects get a boost, sound plans and preparations are made. Financial systems work fluidly.

On Wednesday the 12th of November Mercury and Mars form a conjunction, describing vigorous mental energy and very frank and forthright expression of views and opinions. Mercury conjunct Mars is potentially very skillful and dynamic, but prone to irrritability and tactlessness.

☉ Sunday

9

☿ SR	19:01
☽△☉	20:25

☽ Monday

10

☽ VOC	17:22
☽→♌	17:33

☽☌♃	9:09
☽△♄	9:39
☽△♆	16:53
☽✶♅	17:22
☽☍♀	20:16

♂ Tuesday

11

☽△♂	1:48
☽□♀	2:43
☽△☿	5:21
♃ SR	15:50

November 2025

Mercury is retrograde from the 9th of Nov. (6°52'♐) through the 29th of Nov. (20°42'♏).

☿ Wednesday

12

☽ VOC 23:29
☽→♍ 23:52

● Last Quarter
20°♌05

☽□☉ 5:28
☿☌♂ 23:15
☽□♅ 23:29

♃ Thursday

13

☽□♀ 10:49
☽□♂ 12:03
☽⚹♀ 15:47

♀ Friday

14

☽⚹☉ 19:20

♄ Saturday

15

☽ VOC 9:08
☽→♎ 9:43

☽⚹♃ 0:09
☽☍♄ 0:30
☽☍♆ 8:50
☽△♅ 9:08
☽△♇ 12:55
☽⚹☿ 17:40

Regulus 2025 Astrological Planner

♏ Scorpio

On Monday the 17th of November the Sun forms a grand trine configuration with Jupiter and Saturn placing an emphasis on economic progress and large scale plans and projects that require both vision and practical realism. On Tuesday the 18th of November Mars will be sesquiquadrate Jupiter, so there's a spirit of adventure and conquest. People get fired up about their beliefs and principles.

Then on the 20th of November we have a New Moon at 28 degrees Scorpio with the Sun and Moon conjunct Mercury and this whole trio in opposition to Uranus! All bets are off. Anything can and will happen and the tempo will be brisk. Messages and information come out of the blue; it's startling and sudden.

There's also a Sun-Neptune trine on Friday the 21st of November describing a delicate attunement to spiritual forces. There's compassion and a willingness to make sacrifices for the benefit of others.

Mercury is trine both Jupiter and Saturn on Saturday the the 22nd of November indicating that there is a constructive use of information, careful and diligent planning and important negotiations and formal agreements.

☉ Sunday
16

☽ Monday
17

☽⚹♂ 2:16
☽ VOC 11:51
☽→♏ 21:44

♂ Tuesday
18

☉△♃ 5:07
☉△♄ 8:56
☽□♃ 11:51
☿⚹♇ 20:35

☽□♇ 1:05

172 GMT

November 2025

Mercury is retrograde from the 9th of Nov. (6°52'♐) through the 29th of Nov. (20°42'♏).

☿ Wednesday
19

☿→♏	3:20
☽☌♀	4:49
☿☍♅	11:44
☿△♆	12:21

♃ Thursday
20

New Moon
28♏12

☽VOC	9:24
☽→♐	10:26
☽△♃	0:23
☽△♄	0:45
☽☌☉	6:47
☽☌☿	7:15
☿☌☉	9:23
☽△♆	9:23
☽☍♅	9:24
☽✶♇	13:52
♅✶♆	14:38

♀ Friday
21

☽☌☿	11:13
☉☍♅	12:25
☉△♆	13:05

♄ Saturday
22

☽VOC	21:47
☽→♑	22:52
☉→♐	1:35
☽□♄	13:13
☿△♄	18:45
☽□♆	21:47
☿△♃	23:37

Regulus 2025 Astrological Planner

♐ Sagittarius

The week begins with Sun sextile Pluto which makes for clarity of purpose and intention. Collective goals are pursued with determination and concentrated effort.

One the 26th of November Venus forms a trine to both Jupiter and Saturn creating a grand trine configuration. Personal relationships are focussed on concrete long term goals rather than more transient immediate concerns. Commitments in relationships are taken seriously and this opens up possibilities for creating long term financial and social security.

Saturn turns direct on the 28th of November at 25° of Pisces suggesting changes and adjustments in order to move projects forward.

☉ Sunday

23

☉⚹♇ 19:19

☽ Monday

24

☽⚹♀ 19:24
☽⚹☿ 20:28

♂ Tuesday

25

☽ VOC 9:09
☽→♒ 10:15

☽☍♃ 0:12
☽⚹♄ 0:48
☿☌♀ 1:51
☽△♅ 8:52
☽⚹♆ 9:09
☽☌♇ 13:45
☽⚹☉ 17:27

GMT

November 2025

☿ Wednesday
26

♀△♃ 16:31
☽⚹♂ 17:21
♀△♄ 23:48

♃ Thursday
27

☽ VOC 17:53
☽→♓ 19:23

☽□☿ 3:12
☽□♀ 11:32
☽□♅ 17:53

♀ Friday
28

◐
First Quarter
06 ♓ 18

♄ SD 4:04
☽□☉ 6:59

♄ Saturday
29

☽□♂ 3:58
☽△☿ 8:54
☽△♃ 15:45
☽☌♄ 16:42
☿ SD 17:38
☽△♀ 23:12
☽⚹♅ 23:33

Regulus 2025 Astrological Planner

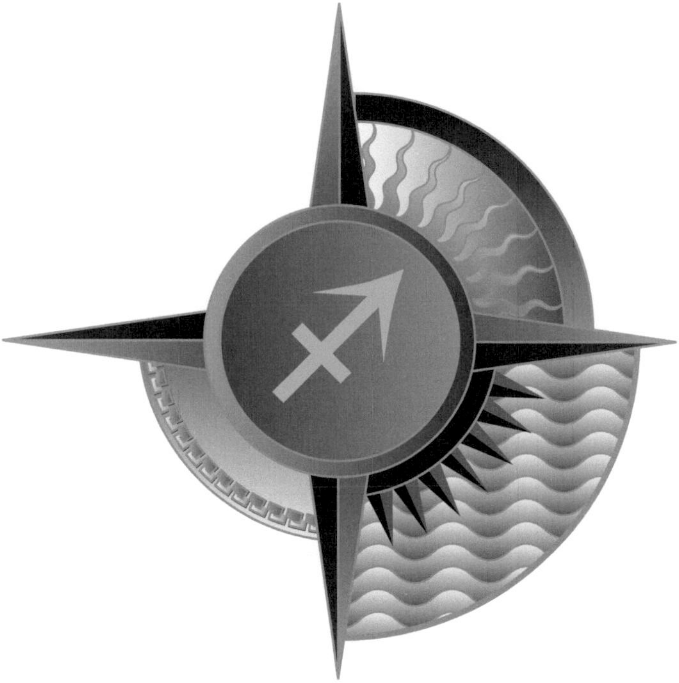

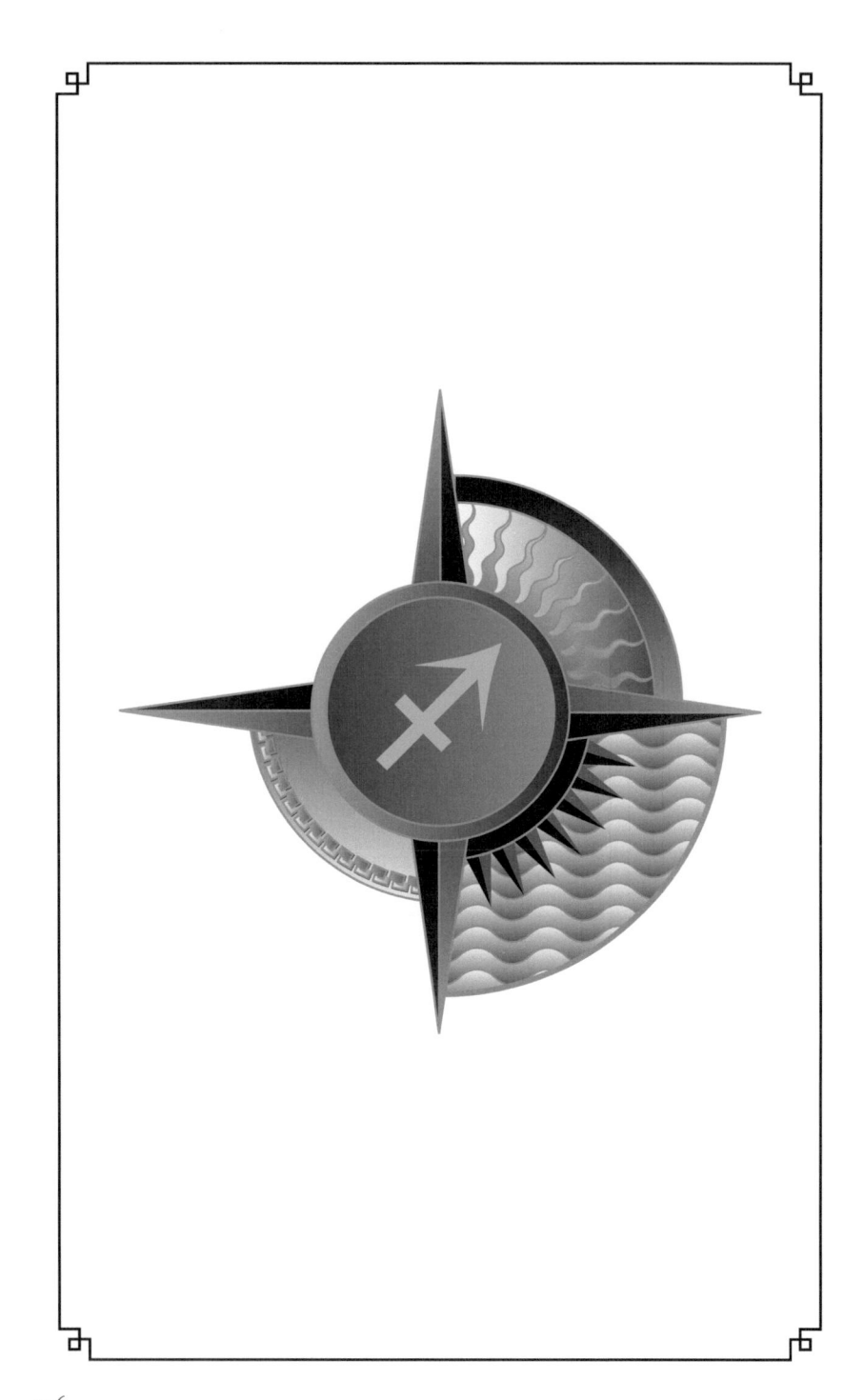

Ephemeris for December 2025, set at Midnight GMT.

December 2025

Day	☉	☽	True ☊	☿	♀	♂	♃	♄	♅	♆	♇
01	09 ♐ 02 24	13 ♈ 27 36	14 ♓ 17 ℞	20 ♏ 51 D	00 ♐ 12 D	19 ♐ 18 D	24 ♋ 32 ℞	25 ♓ 10 D	29 ♉ 03 ℞	29 ♓ 24 ℞	01 ♒ 54 D
02	10 03 11	28 01 13	14 13	21 08	01 27	20 02	24 28	25 10	29 01	29 24	01 55
03	11 04 00	12 ♉ 58 41	14 05	21 35	02 43	20 47	24 24	25 11	28 58	29 23	01 57
04	12 04 50	28 12 48	13 55	22 10	03 58	21 31	24 20	25 11	28 56	29 23	01 58
05	13 05 41	13 ♊ 33 12	13 43	22 52	05 14	22 16	24 15	25 12	28 53	29 23	01 59
06	14 06 33	28 48 08	13 31	23 40	06 29	23 01	24 11	25 13	28 51	29 23	02 01
07	15 07 26	13 ♋ 46 32	13 21	24 33	07 45	23 46	24 06	25 14	28 49	29 23	02 02
08	16 08 20	28 20 02	13 13	25 32	09 00	24 30	24 01	25 15	28 46	29 22	02 04
09	17 09 15	12 ♌ 23 58	13 08	26 35	10 16	25 15	23 56	25 16	28 44	29 22	02 05
10	18 10 12	25 57 22	13 05	27 42	11 31	26 00	23 51	25 17	28 41	29 22	02 07
11	19 11 09	09 ♍ 02 13	13 04	28 51	12 47	26 45	23 45	25 18	28 39	29 22 D	02 08
12	20 12 08	21 42 27	13 04	00 ♐ 04	14 02	27 30	23 40	25 20	28 37	29 22	02 10
13	21 13 08	04 ♎ 03 00	13 04	01 19	15 18	28 15	23 34	25 21	28 35	29 22	02 11
14	22 14 09	16 09 04	13 02	02 36	16 33	29 01	23 28	25 23	28 32	29 23	02 13
15	23 15 11	28 05 38	12 57	03 56	17 49	29 46	23 22	25 25	28 30	29 23	02 14
16	24 16 14	09 ♏ 57 05	12 49	05 16	19 04	00 ♑ 31	23 16	25 27	28 28	29 23	02 16
17	25 17 18	21 47 05	12 39	06 38	20 20	01 16	23 10	25 29	28 26	29 23	02 17
18	26 18 22	03 ♐ 38 30	12 28	08 01	21 35	02 02	23 03	25 31	28 24	29 23	02 19
19	27 19 28	15 33 23	12 12	09 26	22 51	02 47	22 57	25 33	28 21	29 24	02 21
20	28 20 34	27 33 11	11 57	10 51	24 06	03 33	22 50	25 35	28 19	29 24	02 22
21	29 21 41	09 ♑ 38 57	11 44	12 17	25 22	04 18	22 43	25 37	28 17	29 24	02 24
22	00 ♑ 22 48	21 51 35	11 32	13 44	26 37	05 04	22 36	25 40	28 15	29 25	02 26
23	01 23 56	04 ♒ 12 08	11 24	15 11	27 53	05 49	22 29	25 42	28 13	29 25	02 27
24	02 25 03	16 42 04	11 18	16 39	29 08	06 35	22 22	25 45	28 11	29 26	02 29
25	03 26 11	29 23 24	11 16	18 08	00 ♑ 24	07 20	22 15	25 48	28 09	29 26	02 31
26	04 27 19	12 ♓ 18 41	11 15 D	19 37	01 39	08 06	22 07	25 51	28 08	29 27	02 32
27	05 28 27	25 30 50	11 15	21 06	02 55	08 52	22 00	25 54	28 06	29 27	02 34
28	06 29 36	09 ♈ 02 41	11 16 ℞	22 36	04 10	09 38	21 52	25 57	28 04	29 28	02 36
29	07 30 44	22 56 23	11 14	24 06	05 26	10 24	21 45	26 00	28 02	29 29	02 38
30	08 31 52	07 ♉ 12 37	11 11	25 37	06 41	11 09	21 37	26 03	28 00	29 29	02 40
31	09 33 00	21 49 42	11 05	27 08	07 57	11 55	21 29	26 07	27 59	29 30	02 41

Declination

Day	☉	☽	True ☊	☿	♀	♂	♃	♄	♅	♆	♇
1	-21°53'	+10°50'	-06°11'	-15°29'	-19°39'	-23°42'	+21°23'	-04°06'	+19°44'	-01°29'	-23°24'
3	-22°10'	+22°19'	-06°17'	-15°43'	-20°13'	-23°50'	+21°24'	-04°05'	+19°43'	-01°29'	-23°23'
5	-22°26'	+28°06'	-06°25'	-16°09'	-20°45'	-23°56'	+21°26'	-04°04'	+19°42'	-01°29'	-23°23'
7	-22°40'	+25°42'	-06°33'	-16°44'	-21°15'	-24°01'	+21°28'	-04°03'	+19°41'	-01°29'	-23°22'
9	-22°52'	+16°59'	-06°38'	-17°24'	-21°42'	-24°06'	+21°30'	-04°01'	+19°40'	-01°29'	-23°21'
11	-23°02'	+05°33'	-06°40'	-18°07'	-22°06'	-24°09'	+21°32'	-04°00'	+19°39'	-01°29'	-23°21'
13	-23°11'	-06°07'	-06°40'	-18°52'	-22°28'	-24°12'	+21°35'	-03°58'	+19°38'	-01°29'	-23°20'
15	-23°17'	-16°33'	-06°44'	-19°36'	-22°47'	-24°13'	+21°37'	-03°57'	+19°37'	-01°29'	-23°19'
17	-23°22'	-24°02'	-06°51'	-20°20'	-23°04'	-24°13'	+21°40'	-03°55'	+19°37'	-01°28'	-23°19'
19	-23°25'	-28°06'	-07°02'	-21°01'	-23°18'	-24°12'	+21°42'	-03°52'	+19°36'	-01°28'	-23°18'
21	-23°26'	-26°39'	-07°11'	-21°40'	-23°28'	-24°11'	+21°45'	-03°50'	+19°35'	-01°28'	-23°17'
23	-23°25'	-20°08'	-07°17'	-22°15'	-23°36'	-24°08'	+21°47'	-03°48'	+19°34'	-01°27'	-23°16'
25	-23°23'	-09°50'	-07°19'	-22°47'	-23°41'	-24°04'	+21°50'	-03°45'	+19°33'	-01°27'	-23°16'
27	-23°18'	+02°33'	-07°19'	-23°14'	-23°43'	-23°59'	+21°53'	-03°42'	+19°32'	-01°26'	-23°15'
29	-23°12'	+15°03'	-07°20'	-23°37'	-23°43'	-23°52'	+21°55'	-03°40'	+19°31'	-01°26'	-23°14'
31	-23°03'	+24°49'	-07°25'	-23°56'	-23°39'	-23°45'	+21°58'	-03°37'	+19°31'	-01°25'	-23°13'

December, 2025

Degree of
Key Aspects

2 Dec 2025
♀ ⚹ ♇ 1♐56 1♒56

6 Dec 2025
☿ △ ♃℞ 24♏08 24♋08

7 Dec 2025
☿ △ ♄ 25♏14 25♓14

9 Dec 2025
♂ □ ♄ 25♐16 25♓16

10 Dec 2025
♆D 29♓22
☿ ☍ ♅℞ 28♏40 28♉40

11 Dec 2025
☿ △ ♆ 29♏22 29♓22

13 Dec 2025
☿ ⚹ ♇ 2♐12 2♒12

14 Dec 2025
♂ □ ♆ 29♐23 29♓23

17 Dec 2025
☉ □ ♄ 25♐29 25♓29

21 Dec 2025
☉ □ ♆ 29♐24 29♓24
♀ □ ♄ 25♐38 25♓38

24 Dec 2025
♀ □ ♆ 29♐26 29♓26

30 Dec 2025
☿ □ ♄ 26♐04 26♓04

SAGITTARIUS

Sunday	Monday	Tuesday
30 ☽ voc 0:05 ☽→♈ 1:07 ☽☌♆ 0:05 ♀☍♅ 2:48 ☽⚹♇ 4:22 ♀△♆ 8:48 ☽△☉ 15:59 ♀→♐ 20:13	**1** ☽ voc 18:14 ☽△♂ 10:14 ☽□♃ 18:14	**2** ☽→♉ 3:13 ☽□♇ 6:20 ♀⚹♇ 9:07
7 ☽☌♃ 16:51 ☿△♄ 16:57 ☽△♄ 18:50 ☽△☿ 18:58 ☽⚹♅ 0:44 ☽△♆ 1:45	**8** ☽ voc 1:45 ☽→♌ 2:48 ☽☍♇ 6:17 ☽△♀ 19:55	**9** ♂□♄ 0:15 ☽△☉ 8:59
14 ☽⚹♀ 0:53 ♂□♆ 11:43 ☽⚹☉ 13:20 ☽□♃ 14:33	**15** ☽ voc 3:36 ☽→♏ 3:51 ☽⚹♂ 3:36 ♂→♑ 7:34 ☽□♇ 8:24	**16**
21 ☉□♆ 1:02 ♀□♄ 5:09 ☉→♑ 15:03	**22** ☽ voc 14:43 ☽→♒ 15:52 ☽☍♃ 1:26 ☽⚹♄ 7:27 ☽△♅ 12:26 ☽⚹♆ 14:43 ☽☌♇ 20:37	**23** ☽⚹☿ 23:54
28 ☽□♂ 1:05 ☽□♃ 21:59	**29** ☽ voc 2:13 ☽→♒ 11:57 ☽△☿ 2:13 ☽□♇ 16:24 ☽△♀ 23:03	**30** ☽△☉ 2:21 ☽△♂ 6:54 ☿□♄ 7:15 ☽⚹♃ 23:27

Charts cast with Natural House System in GMT

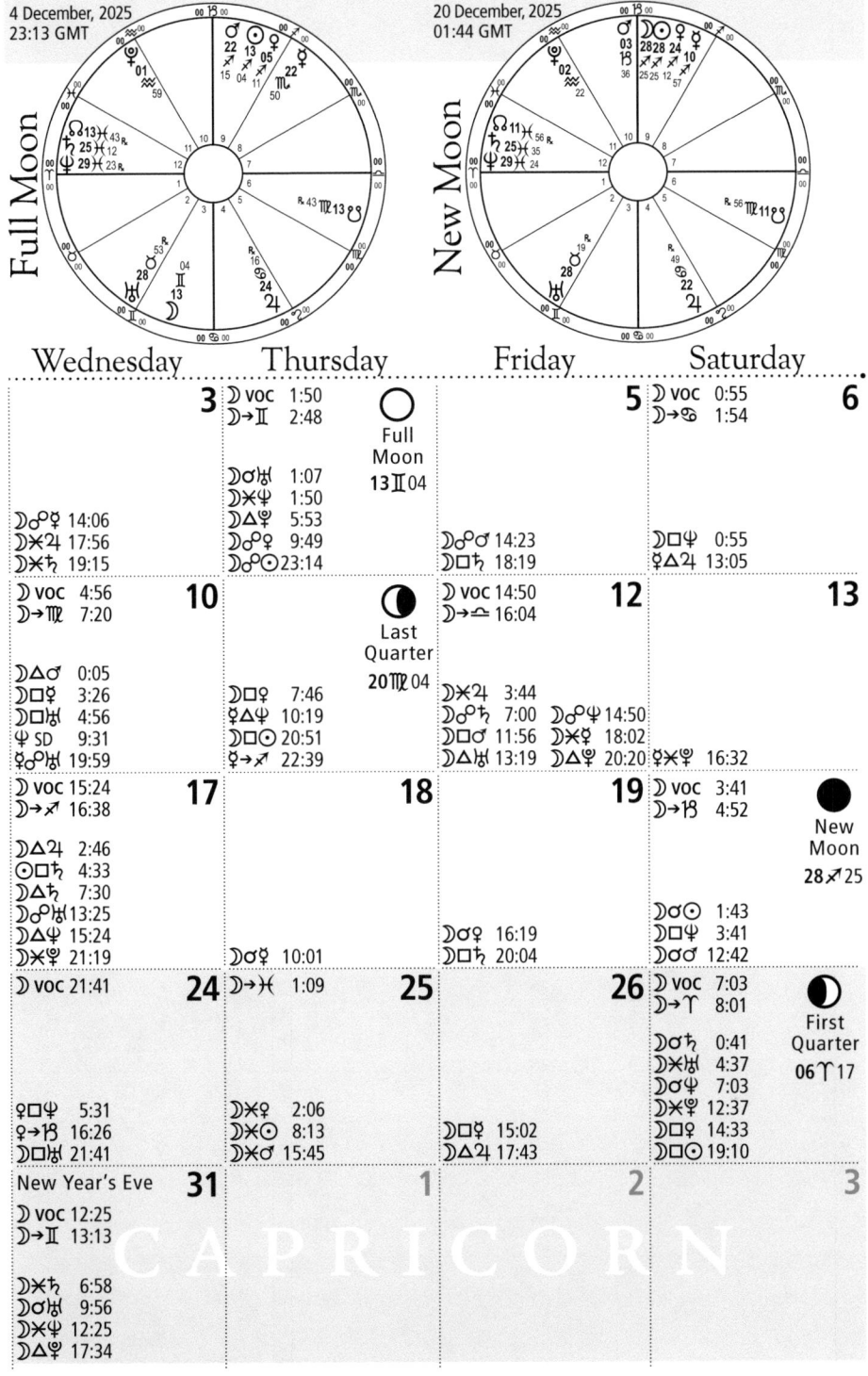

4 December, 2025
23:13 GMT

Full Moon

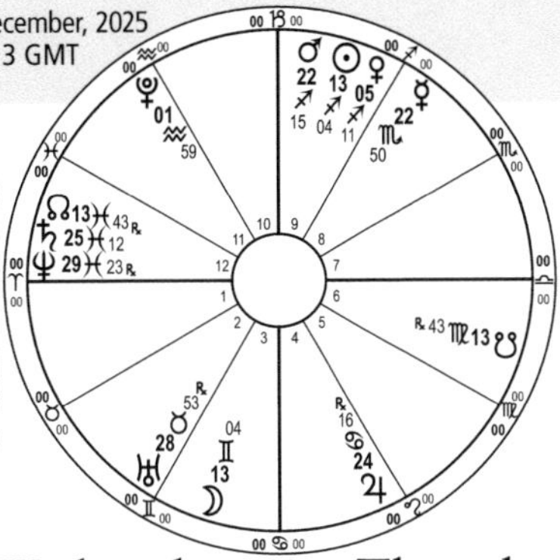

20 December, 2025
01:44 GMT

New Moon

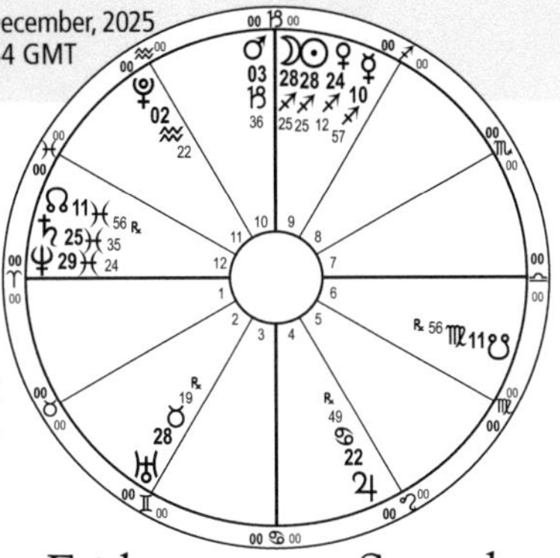

Wednesday	Thursday	Friday	Saturday
3 ☽☍☿ 14:06 ☽⚹♃ 17:56 ☽⚹♄ 19:15	☽ voc 1:50 ☽→♊ 2:48 ○ Full Moon **13**♊04 ☽☌♅ 1:07 ☽⚹♆ 1:50 ☽△♇ 5:53 ☽☍♀ 9:49 ☽☍☉ 23:14	**5** ☽☍♂ 14:23 ☽□♄ 18:19	**6** ☽ voc 0:55 ☽→♋ 1:54 ☽□♆ 0:55 ☿△♃ 13:05
10 ☽ voc 4:56 ☽→♍ 7:20 ☽△♂ 0:05 ☽□☿ 3:26 ☽□♅ 4:56 ♆ SD 9:31 ☿☍♅ 19:59	◑ Last Quarter **20**♍04 ☽□♀ 7:46 ☿△♆ 10:19 ☽□☉ 20:51 ☿→♐ 22:39	**12** ☽ voc 14:50 ☽→♎ 16:04 ☽⚹♃ 3:44 ☽☍♄ 7:00 ☽□♂ 11:56 ☽△♅ 13:19 ☽☍♆ 14:50 ☽⚹☿ 18:02 ☽△♇ 20:20	**13** ☿⚹♇ 16:32
17 ☽ voc 15:24 ☽→♐ 16:38 ☽△♃ 2:46 ☉□♄ 4:33 ☽△♄ 7:30 ☽☍♅ 13:25 ☽△♆ 15:24 ☽⚹♇ 21:19	**18** ☽☌☿ 10:01	**19** ☽☌♀ 16:19 ☽□♄ 20:04	☽ voc 3:41 ☽→♑ 4:52 ● New Moon **28**♐25 ☽☌☉ 1:43 ☽□♆ 3:41 ☽☌♂ 12:42
24 ☽ voc 21:41 ♀□♆ 5:31 ♀→♑ 16:26 ☽□♅ 21:41	**25** ☽→♓ 1:09 ☽⚹♀ 2:06 ☽⚹☉ 8:13 ☽⚹♂ 15:45	**26** ☽□☿ 15:02 ☽△♃ 17:43	☽ voc 7:03 ☽→♈ 8:01 ◐ First Quarter **06**♈17 ☽☌♄ 0:41 ☽⚹♅ 4:37 ☽☌♆ 7:03 ☽⚹♇ 12:37 ☽□♀ 14:33 ☽□☉ 19:10
New Year's Eve **31** ☽ voc 12:25 ☽→♊ 13:13 ☽⚹♄ 6:58 ☽☌♅ 9:56 ☽⚹♆ 12:25 ☽△♇ 17:34	1	2	3

CAPRICORN

♐ Sagittarius

On Sunday Venus forms an opposition to Uranus and a trine to Neptune suggesting sudden changes of feeling and perspective in personal relationships. At best this can be liberating, enabling friends and lovers to see each other and their relationship in a fresh and unencumbered way.

On Tuesday the 2nd of December Venus forms a sextile to Pluto which deepens and intensifies the connection between friends and lovers. Sometimes even slightly uncomfortable emotions can help us appreciate how important and meaningful our personal relationships are.

The Full Moon of 4 December occurs at 13 degrees Gemini in relatively close alignment with the Venus-Mars midpoint, so this could be a time of romantic passion and assertiveness within personal relationships.

On Saturday the 6th of December Mercury will be trine Jupiter and then trine Saturn the following day. This is a recurrence of a combination that occurred on the 22nd of November. There is a constructive use of information, careful and diligent planning and important negotiations and formal agreements.

☉ Sunday

30

☽ VOC	0:05
☽→♈	1:07

☽☌♆	0:05
♀☍♅	2:48
☽⚹♇	4:22
♀△♆	8:48
☽△☉	15:59
♀→♐	20:13

☽ Monday

1 December

☽ VOC	18:14

☽△♂	10:14
☽□♃	18:14

♂ Tuesday

2

☽→♉	3:13

☽□♇	6:20
♀⚹♇	9:07

GMT

December 2025

☿ Wednesday

3

☽ ☍ ☿	14:06
☽ ✶ ♃	17:56
☽ ✶ ♄	19:15

♃ Thursday

4

☽ VOC   1:50
☽ → ♊   2:48

○
Full Moon
13 ♊ 04

☽ ☌ ♅	1:07
☽ ✶ ♆	1:50
☽ △ ♇	5:53
☽ ☍ ♀	9:49
☽ ☍ ☉	23:14

♀ Friday

5

☽ ☍ ♂	14:23
☽ □ ♄	18:19
☽ □ ♆	0:55

♄ Saturday

6

☽ VOC   0:55
☽ → ♋   1:54

☿ △ ♃   13:05

Regulus 2025 Astrological Planner

♐ Sagittarius

Mars is quincunx Jupiter on Sunday the 7th of November pointing to vigorous work and industriousness. It may also describe demands for better working conditions or better terms in financial agreements.

Then Mars forms a square to Saturn on Tuesday the 9th of November and this is an even more intense type of hard work and effort. There may even be acute tension and frustration that can lead to conflict and obstructive actions.

Around 10-11 November Mercury will be opposite Uranus and then trine Neptune, a combination that could manifest as metaphysical studies or extraordinary new information or new and novel forms of communication.

Mercury goes on to form a sextile to Pluto on Saturday the 13th of November, pointing to thorough research and investigation and communication that is forthright, deep and serious.

☉ Sunday

7

☽☌♃	16:51
☿△♄	16:57
☽△♄	18:50
☽△♀	18:58

☽ Monday

8

| ☽ VOC | 1:45 |
| ☽→♌ | 2:48 |

☽✶♅	0:44
☽△♆	1:45
☽☍♇	6:17
☽△♀	19:55

♂ Tuesday

9

| ♂□♄ | 0:15 |
| ☽△☉ | 8:59 |

GMT

December 2025

☿ Wednesday

10

☽ VOC 4:56
☽→♍ 7:20

☽△♂ 0:05
☽□☿ 3:26
☽□♅ 4:56
♆ SD 9:31
☿☍♅ 19:59

♃ Thursday

11

◐
Last Quarter
20♍04

☽□♀ 7:46
☿△♆ 10:19
☽□☉ 20:51
♀→♐ 22:39

♀ Friday

12

☽ VOC 14:50
☽→♎ 16:04

☽✶♃ 3:44
☽☍♄ 7:00
☽□♂ 11:56
☽△♅ 13:19
☽☍♆ 14:50
☽✶☿ 18:02
☽△♇ 20:20

♄ Saturday

13

☿✶♇ 16:32

Regulus 2025 Astrological Planner   183

♐ Sagittarius

On Sunday the 14th of December Mars is square Neptune, so there's potential for exhaustion or a lack of focus and follow through. Intentions are not clear and transparent, the warrior is confused or misguided about the target of his attack.

The New Moon on the 20th of December occurs at 28 degrees Sagittarius, quincunx Uranus and square Neptune. Spiritual aspirations and ideals are stimulated but there is also some element of escapism and carelessness implied.

☉ Sunday

14

☽✶♀	0:53
♂□♆	11:43
☽✶☉	13:20
☽□♃	14:33

☽ Monday

15

☽ VOC	3:36
☽→♏	3:51

♂ Tuesday

16

☽✶♂	3:36
♂→♑	7:34
☽□♀	8:24

184　　　　　　　　　　　　　　　　　　　　　　　GMT

December 2025

☿ Wednesday
17

☽ VOC 15:24
☽→♐ 16:38

☽△♃ 2:46
☉□♄ 4:33
☽△♄ 7:30
☽☌♅ 13:25
☽△♆ 15:24
☽✶♇ 21:19

♃ Thursday
18

☽☌☿ 10:01

♀ Friday
19

☽☌♀ 16:19
☽□♄ 20:04

♄ Saturday
20

● New Moon
28♐25

☽ VOC 3:41
☽→♑ 4:52

☽☌☉ 1:43
☽□♆ 3:41
☽☌♂ 12:42

Regulus 2025 Astrological Planner   185

♑ Capricorn

Venus forms a square aspect to Saturn on Sunday the 21st of December (which happens to be the solstice, marking the Sun's ingress into Capricorn). There is distance in personal relationships, either due to unavoidable practical circumstances or due to a more internal feeling of disillusionment in the connection. The focus is on the duty in relationships rather than the joy.

Venus goes on to form a square to Neptune on Wednesday the 24th of November and so friends and lovers are in a dreamy and idealistic mood. This can either make for a deeper level of acceptance and compassion in personal relationships, or there can be disorientation and uncertainty about the solidity of the connection.

☉ Sunday

21

Winter Solstice

☉□♆	1:02
♀□♄	5:09
☉→♑	15:03

☽ Monday

22

☽ VOC	14:43
☽→♒	15:52

☽☌♃	1:26
☽✶♄	7:27
☽△♅	12:26
☽✶♆	14:43
☽☌♇	20:37

♂ Tuesday

23

☽✶☿	23:54

GMT

December 2025

☿ Wednesday
24

☽ VOC 21:41

♀□♆ 5:31
♀→♑ 16:26
☽□♅ 21:41

♃ Thursday
25

☽→♓ 1:09

☽⚹♀ 2:06
☽⚹☉ 8:13
☽⚹♂ 15:45

♀ Friday
26

☽□☿ 15:02
☽△♃ 17:43

♄ Saturday
27

☽ VOC 7:03
☽→♈ 8:01

◐ First Quarter
06♈17

☽☌♄ 0:41
☽⚹♅ 4:37
☽☌♆ 7:03
☽⚹♇ 12:37
☽□♀ 14:33
☽□☉ 19:10

Regulus 2025 Astrological Planner

♑ Capricorn

Mercury forms a square to Saturn on the 30th of December, and so the tone of communication is deep and serious and focussed on practical matters.

Then on the 1st of January 2026 Mercury will be square Neptune and communication becomes far more richly imbued with emotions. This could be poetic or abstract ideas. Not the ideal energy for mental tasks requiring precision and strict accuracy.

☉ Sunday
28

☽ Monday
29

☽□♂	1:05
☽□♃	21:59
☽ VOC	2:13
☽→♉	11:57

♂ Tuesday
30

☽△☿	2:13
☽□♆	16:24
☽△♀	23:03
☽△☉	2:21
☽△♂	6:54
☿□♄	7:15
☽⚹♃	23:27

GMT

January 2026

☿ Wednesday ☽VOC 12:25
☽→♊ 13:13

31

☽⚹♄ 6:58
☽☌♅ 9:56
☽⚹♆ 12:25
☽△♇ 17:34

♃ Thursday

1 January

☿□♆ 13:33
☿→♑ 21:10

♀ Friday ☽VOC 12:23
☽→♋ 13:09

2

☽□♄ 7:09
☽□♆ 12:23
☽☍♀ 14:58

♄ Saturday

3

○
Full Moon
13♋02

☽☍♀ 8:40
☽☍☉ 10:03
☽☍♂ 12:37
☽☌♃ 22:54

Regulus 2025 Astrological Planner

January, 2026

Degree of
Key Aspects

1 Jan 2026
☿ □ ♆ 29♐31 29♓31
6 Jan 2026
☉ ☌ ♀ 16♑22 16♑22
8 Jan 2026
♀ ☌ ♂ 18♑09 18♑09
9 Jan 2026
☉ ☌ ♂ 19♑13 19♑13
♀ ☍ ♃℞ 20♑12 20♋12
10 Jan 2026
☉ ☍ ♃℞ 20♑06 20♋06
♂ ☍ ♃℞ 20♑05 20♋05
14 Jan 2026
☿ ☍ ♃℞ 19♑34 19♋34
15 Jan 2026
♀ △ ♅℞ 27♑37 27♉37
17 Jan 2026
☉ △ ♅℞ 27♑35 27♉35
18 Jan 2026
☿ ☌ ♂ 26♑03 26♑03
19 Jan 2026
☿ △ ♅℞ 27♑34 27♉34
20 Jan 2026
♀ ☌ ♇ 3♒19 3♒19
♂ △ ♅℞ 27♑33 27♉33
21 Jan 2026
☉ ☌ ☿ 1♒37 1♒37
22 Jan 2026
☿ ☌ ♇ 3♒24 3♒24
23 Jan 2026
☉ ☌ ♇ 3♒25 3♒25
27 Jan 2026
♂ ☌ ♇ 3♒34 3♒34
29 Jan 2026
☿ ☌ ♀ 14♒57 14♒57

Sunday	Monday	Tuesday
28	29	30
CAPRICORN		
4 ☽ voc 12:59 ☽→♌ 13:43 ☽△♄ 7:44 ☽⚹♅ 10:11 ☽△♆ 12:59 ☽☍♇ 18:25	5	6 ☽ voc 13:04 ☽→♍ 16:56 ☽□♅ 13:04 ♀☌☉ 16:36
11 ☽→♏ 10:55 ☽□♇ 17:02	12 ☽⚹☿ 21:44	13 ☽ voc 22:59 ☽→♐ 23:34 ☽△♃ 2:46 ☽⚹♂ 7:43 ☽⚹☉ 9:48 ☽⚹♀ 13:27 ☽△♄ 17:32 ☽☍♅ 18:49 ☽△♆ 22:59
☽ voc 21:56 ☽→♒ 22:18 New Moon 28♑44 ☽☍♃ 1:13 ☿☌♂ 7:40 ☽☌♂ 15:11 ☽☌☿ 15:48 ☽⚹♄ 17:22 ☽△♅ 17:38 ☽☌☉ 19:52 ☽⚹♆ 21:56	19 ☽☌♀ 2:02 ☿⚹♄ 4:09 ☽☌♇ 4:35 ☿△♅ 5:37 ☉⚹♆ 21:54	20 ☉→♒ 1:45 ♀☌♇ 4:04 ♄⚹♅ 5:18 ♂△♅ 5:56 ♂⚹♄ 6:02 ☿⚹♆ 14:34 ☿→♒ 16:41
25 ☽→♉ 18:05 ☽□♂ 21:27	First Quarter 06♉14 ☽□♇ 0:07 ☽□☉ 4:47 ☽□☿ 10:50 ☽□♀ 13:31 ♆→♈ 17:38	27 ☽ voc 17:57 ☽→♊ 20:55 ☽⚹♃ 0:40 ☽☌♅ 16:42 ☽⚹♄ 17:57 ☽⚹♆ 20:58 ♂☌♇ 23:02

Charts cast with Natural House System in GMT

Full Moon

3 January, 2026
10:02 GMT

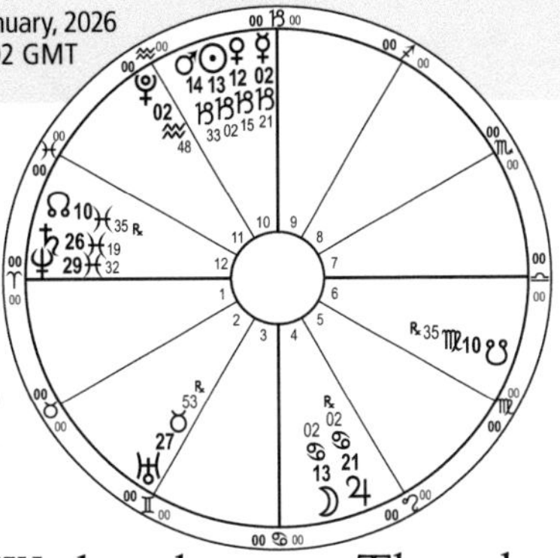

New Moon

18 January, 2026
19:52 GMT

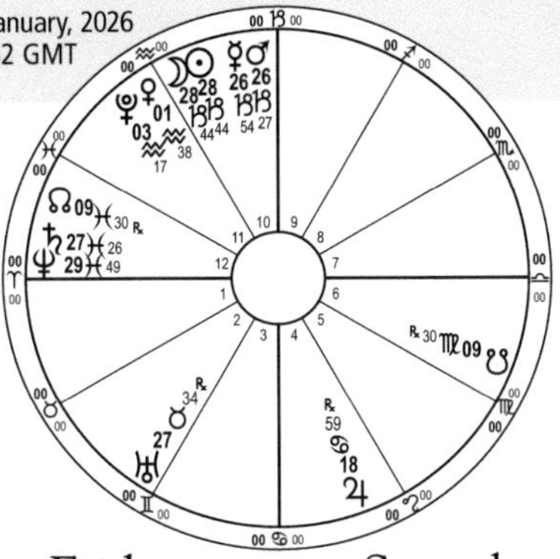

Wednesday	Thursday	Friday	Saturday
31	1 ☿□♆ 13:33 ☿→♑ 21:10	2 ☽ voc 12:23 ☽→♋ 13:09 ☽□♄ 7:09 ☽□♆ 12:23 ☽☍☿ 14:58	○ Full Moon 13♋02 ☽☍♀ 8:40 ☽☍☉ 10:03 ☽☍♂ 12:37 ☽☌♃ 22:54
7 ☽△☿ 8:02	8 ☽ voc 23:22 ☽△☉ 1:04 ☽△♀ 1:44 ☽△♂ 1:46 ♀☌♂ 2:43 ☽⚹♃ 5:59 ☽☍♄ 17:45 ☽△♅ 19:49 ☽☍♆ 23:22	9 ☽→♎ 0:05 ☽△♇ 5:47 ☉☌♂ 11:41 ♀☍♃ 17:35	☽ voc 17:54 ◑ Last Quarter 20♎25 ☽□☿ 0:33 ☉☍♃ 8:42 ♂☍♃ 14:24 ☽□♃ 15:08 ☽□♂ 15:11 ☽□☉ 15:48 ☽□♀ 17:54
14 ☽⚹♇ 5:54 ☿☍♃ 8:17	15 ♀⚹♄ 6:18 ♀△♅ 15:22	16 ☽ voc 11:19 ☽→♑ 11:47 ☽□♄ 6:17 ☽□♆ 11:19	17 ♀⚹♆ 8:33 ☉⚹♄ 10:41 ♀→♒ 12:43 ☉△♅ 16:58
21 ☽ voc 2:16 ☽→♓ 6:49 ☽□♅ 2:16 ☿☌☉ 15:49	22 ☽△♃ 16:41 ☿☌♇ 17:15	23 ☽ voc 13:17 ☽→♈ 13:25 ♂⚹♆ 6:39 ☽⚹♅ 8:59 ♂→♒ 9:17 ☽☌♄ 9:33 ☉☌♇ 10:28 ☽☌♆ 13:17 ☽⚹♂ 13:41 ☽⚹♇ 19:33 ☽⚹☉ 20:16 ☽⚹☿ 23:16	24 ☽ voc 21:36 ☽⚹♀ 4:17 ☽□♃ 21:36
28 ☽△♇ 2:52 ☽△♂ 3:05 ☽△☉ 11:06 ☽△☿ 20:00 ☽△♀ 20:32	29 ☽ voc 19:56 ☽→♋ 22:31 ☿☌♀ 10:17 ☽□♄ 19:56 ☽□♆ 22:40	30	31 ☽ voc 21:52 ☽→♌ 0:09 ☽☌♃ 3:18 ☽⚹♅ 19:55 ☽△♄ 21:52

AQUARIUS

♑ Capricorn

☉ Sunday
4

☽VOC 12:59
☽→♌ 13:43

☽ Monday
5

☽△♄ 7:44
☽✶♅ 10:11
☽△♆ 12:59
☽☍♇ 18:25

♂ Tuesday
6

☽VOC 13:04
☽→♍ 16:56

☽□♅ 13:04
♀☌☉ 16:36

GMT

January 2026

☿ Wednesday

7

☽△☿	8:02

♃ Thursday

8

☽VOC	23:22
☽△☉	1:04
☽△♀	1:44
☽△♂	1:46
♀☌♂	2:43
☽✷♃	5:59
☽☍♄	17:45
☽△♅	19:49
☽☍♆	23:22

♀ Friday

9

☽→♎	0:05
☽△♇	5:47
☉☌♂	11:41
♀☍♃	17:35

♄ Saturday

10

◐ Last Quarter
20♎25

☽VOC	17:54
☽□☿	0:33
☉☍♃	8:42
♂☍♃	14:24
☽□♃	15:08
☽□♂	15:11
☽□☉	15:48
☽□♀	17:54

Regulus 2025 Astrological Planner

193

♑ Capricorn

☉ Sunday
11

☽→♏ 10:55

☽ Monday
12

☽□♇ 17:02

♂ Tuesday
13

☽⚹♀ 21:44
☽VOC 22:59
☽→♐ 23:34

☽△♃ 2:46
☽⚹♂ 7:43
☽⚹☉ 9:48
☽⚹☿ 13:27
☽△♄ 17:32
☽☌♅ 18:49
☽△♆ 22:59

GMT

January 2026

☿ Wednesday

14

☽✶♇	5:54
☿☌♃	8:17

♃ Thursday

15

♀✶♄	6:18
♀△♅	15:22

♀ Friday

16

☽ VOC	11:19
☽→♑	11:47

☽□♄	6:17
☽□♆	11:19

♄ Saturday

17

♀✶♆	8:33
☉✶♄	10:41
♀→♒	12:43
☉△♅	16:58

Regulus 2025 Astrological Planner

☉ Sunday

18

New Moon
28♑44

☽VOC 21:56
☽→♒ 22:18

☽☍♃ 1:13
☿☌♂ 7:40
☽☌♂ 15:11
☽☌☿ 15:48
☽⚹♄ 17:22
☽△♅ 17:38
☽☌☉ 19:52
☽⚹♆ 21:56

☽ Monday

19

☽☌♀ 2:02
☿⚹♄ 4:09
☽☌♇ 4:35
☿△♅ 5:37
☉⚹♆ 21:54

♂ Tuesday

20

☉→♒ 1:45
♀☌♇ 4:04
♄⚹♅ 5:18
♂△♅ 5:56
♂⚹♄ 6:02
☿⚹♆ 14:34
☿→♒ 16:41

January 2026

☿ **Wednesday**

21

☽VOC 2:16
☽→♈ 6:49

☽□♅ 2:16
☿☌☉ 15:49

♃ **Thursday**

22

☽△♃ 16:41
☿☌♇ 17:15

♀ **Friday**

23

☽VOC 13:17
☽→♈ 13:25

♂⚹♆	6:39	☽☌♆	13:17
☽⚹♅	8:59	☽⚹♂	13:41
♂→♒	9:17	☽⚹♇	19:33
☽☌♄	9:33	☽⚹☉	20:16
☉☌♇	10:28	☽⚹☿	23:16

♄ **Saturday**

24

☽VOC 21:36

☽⚹♀ 4:17
☽□♃ 21:36

Regulus 2025 Astrological Planner

♒ Aquarius

☉ Sunday
25

☽→♉ 18:05

☽ Monday
26

☽□♂ 21:27

◐
First Quarter
06 ♉ 14

♂ Tuesday
27

☽□♆ 0:07
☽□☉ 4:47
☽□☿ 10:50
☽□♀ 13:31
♆→♈ 17:38

☽ VOC 17:57
☽→♊ 20:55

☽✶♃ 0:40
☽☌♅ 16:42
☽✶♄ 17:57
☽✶♆ 20:58
♂☌♀ 23:02

198   GMT

January 2026

☿ Wednesday
28

☽△♇ 2:52
☽△♂ 3:05
☽△☉ 11:06
☽△☿ 20:00
☽△♀ 20:32

♃ Thursday
29

☽VOC 19:56
☽→♋ 22:31

♀ Friday
30

☿♂♀ 10:17
☽□♄ 19:56
☽□♆ 22:40

♄ Saturday
31

☽VOC 21:52
☽→♌ 0:09

☽♂♃ 3:18
☽✶♅ 19:55
☽△♄ 21:52

Annotations

Annotations

Annotations

Annotations

Natal Chart

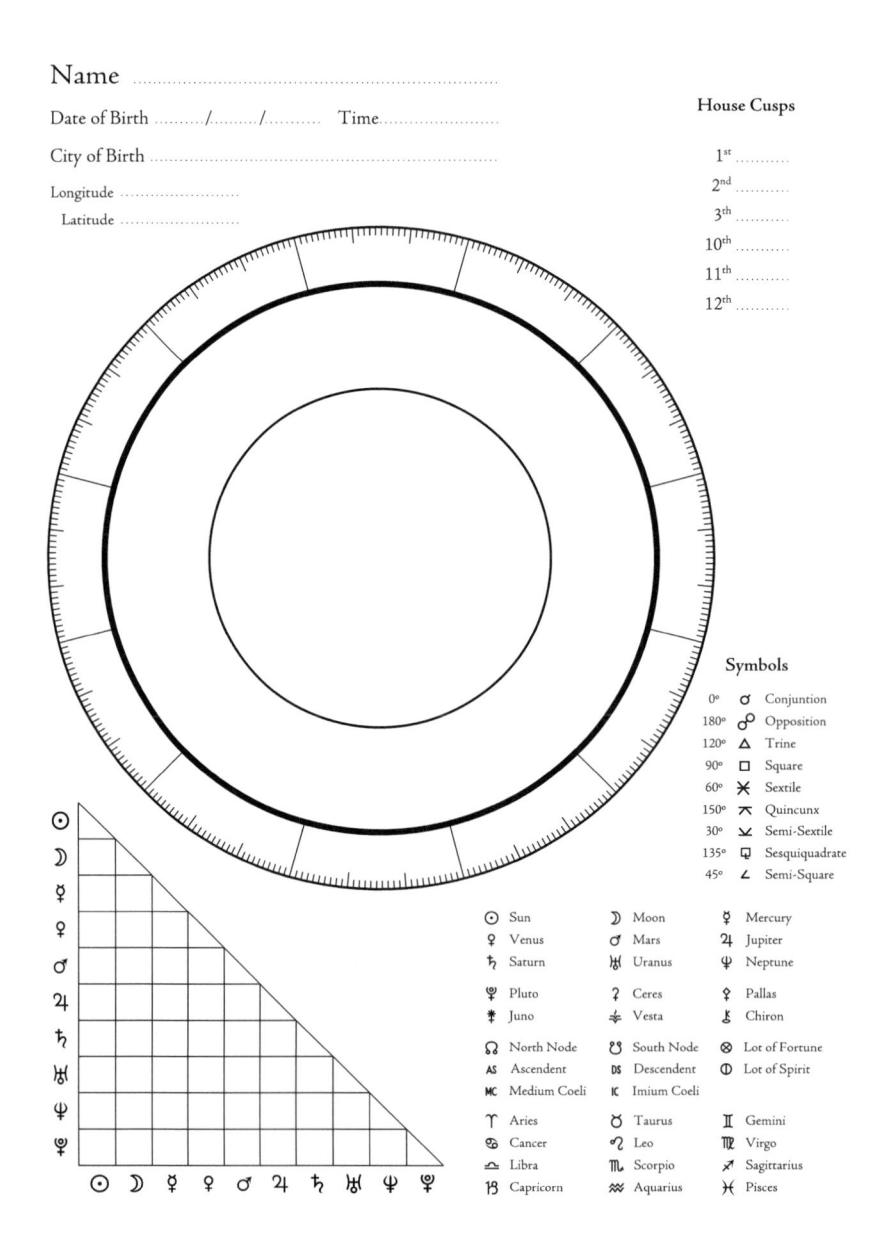

Name ....

Date of Birth ..../.........../........... Time ....

City of Birth ....

Longitude ....

Latitude ....

House Cusps

1st ....
2nd ....
3rd ....
10th ....
11th ....
12th ....

Symbols

0°	☌	Conjunction
180°	☍	Opposition
120°	△	Trine
90°	□	Square
60°	✶	Sextile
150°	⚻	Quincunx
30°	⚺	Semi-Sextile
135°	⚼	Sesquiquadrate
45°	∠	Semi-Square

☉ Sun	☽ Moon	☿ Mercury
♀ Venus	♂ Mars	♃ Jupiter
♄ Saturn	♅ Uranus	♆ Neptune
♇ Pluto	⚳ Ceres	⚴ Pallas
⚵ Juno	⚶ Vesta	⚷ Chiron
☊ North Node	☋ South Node	⊗ Lot of Fortune
AS Ascendent	DS Descendent	⊕ Lot of Spirit
MC Medium Coeli	IC Imum Coeli	

♈ Aries	♉ Taurus	♊ Gemini
♋ Cancer	♌ Leo	♍ Virgo
♎ Libra	♏ Scorpio	♐ Sagittarius
♑ Capricorn	♒ Aquarius	♓ Pisces

Legend

Signs

♈	Aries Fire Cardinal		♎	Libra Air Cardinal
♉	Taurus Earth Fixed		♏	Scorpio Water Fixed
♊	Gemini Air Mutable		♐	Sagittarius Fire Mutable
♋	Cancer Water Cardinal		♑	Capricorn Earth Cardinal
♌	Leo Fire Fixed		♒	Aquarius Air Fixed
♍	Virgo Earth Mutable		♓	Pisces Water Mutable

☽	Moon Luna Goddess		☉	Sun Sol Invictus
☿	Mercury Messenger of the Gods		♀	Venus Goddess of Love
♂	Mars God of War		♃	Jupiter King of the Gods
♄	Saturn The Nature of Time		♅	Uranus God of the Sky
♆	Neptune God of the Oceans		♇	Pluto Lord of the Underworld

Asteroids

⚷	Kiron	The Healer
⚴	Pallas	The Warrior Queen
⚵	Juno	Goddess of Union
⚳	Ceres	The Great Mother
⚶	Vesta	The Flame Keeper

Major Aspects (Ptolomaic)

☌	Conjunction	0°
☍	Oposition	180°
△	Trine	120°
□	Square	90°
✶	Sextile	60°

Secondary Aspects

⌄	Semi-Sextile	30°
∠	Semi-Square	45°
⚼	Sesquisquare	135°
⊼	Quincunx	150°

Minor Aspects

✶	Septile	51.2°
⋈	Novile	40°
Q	Quintile	72°
Q	Quindecile	15°

Regulus 2025 Astrological Planner. Produced by Paula Belluomini and Richard Fidler. Published by Regulus Publishing. Astrological data generated in partby Matrix Search Inc Software. Astronomical data and information about the visibility of the Eclipse: <http://sunearth.gsf.nasa.gov/>. No part of this publication may be reproduced or transmitted in any form or by any means, electronic or mechanical, without prior authorization from Regulus Publishing. www.reguluspublishing.com - email: reguluspublishing@gmail.com. Learn more about the Astrologers: Paula Belluomini's website www.astropaula.com / Richard Fidler's website www.richardfidler.com.

World Map with Time Zones

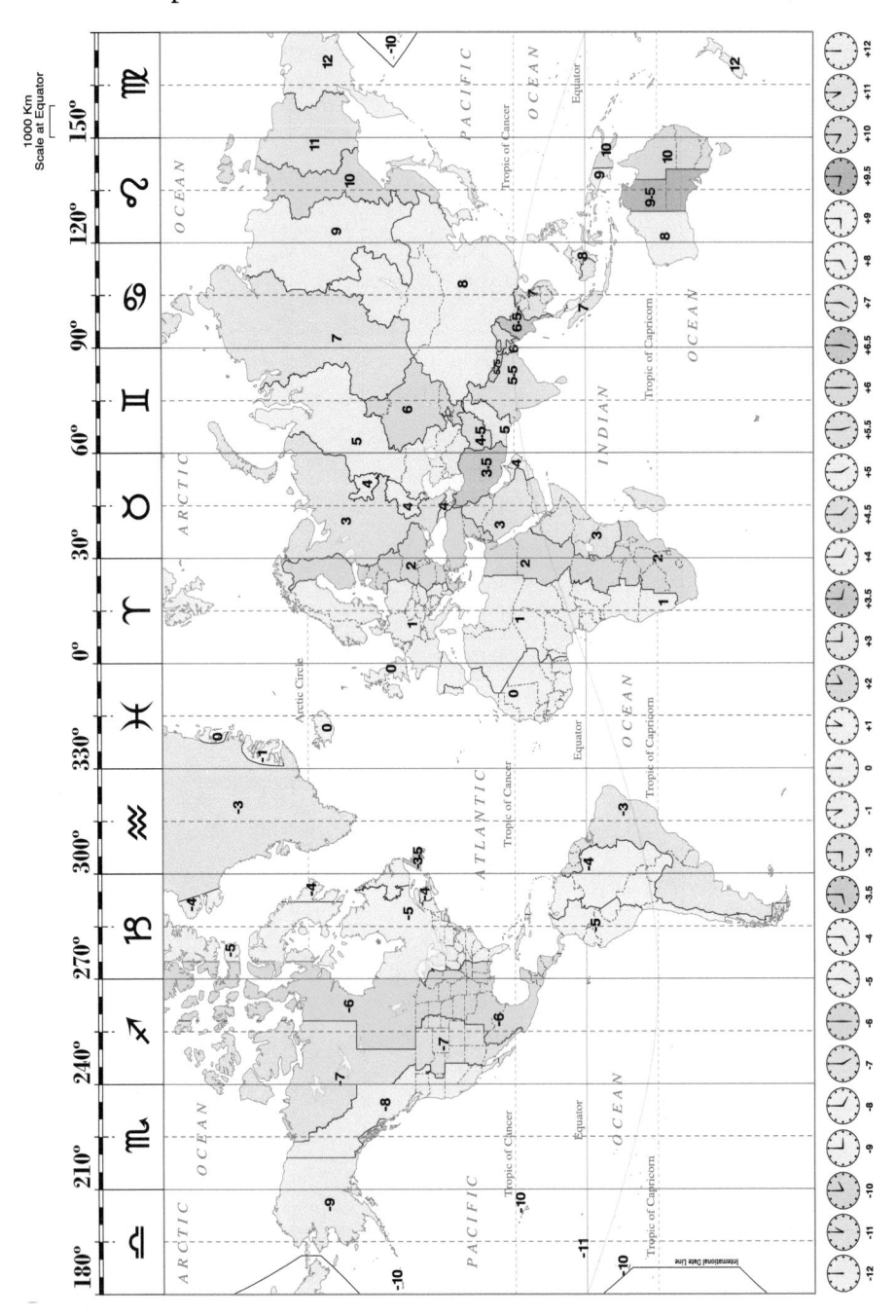